Observed Correction

Oxford Studies in Digital Politics

Founder and Series Editor: Andrew Chadwick, Professor of Political Communication and Director of the Online Civic Culture Centre (O3C) in the Department of Communication and Media, Loughborough University

Observed
Correction

HOW WE CAN ALL RESPOND TO
MISINFORMATION ON SOCIAL MEDIA

LETICIA BODE
EMILY K. VRAGA

OXFORD
UNIVERSITY PRESS

Oxford University Press is a department of the University of Oxford.
It furthers the University's objective of excellence in research, scholarship,
and education by publishing worldwide. Oxford is a registered trade mark of
Oxford University Press in the UK and in certain other countries.

Published in the United States of America by Oxford University Press
198 Madison Avenue, New York, NY 10016, United States of America.

© Leticia Bode and Emily K. Vraga 2025

For additional information about our data and methods, please visit https://bode.vraga.org/

CIP data is on file at the Library of Congress

ISBN 9780197565902

ISBN 9780197565896 (hbk.)

DOI: 10.1093/oso/9780197565896.001.0001

Paperback Printed by Integrated Books International, United States of America
Hardback Printed by Bridgeport National Bindery, Inc., United States of America

The manufacturer's authorized representative in the EU for product safety is Oxford
University Press España S.A., Parque Empresarial San Fernando de Henares,
Avenida de Castilla, 2–28830 Madrid (www.oup.es/en).

MIX
Paper
FSC   FSC® C183721

Contents

List of Figures

List of Tables

Acknowledgments

We worked on this book for a long time. Like a really long time. And we never would have made it across the finish line without the help of a lot of people. We owe thanks to so many people, and we feel so lucky to have the support that we do to take on crazy projects like this book.

First, we want to thank Andy Chadwick for encouraging us to write this book in the first place. We didn't think we were book writers (and at least one of us still doesn't!), but Andy went out of his way to encourage us to think about how to weave our existing work into a larger project. We're so grateful for this push, and we are motivated to push others in the same helpful way as we go forward.

Likewise, we are thankful to Oxford University Press and especially Angela Chnapko for a smooth process, for the utmost understanding of our multiple delays (a baby! COVID! another baby!), and for always answering our sometimes-trivial-but-important-to-us questions.

We are also grateful to the many respondents who participated in our interviews, surveys, and experiments over the last decade to produce the evidence we rely on in this book. Particular thanks go to the interview participants, who spent so much of their time with us to make sure we understood their motivations and constraints.

In addition, we are so very lucky to thank the veritable army of research assistants who have contributed to this book, in ways large and small, including Danel Akhmetova, Hyland Brown, Benedetta Burston, Jialin Chen, Troy Cheng, Amanda Chu, Dhriti Gupta, Meghan Landsberg, Yuwei Ma, Ellen Naughton, Eleanor Plaunt, Kavya Shah, Olivia Stevens, Jikai Sun, Rutvi Zamre, and Linpei Zhang, as well as to our respective institutions (Georgetown and Minnesota, including the Don R. and Carole J. Larson Professorship in Health Communication) for supporting this work. Special thanks to Rowan McMullen Cheng, who masterfully conducted all of the interviews with members of the public, and Rita Tang, who continues to support this book and our work in so many ways we can't even name them.

Finally, we are grateful for all those that gave feedback on this book, or on pieces of it, including those at the University of Wisconsin Communication and Civic Life Amid Contention Conference, the University of Pennsylvania Social Action Lab, the 2022 annual conference of the International Fact-Checking Network, the 2022 annual conference of the Association for Education in Journalism and Mass Communication, the How COVID Has Changed Health Communication: A New Path Forward in October 2022, the 2022 annual conference of the American Political Science Association, the 2023 annual conference of the Southern Political Science Association, the 2023 conference on Misinformation and Its Consequences for American Democracy hosted by the Jack Citrin Center for Public Opinion Research at UC-Berkeley, and the 2023 Harvard/Northeastern Misinformation Speaker Series Harvard University and Northeastern University. In addition, we want to thank those at the Media and Politics Research Group at Minnesota in February 2023 for their feedback on Chapter 2 (even though it no longer exists). LATIS Research Services at the University of Minnesota was an incredible resource to help us create figures, especially Alicia Hofelich Mohr.

We also have several individuals who deserve special acknowledgment. Thank you to Matt Carlson, for reading our first draft of the proposal way back in 2019 and offering so much thoughtful feedback and support. We will always be grateful to Stephanie Edgerly, Kjerstin Thorson, and Melissa Tully, our dear friends who read the endlessly long and often tedious first draft of this book and expertly helped us find the good stuff and leave the rest behind. Extra thanks for coming to Minnesota in February.

And big thanks to our second book workshop participants, including Lisa Fazio, Lucas Graves, Ethan Porter, Briony Swire-Thompson, and Emily Thorson, who took time out of their enormously busy lives to give thoughtful and detailed feedback on the book, and did so with humor, candor, and grace.

Leticia: First and foremost, I have to thank Emily. I can't count how many times I've told you that I'll never write a book again, and it's equally true that there's no way I would have ever finished this one without you. You are brilliant, patient, share my love of peanut butter M&Ms, laugh at most of my bad jokes, nudge me just the right amount to get my shit done, always run the analysis, pick the best sushi places, and (usually) accept it when I demand we stop collecting more data. More importantly, you are one of my best friends and I'm so glad we've had this time together.

I'm also thankful to my academic peers, mentors, and supporters, including everyone at Wisconsin that saw any glimmer of promise in me all those years ago, and everyone at Georgetown who has supported me and given me a place to be weird and flourish anyway.

Thanks also go to my parents, even if you do ask about the book every damn week. I have done weird things with my life, and taken a path that probably never made much sense to you, but in every single moment you have supported me 100%. I couldn't ask for anything more.

I'm also so grateful to my kids. Parenting has given me a new perspective on work and life, and it's all for the better. You have given me a cute face in Zoom meetings, a remedy to a workaholic lifestyle, and a crash course in task switching. I love you so so much and love that you are more important than any work project. But I hope that when I take on big projects like this it reminds you that you can too.

Finally, saving the best for last, to Dave. My partner, my coparent, my person. No one makes me better than you do. You're always ready with a many-bullet-point-list of why I can do a thing, you find ways to make impossible logistics work, and when everything gets hard you remind me that I should probably eat something. Thank you for always making our book summits work (there were at least 10, but I've lost count), for showing the kids all of the flamingo pictures, and for being the best at welcoming me home. For this and everything, I am so lucky.

Emily: Leticia—we did it! There were definitely moments when I questioned our sanity and whether we would ever finish this book. I still can't quite believe that this is the outcome of over a decade of work together; a decade that has seen so many changes in both of our lives. Our friendship has grown from the weekly "Shut Up and Write" sessions in DC and Virginia, where we did write but rarely shut up, commiserating over all the vagaries of academic life, and juggling professional goals with being a parent—you've always had my back and been my sounding board. I'm so grateful to have you in my life and I can't imagine writing my first book with anyone else.

To my parents: I've finally written a book as you always said I would, even if it's not the novel you envisioned me writing. Thank you for always supporting my professional goals, even when you didn't understand them (no, grad school is not the fast track to being an anchor like Tom Brokaw).

To my kids—I love you more than words can say. Watching you grow and getting to know you as the wonderful people that you are is the most important privilege of my life.

And to my husband Hans—thank you. From changing your name to changing where we live (multiple times!), you've always supported me. It may be impossible to truly have it all as a wife, a mother, and a professional, but you've always done your best to get me as close to that ideal as possible. I love you.

Chapter 1

Introduction

Once upon a time, there was an r/baseball subreddit where people were complaining about a play they thought had been called incorrectly. A retired umpire weighed in, screenshotted the relevant rule, translated each part of its jargon, and explained how each piece of the rule applied to the play in question. Other users on reddit upvoted that comment, so that it became the top comment—shown at the very top of the feed—and essentially served as *the* answer to the debate (as shown in Figure 1.1).

This story, described to Leticia by Benjamin Burnley, can be thought of as a sort of Platonic ideal of what we'll call "observed correction"—the focus of this book. In response to someone sharing information, someone else (the umpire) acted to directly respond with accurate information to the misinformation that the call on the field was wrong (correction). That conversation was public and other people therefore witnessed the exchange (observed correction). For this correction to be more effective, people also agreed on who was an appropriate expert (an umpire whose expertise derives from his former occupation) and acted to promote (upvote) that correction and the information (evidence) it contained. The platform (reddit) didn't just allow but facilitated this. As others have noted,[1] the affordances of reddit make it among the more democratic of platforms by creating elaborate threads of many replies, giving users the ability to collectively promote some comments—the ones they consider "best"—over others, bringing it closer to being a true marketplace of ideas.[2]

To help this ideal of observed correction come to life, consider some of our personal experiences with observed correction on social media. On reddit, I (Emily) came across a post to r/politicalhumor[3] in early 2023 with a purported tweet from famed US journalist Bob Woodward claiming to reveal that former president Donald Trump wears adult diapers (Figure 1.2). The top post in

Observed Correction. Leticia Bode and Emily K. Vraga, Oxford University Press.
© Leticia Bode and Emily K. Vraga (2025). DOI: 10.1093/oso/9780197565896.003.0001

Figure 1.1   Platonic example of observed correction. Credit: Meg Leta Jones, 2024.

response is a reminder from the moderators that the subreddit is devoted to satire and that the post is (in his words) obviously a joke. In addition, the top comment, upvoted over 2,000 times, was from an anonymous user sharing links to two fact-checking sites, both of which showed that this tweet was fabricated. Much like in our Platonic ideal, I experienced observed correction: I knew the post was

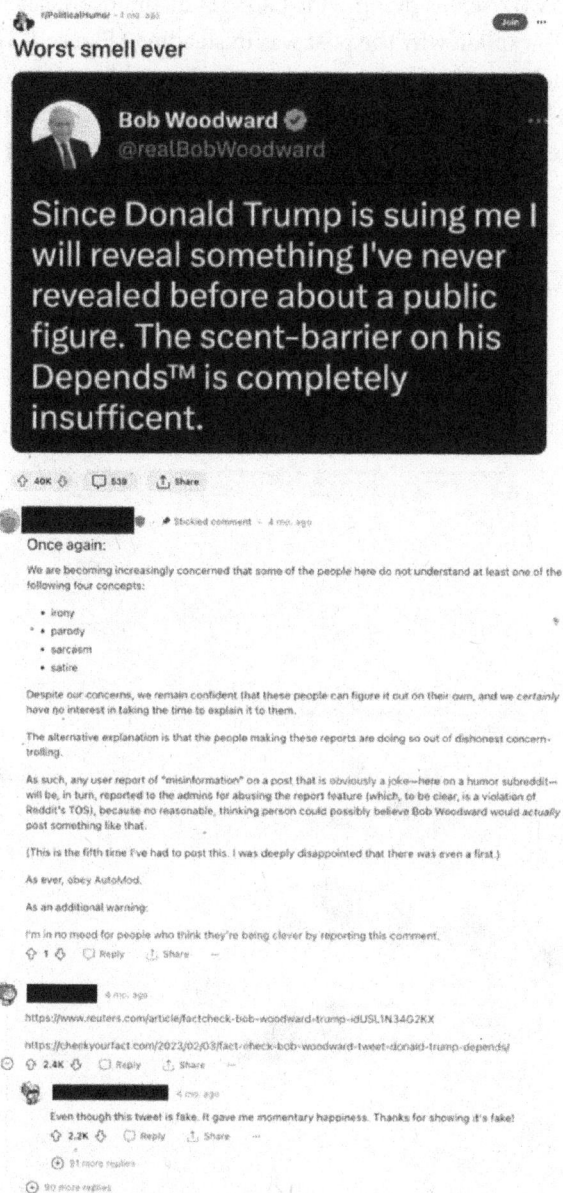

Figure 1.2 reddit example of observed correction.

false because the community had worked together to provide and promote clear corrective evidence to the misinformation.

This experience of observed correction happens on many social media platforms beyond reddit. When an acquaintance of mine (Leticia) shared a post on Facebook in August 2020 claiming that only 6% of COVID-19 deaths were due to COVID itself rather than some other cause (the infamous dying-from-COVID versus dying-with-COVID distinction), several other people weighed in to explain why the post was misleading (Figure 1.3). One person shared a personal narrative, one pointed out the logical flaw in how the post was thinking about "other" deaths, and one shared an article describing how many more deaths the US had that year compared to an average year. All of these users

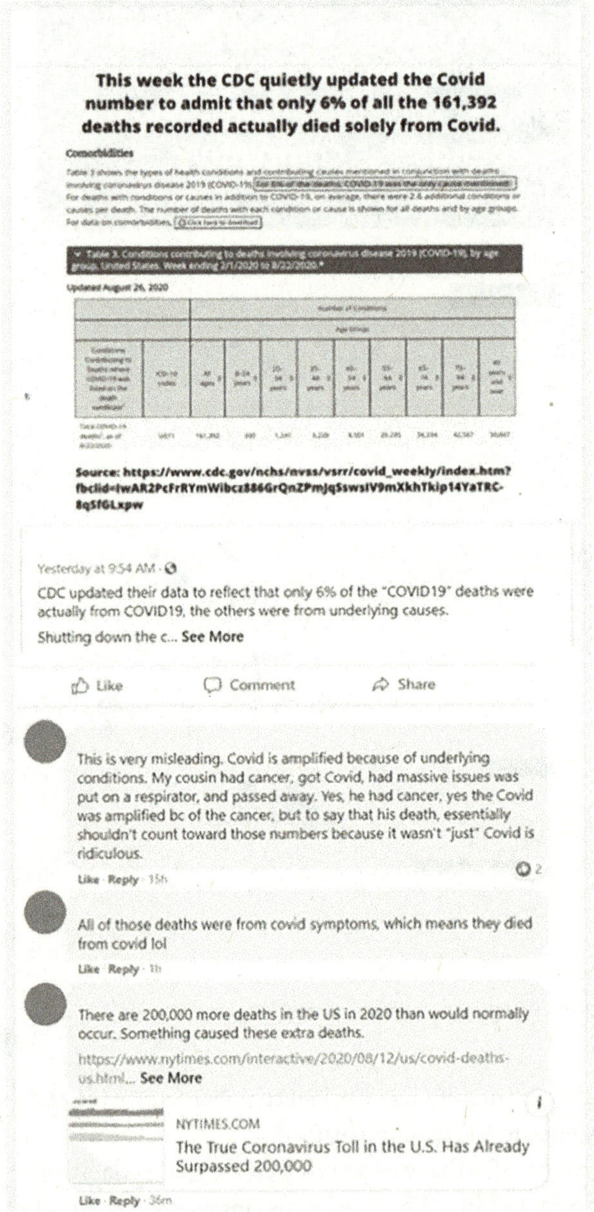

Figure 1.3 Facebook example of observed correction.

engaged in correction of the misinformation in the original post, and I got to witness it—another example of observed correction.

We both saw the next example, which made the rounds on Twitter[4] in early 2021 (Figure 1.4). When the original poster claimed that a $15 per hour minimum wage would lead to $38 burritos at Taco Bell, a poster from Washington, DC noted that their minimum wage is already that high, and Taco Bell prices are still quite low.

Observed correction has even crept into my (Leticia) neighborhood email list (Figure 1.5). When the city proposed to install new bike lanes on a well-traveled road in our neighborhood, one neighbor said that he "highly doubt[ed]" that building bike lanes would encourage more people to bike, and another neighbor replied—with a peer-reviewed study—indicating that building bike lanes tends to have just that effect. While email is often a private communication platform—one person emailing one other person—in this case, because the hundreds of people who subscribe to my neighborhood list also saw the emails, it still constitutes observed correction.

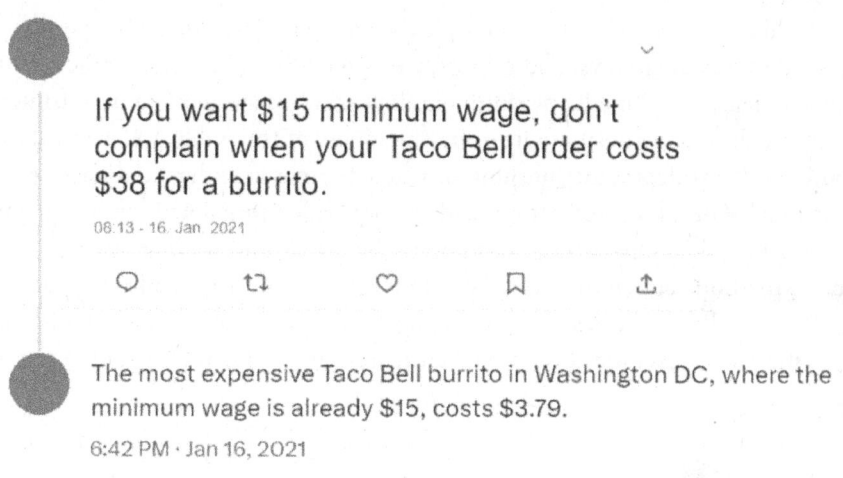

Figure 1.4   Twitter example of observed correction.

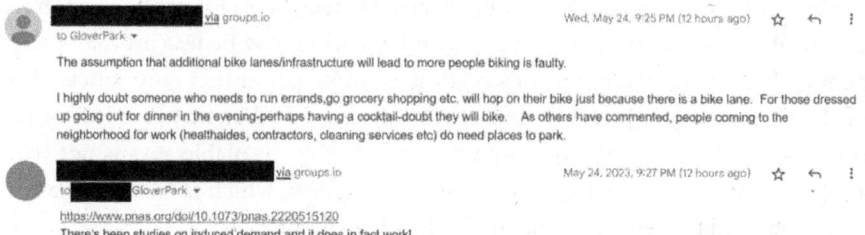

Figure 1.5   Email example of observed correction.

We could go on and on; we've both seen examples on YouTube, TikTok, WhatsApp, and many other platforms. And it's not just us: observed correction is a lived experience that happens at least on occasion for many people. In this book, we'll make an argument for why observed correction—when misinformation is corrected in public—is a useful strategy for addressing misinformation on social media. We'll offer evidence that observed correction makes people more accurate, especially when they remember the corrections, and that emerging norms support the value of correction on social media. We'll also describe how lots of people—social media users, public health experts, and fact checkers among them—are conflicted or constrained correctors: they think correction is valuable and want to do it well, even as they raise real concerns about the risks and downsides of doing so. Sometimes, simple messages addressing these concerns make people more willing to respond to misinformation; to mitigate other concerns will require real changes to the structure of social media and society. Fundamentally, our argument is that observed correction is an important tool in the fight against misinformation because it is effective and can be scalable if more people are willing to do it.

To do all this we'll leverage multiple data sources, including 11 experimental studies, seven surveys, and 60 interviews with fact checkers, public health professionals, social media platform employees who have worked on misinformation policy, and social media users (members of the public). Each of these sources of data offers something unique when it comes to understanding the phenomenon of observed correction, and we'll provide more details about each of these data collections as they come up in the book (and we have an extensive online methods appendix if you want to read more, https://bode.vraga.org/). But first, we'll use the rest of this chapter to explain what we mean by misinformation and observed correction, before describing the outline for the rest of the book.

Why Misinformation Is a Problem

Misinformation is obviously a problem that has received a lot of attention, both on social media and offline,[5] even if misinformation may be less prevalent than people think.[6] We define misinformation as information that contradicts clear evidence, and, when possible, expert consensus.[7] In other words, misinformation is something that the best information we have available says is not true, and stands in direct contrast to *accurate* information, which is based on expert consensus and the weight of the best available evidence.

We use the term "misinformation" as an umbrella category, which can capture a lot of ways in which information is untrue. For example, many people distinguish between misinformation and disinformation, which is deliberately created or shared to advance an economic, political, or social strategic goal.[8] Folks working in national security often combine misinformation and disinformation with a third category of malinformation—that is, information that is roughly true but taken out of context or otherwise misleading—using the abbreviation MDM to describe these three types.[9] Those working in computer science and political communication often investigate what they call rumors[10]—which sometimes means information that is not yet verified, but can also include information that doesn't align with available data and expert consensus (what we call misinformation).

In practice, the distinction between these types of content can be opaque. On social media, intent is usually unknowable; that is, when we see a post on social media, we do not know *why* someone chose to share it or whether they believe it. Additionally, observed correction should theoretically be valuable in responding to all these types of bad information—it can help people become more accurate, whether they are seeing something that is deliberately false, misleading, or unverified, by providing the most accurate information in response. Therefore, we use the broader term "misinformation" throughout this book.

So why is this book focused on misinformation and accuracy? First, we care about misinformation on principle. Even if misinformation did not affect anyone's beliefs, attitudes, or behaviors, we would prefer that information circulating in the marketplace of ideas be reliable and accurate. Fundamentally, we think that truth is important.

Second, we also know that misinformation can often cause harm. In the context of politics, misinformation can lead to misperceptions about wealth distribution and refugee policy,[11] affect people's choice whether or not to vote[12] and who to vote for,[13] erode trust in the political system,[14] intensify ideological polarization,[15] increase racial discrimination,[16] and facilitate crime,[17] violence,[18] and even genocide.[19] In the context of health, misinformation has been linked to decisions about smoking,[20] the refusal to wear a mask or social distance during the COVID-19 pandemic,[21] wariness about contraception use,[22] rejection of cancer treatment,[23] and decreased intentions to take a variety of vaccines.[24] Health and politics are only two domains in which misinformation spreads, but it has the potential to be especially detrimental to society in these cases because many health and political decisions involve both personal and societal risk or harm. Therefore, this book will focus mostly on health and political examples.

We do not wish to be hyperbolic here—plenty of misinformation has no meaningful impact on anyone. In 2022, a series of videos depicting cooking chicken in Nyquil as a tasty treat swept through TikTok. To be clear, this is misinformation, and cooking chicken (or anything, really) in Nyquil is also a terrible idea! But as far as we can tell, it was always done as a joke, everyone got the joke, and no one was ever injured by it as a result.[25] This sort of nothingburger of a misinformation story happens a lot.

But research is not great at predicting when misinformation leads to harmful behaviors and when it doesn't. And today's harmless weird conspiracy theory may well be tomorrow's hate crime, murder, or insurrection. Many dismissed the "pizzagate" conspiracy theory until someone took it seriously enough to bring a gun to a pizza place full of families.[26] While misinformation related to raw milk is so-called evergreen (it doesn't really go away), it has largely been seen as innocuous. Most people buy milk from the grocery store, and that milk is pasteurized because of federal food safety protections. So even if they think raw milk would be more nutritious (it wouldn't be[27]), they don't even have an opportunity to act on that belief. Even among those who do actively seek out raw milk to drink, while it may well make them very sick,[28] it is unlikely to have fatal consequences (E. coli and salmonella are both transmitted through unpasteurized milk, but they are usually not seriously dangerous for most healthy people[29]). So you might conclude that raw milk is not a misinformation issue worth focusing on. In the spring of 2024, however, a strain of avian flu (H5N1) started circulating in cows, which can pass to their milk. While it occurs in both raw and pasteurized milk, it doesn't reproduce in pasteurized milk.[30] Misinformation about the value of raw milk, then, could lead to increased public demand for such milk and therefore contribute to the spread of a dangerous pathogen, a severe public health risk. While this is just one example, our overall point is that it is often difficult to tell a serious issue from one that may not really affect meaningful behaviors or outcomes. Until we can predict the relationships between misinformation, misperceptions, and behaviors with more confidence, we think it's prudent to study—and attempt to mitigate—all types of misinformation, even if not all of them require equal urgency.[31]

Defining Observed Correction

In this book, we focus specifically on *observed correction* as one particularly useful approach to mitigating the impact of misinformation on social media. As we're about to spend an entire book talking about it, we want to be as clear as possible about what we mean by observed correction. We define observed correction as happening when an individual sees another person corrected.[32] Observed correction requires three components (Figure 1.6). First, it must directly respond to misinformation (or misleading information, as we mentioned above).[33] Second, it must contain accurate information correcting the misinformation. And third, the feature of observed correction that really sets it apart from

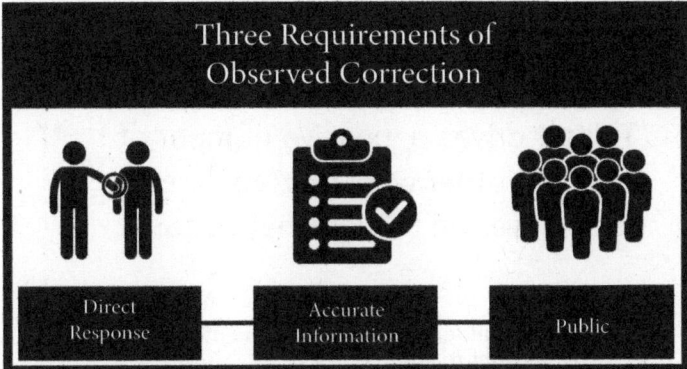

Figure 1.6 Three requirements of observed correction.

other types of correction is that it must be *public*—that is, at least one other person, besides the original poster, must be able to see the interaction. These three key features lay the groundwork for observed correction to happen; but observed correction only takes place when someone actually witnesses the public correction.

Notably, observed correction can come from a variety of sources. For example, when President Trump retweeted misinformation on Twitter in 2017 claiming a video depicted a Muslim migrant attacking a young boy on crutches, the Embassy of the Netherlands (a governmental organization) corrected one of his tweets, clarifying that the perpetrator of the violence was a non-Muslim Dutch citizen (a nonmigrant) who was convicted under Dutch law.[34] More recently, in November of 2022 Elon Musk posted on Twitter about the proportion of links that originate from Twitter versus other social media platforms; his tweet was corrected by a combination of platforms and people through the community notes feature (see Figure 1.7).

As these examples suggest, many different actors, which we'll describe as the 5 Ps of people, platforms, policymakers, professionals, and the press in the next chapter, can create the conditions for observed correction, so long as the three criteria are met: that it is a 1) direct 2) correction of misinformation that 3) could be witnessed by other actors not involved in the exchange. Our previous research has suggested that corrections from any of those sources can increase the accuracy of the people witnessing the interaction,[35] and we'll expand upon this research to look across a range of misinformation topics, correction sources, and social media platforms in Chapter 3.

While we have been focusing on the importance of observed correction for social media, observed correction can also happen in offline spaces. If, during a conversation around the coffeemaker at work, a group of colleagues hears one coworker debunking another who says they heard that Jimmy Fallon has died,[36]

Elon Musk ✓
@elonmusk

Twitter drives a massive number of clicks to other websites/apps. Biggest click driver on the Internet by far.

◎ **Readers added context they thought people might want to know**

The reverse is true. Twitter drives 7% of web traffic referrals. Facebook drives 74%. Pinterest drives 7%
datareportal.com/reports/digita...

Do you find this helpful?   Rate it

Context is written by people who use Twitter, and appears when rated helpful by others. Find out more.

7:17 PM · 11/12/22 · Twitter for iPhone

Figure 1.7   Twitter community notes example of observed correction on Twitter.

or in line at the pharmacy, someone hears the pharmacist explaining that the flu shot cannot give you the flu in response to another customer's concerns, this too counts as observed correction. For example, when my (Leticia's) mom got sick at a family reunion, my sister claimed that you can't get strep throat if you've had your tonsils removed (mom has). My sister then looked it up on her phone and announced to the family that this was a myth—while tonsil removal decreases your susceptibility to strep, it doesn't make you immune.[37] In this case, the source of the misinformation and the correction were the same. My (Leticia's) sister said something false, realized it might not be true, and publicly corrected herself. This still counts as observed correction because it meets our three criteria of a direct response to misinformation with accurate information, witnessed by others. As a result, the whole family experienced observed correction, and now know the truth.

Many of the theoretical mechanisms for why observed correction increases accuracy among this secondary viewing audience should also apply offline. However, we expect offline observed correction to be less scalable because there are fewer interactions where corrections can be offered and because the size of the audience is smaller (we just don't tend to interact with very large groups much in an offline setting). Even my family reunion was only 14 people, a number that is easily dwarfed in many social media contexts where hundreds or even many thousands can experience observed correction (for example, with the Musk tweet above).

Importantly, it's worth clarifying that no one can engage in observed correction; they simply correct someone. Correction turns into observed correction when someone is directly responding to misinformation and an audience is added, but no additional content or intent is required on the part of the corrector. This means that sometimes we'll actually be talking about and trying to measure *observed* correction (as we do in Chapters 3, 4, and 5, when we talk about the frequency and effects of seeing these public corrections), but other times we focus on those engaging (or not) in correction (especially in Chapters 6, 7, and 8, where we talk with people about why they do or don't correct others publicly), because without someone engaging in public correction, there can be no observed correction.

In summary, our definition of observed correction requires 1) a direct response to misinformation 2) that provides accurate information and 3) that happens in a public space. This definition may feel overly narrow, but by removing any of the requirements, we would end up with a definition that contains almost all conversations. If we remove the first requirement of direct response, then we can't be sure any given post containing accurate information is targeted at a particular piece of untrue or misleading content. If I (Emily) shared that Minneapolis is expecting over two feet of snow in the next few days (yes, really),[38] it could potentially be corrective if I knew that someone else believed the weather in Minnesota was going to be 40 degrees and sunny. But we can't tell from my post whether I meant it as a correction or not. Indeed, a different user might post the same exact information just wanting to share the information about the potential for a lot of snow, not having anything to do with someone else sharing or believing misinformation. Just like with misinformation, intent is unknowable. Therefore, we classify simply posting accurate information on social media as being outside our definition of correction, even though some of those posts are likely intended as indirect corrections. But to be clear, accurate posts, no matter their intent, are still valuable to the information ecosystem and sometimes produce corrective effects.

If we remove the second requirement—accurate information in response to misinformation—then any conversation happening would qualify, whether the information shared by either party was true or not. For example, if two people are debating whether marijuana should be legal, their responses to each other could contain accurate information, but could also offer opinions or share personal experiences. And without the presence of misinformation (or at least misleading or unverified information), *correction* would not be occurring. This would instead represent a kind of cross-cutting conversation that has its own value[39] but does not implicate *truth* and is not observed correction.

If we remove the third requirement of publicness, we would lose our focus on the secondary audience of those witnessing the correction, which is one of the things that makes observed correction novel and scalable. For example, we (Emily and Leticia) have a private WhatsApp group. With only the two of us, observed correction is not possible, even if we were to correct each other, because there is no audience to witness the correction. In contrast, we also have a WhatsApp group with Emily's husband, creating opportunities for observed correction. So when Leticia was wrong about a flight time in the WhatsApp group, Emily's husband gave the right time, and Emily witnessed the interaction, so everyone knew exactly when the flight took off. Of course, private (one-on-one) corrections can be effective—and sometimes, may work even better by allowing more of an ongoing and responsive conversation to someone holding misperceptions[40] (something we'll hear more about in Chapter 6). But several features of being a *witness* rather than a *participant* in correction make it even more powerful (as we'll discuss in Chapter 2) and by thinking about the potential to correct many witnesses rather than a single person, observed correction is uniquely scalable.

The Potential of Observed Correction

People offer a *lot* of different solutions to address misinformation, including prebunking against common misinformation tactics,[41] increasing media literacy among the public,[42] rebuilding trust in institutions,[43] producing high-quality information,[44] priming people to think about accuracy,[45] offering contextual credibility cues,[46] reducing misinformation supply,[47] and policy or regulation-based approaches.[48]

These are all important solutions. Mitigating misinformation is not a winner-take-all scenario. It requires lots of different tools, techniques, and stakeholders, offering a layered approach of protection[49] to catch misinformation at different stages of its production, dissemination, and impact. Some have referred to this idea of layered protection in other contexts[50] as the "Swiss cheese model": even if a pathogen is able to evade one layer of protection (sneak through a hole in the first layer of Swiss cheese), multiple layers offer additional defense. This model (see Figure 1.8) also applies to misinformation (i.e. the pathogen): we need a Swiss cheese approach that incorporates all of these different solutions to maximize their collective impact.[51] We deliberately place observed correction as the last slice of cheese in this model. Misinformation has always been and will always be a problem—it just means someone was wrong about something.

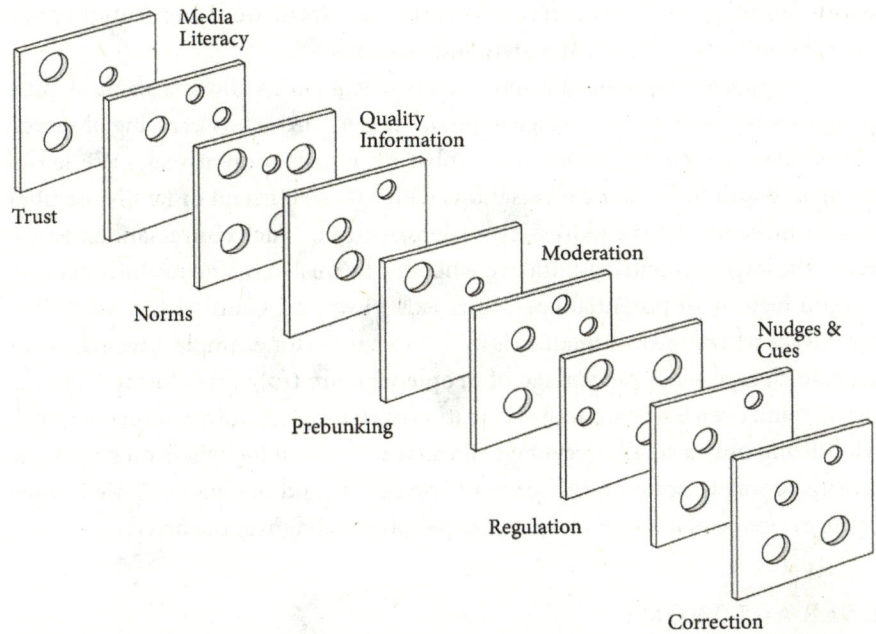

Figure 1.8 The Swiss Cheese approach to misinformation. Credit: Leticia Bode, 2024.

We are all wrong about all sorts of things all the time! So even if we get all the other pieces in place to make misinformation less common, there will always be some that sneaks through—and that's where we need observed correction.

Beyond this reality of the ever-present need for correction, we think observed correction offers several additional advantages as part of the toolbox against misinformation, which we describe next.

EFFECTIVENESS

First and most importantly, observed correction leads the broader community witnessing a correction to become more accurate.[52] Broadly speaking, the academic literature on correction shows it increases accuracy.[53] In Chapters 3 and 4, we'll show that observed correction consistently makes people more accurate, improving accuracy in 22 out of 24 cases.

SCALABILITY

Second, any solution to address misinformation must be able to scale up to the size of the problem, and observed correction has this potential. By one estimate from 2019, 432,000 hours of video are uploaded on YouTube, 60 billion messages are sent on WhatsApp, 95 million pictures are shared on Instagram, 140 million tweets are posted, and 300 million photos are uploaded on Facebook every day,[54] and these numbers have likely continued to grow. Given the enormous scope of content on social media, misinformation interventions must have the ability to be applied widely and broadly.

Leveraging *users* gives us the opportunity to make corrections scalable. If more people using social media engage in public correction—thus enabling observed correction—we are better able to combat misinformation at scale. While ongoing in-depth in-person conversations with a trusted friend or family member may be most effective in addressing misinformation,[55] such conversations do not reach the larger secondary audience who may be misled by the misinformation.

And legions of potential correctors exist. Even on many of the most divisive issues where misinformation is most rampant—for example, vaccination or climate change—the percentage of people who are truly misinformed is quite small,[56] and even fewer are actively creating or sharing misinformation content.[57] Mobilizing only a small percentage of those with accurate beliefs on an issue is a realistic way to scale up the reach of correction, and in Chapter 7 we'll show some evidence of how we can increase people's willingness to correct.

USER AUTONOMY

This scalability argument depends on having a lot of people who are willing to do the work of public correction, something that many people feel conflicted about, as we'll discuss in Chapter 6. Correction is fundamentally a solution that celebrates user autonomy, by which we mean allowing users to make their own decisions and choices, rather than imposing blanket restrictions or mandates on them. This is sometimes called self-determination theory—the idea that autonomy is a psychological need.[58]

We see this as a unique strength of observed correction, in that it places users squarely at the center of the response to misinformation. While platforms can sometimes undermine individual autonomy by design,[59] observed correction allows users to become active agents in mitigating the spread and impact of misinformation, rather than passively responding to contextual cues, nudges, platform affordances, or regulation imposed by others.[60] Observed correction contributes to the marketplace of ideas on social media and allows audiences to decide when and how they want to contribute.

ADAPTABILITY

Finally, it's worth remembering that not all social media platforms are the same, and they're also constantly changing. When we started studying misinformation and correction in 2014, we often thought of the prototypical example of social media as Facebook or Twitter, with a large, semipublic audience that many can see. But social media has changed a lot in the past decade. Solutions that once worked on a particular platform may no longer work as platform affordances, audiences, topics, or tactics change. We can't tell you what the next big social media platform will be (if we could, we probably would use that knowledge to play the stock market), but we do know that it will depend on user-generated content. This may change what public corrections can look like; for instance, the popularity of video-based platforms, especially TikTok, has created new ways (like duets) to directly and publicly correct misinformation. Similarly, we've seen a shift toward end-to-end encryption—meaning that content cannot be viewed by anyone except those directly involved in the conversation, even the platform—which is now an option on WhatsApp, Telegram, Signal, and even Instagram. Therefore, any intervention that requires platforms responding to specific types of content (including our first study on observed correction, which involved using the related stories function on Facebook to debunk misinformation[61]) would not work in these new encrypted environments.

As another example of the changing social media landscape, when we started writing this book in 2020, most social media platforms were actively pursuing a range of policies related to misinformation mitigation (and trust and safety more broadly). Since then, multiple platforms have gutted trust and safety teams in the tech layoffs of almost 300,000 workers in 2022 and 2023,[62] and even reversed some of their previous misinformation mitigation policies. For example, Twitter no longer enforces its COVID-19 policies toward misleading information,[63] and YouTube has stopped removing false information regarding fraud and the US presidential elections.[64] As of spring of 2025, Meta (Facebook, Instagram, and WhatsApp's parent company) abandoned its long partnership with third-party fact checkers, moving instead towards a community notes-style approach to labeling misinformation.[65] Future changes may include a shift toward the metaverse, something in which Meta and other social media companies have heavily invested.[66] Because social media and technology more broadly are so fast-moving, by the time you read this, platform policies, design, and relative popularity will almost certainly have changed. So solutions to misinformation need to be adaptable to constantly evolving social media environments.

Observed correction, which can happen anywhere someone views and chooses to respond to posted misinformation with accurate information, can operate in these often hidden spaces where other efforts can fail. The design choices of the platform matter, including how public content is, and how users are allowed to respond to one another, both of which make observed correction more or less likely, as we'll discuss in Chapters 2 and 4. But all social media designs still fundamentally require user-generated content where one person could (theoretically) correct another and others likely witness it. As platforms increasingly consider ways to protect user privacy and explore yet-unknown changes, solutions that are adaptable to whatever social media looks like in the future will be ever more important. Observed correction is one such solution. Even if platforms become less public and visible, there will still be people who can perform corrections for others to see.

The Key Arguments of the Book

Because observed correction consistently makes people more accurate, offers a scalable response to misinformation, empowers people to be part of the solution, and is adaptable to changing social media platforms, it is a particularly promising approach to mitigating misinformation. After describing the key actors of observed correction—people, professionals, platforms, policymakers, and the press (the 5 Ps)—and developing the theoretical context in which observed correction operates (in Chapter 2), the rest of this book offers evidence in support of five main claims, which we'll briefly outline below.

OBSERVED CORRECTION MAKES PEOPLE MORE ACCURATE

First, Chapter 3 uses experimental data to demonstrate that observed correction works to increase accuracy consistently but modestly for a lot of topics among all sorts of people. When focusing on memorable corrections (discussed in Chapter 4), effects are even stronger. In fact, observed correction leaves people more accurate when they see misinformation followed by correction than if they had seen nothing at all on the topic. And observed correction works for a lot of different social groups—young and old, Democrats and Republicans, and those with more or less formal education. This book offers concrete evidence that observed correction is an effective misinformation mitigation strategy, robust across topics, across platforms, and across individuals.

PEOPLE ARE CONFLICTED CORRECTORS

In Chapter 5, we use survey data to show people have strong perceptions that observed correction is happening on social media and tell us they personally correct other people. These patterns suggest the existence of social norms supporting correction. Our interviews with members of the public about their decision of whether and when to correct misinformation on social media in Chapter 6 reveal that most users are *conflicted correctors*. They see real value in correcting, especially when they think about the potential harm of misinformation, a receptive broader audience for corrections, confidence in their ability to correct, or a sense of duty to respond. At the same time, users express great reluctance to correct others publicly on social media because they are concerned about the effectiveness of such corrections, the risk of damaging personal relationships, the toxic social media environment, and the costs of correction.

RELUCTANCE CAN BE REDUCED

Observed correction is only scalable when a lot of people are willing to do it. In Chapter 7, we address several of the reasons people tell us they are reluctant to correct others on social media. Even short messages telling people key findings of this book—that observed correction improves accuracy and that people tend to like it and to do it—make people say they are more willing to correct misinformation on their social media feeds. Informational campaigns to communicate the effectiveness of correction and bolster the emerging social norms in support of correction can help involve more people in doing correction.

EXPERTS PRIORITIZE SUPPLYING ACCURATE CURATED EVIDENCE

But of course, members of the public are not the only possible correctors. In Chapter 8 we describe what we learned speaking with three kinds of experts: fact-checking journalists, communication professionals at public health organizations, and platform employees focused on trust and safety. Overall, the experts we spoke with were *constrained correctors*. Like users, they worried that corrections would be ineffective and were concerned about toxic responses and harassment, but were further limited by lack of organizational support and a recognition that their limited resources were needed elsewhere. Those few experts who did correct spoke about the wider audience who would see corrections, the harm misinformation can cause, the positive reinforcement they received after correcting, and their sense of duty to improve information environments. But the experts also all agreed that most of their efforts centered on creating the kinds of information that could be used by others in corrections, and sometimes even explicitly encouraging others to correct. In Chapter 9, we elaborate on the importance of experts creating a supply of accessible curated evidence (ACE). Not only is this role one that fact checkers and health professionals are more comfortable with, but members of the public also use ACE to decide what is true and false, to make correction easier, and to make those corrections more convincing.

IT'S PART OF THE SOLUTION

In the final chapter, we return to the larger information ecosystem of which correction is only one part. We consider how each of the 5 Ps operate in a social media system, as well as how correction interacts with other mitigation approaches to offer more thorough protection against misinformation—an updated version of the Swiss cheese model we described in Figure 1.8. We also describe the limitations of observed correction, and offer principles for making observed correction even more effective, through increasing correction volume, visibility, and value.

Finally, at the end of each chapter, we'll offer a TL; DR section, which stands for "too long; didn't read" and is a common way of offering key takeaways in online conversation. Obviously, we think you should read the whole book! But the TL; DR sections should offer the main points of each chapter in a short and easy-to-digest format.

TL; DR

- Observed correction requires three elements: 1) a direct rebuttal to misinformation 2) that is accurate and 3) that is seen by other people.
- Observed correction is effective, scalable, empowers people to be part of the solution, and is adaptable to changing social media platforms.
- Observed correction is part of a multilayer approach—a Swiss cheese model—to misinformation mitigation on social media.

Chapter 2

The Theory of Observed Correction

Observed correction is an important misinformation mitigation strategy because it takes advantage of key features of the broader information system. Correction doesn't happen—nor is it witnessed by others—in isolation, and there are multiple moving pieces in the information environment on social media that facilitate observed correction. In this chapter, we'll spend more time describing 1) the constraints and enablers of correction on social media, 2) the audience for corrections (what turns correction into observed correction), and 3) the ways in which the broader systemic context impacts these interactions. Specifically, policy decisions, media systems, social norms, and platform affordances affect when, how, and whether corrections take place, whether they are seen by others, and how they are perceived by those that do see them. Although most of the data we'll discuss throughout the book come from the United States, this theoretical framework should allow readers to apply these elements to other systems and cultures as well.

The Actors in the System: The 5 Ps

We begin by introducing you to the key actors that operate within this system: the 5 Ps of platforms, policymakers, professionals, the press, and the public (see Figure 2.1).

PLATFORMS

The first P is *platforms.* By this, we're referring to technology platforms that facilitate the transfer of information across networks.[1] For this book, most of the time when we say platforms we'll be thinking specifically about social media

Observed Correction. Leticia Bode and Emily K. Vraga, Oxford University Press.
© Leticia Bode and Emily K. Vraga (2025). DOI: 10.1093/oso/9780197565896.003.0002

Figure 2.1   The 5 Ps of misinformation mitigation. Credit: Dhriti Gupta (2024).

platforms (such as Facebook, Twitter, reddit, YouTube, and TikTok), but they can also include knowledge platforms like search engines (like Google search, which we'll elaborate on more in Chapter 9) and wikis (like Wikipedia). In the baseball example that opened the book, it matters that it occurred on reddit, which explicitly gives users the power to determine what is the "best" comment through upvoting or downvoting. Other social media platforms (like Facebook, Twitter, and TikTok), on the other hand, default to showing comments ranked algorithmically, often without explicitly describing how those rankings work.

Platforms provide a space for users to create content and to interact, but their design choices affect the dynamics of those interactions—a concept we'll discuss in terms of platform affordances below. Additionally, platforms do not just determine the social media landscape where corrections happen, but can also serve as correctors in their own right—for example, if reddit had automatically surfaced a correction to the post, like the related stories function on Facebook[2] or the "community notes" box on Twitter.[3] We'll talk about platforms, and describe nine interviews with current and (mainly) former employees who have worked on misinformation at social media companies, search, and wiki platforms, throughout the book and especially in Chapters 8 and 9. The platforms themselves along with the names of employees we spoke with are masked to protect their privacy, but we'll include each type of platform (search, social media, wiki, or other) parenthetically each time we quote someone. For more information about these interviews, see Table 8.3.

POLICYMAKERS

Second, *policymakers* play a key role in the information ecosystem by deciding the regulatory environment (making the rules) in which all the other actors operate. Depending on the political system, policymakers can look quite different: they may be presidents, legislators, dictators, regulatory agencies, multicountry organizations, or someone else. Their regulatory decisions ripple throughout the information ecosystem, often working indirectly through rules they establish for platforms, professionals, and the press. For example, the current interpretation of Section 230 of the Communication Decency Act (though it was passed in 1996, well before social media even existed) protects social media platforms operating in the US from being sued for allowing harmful content to circulate,[4] but these rules differ in other countries, as we'll discuss more later this chapter in terms of *context*. In the baseball example we opened the book with in Chapter 1, that means reddit does not have to strictly police what content users are posting (for example, misinformation), because they know they're free from liability related to that information. Instead, they can leave it up to the public to determine the "best" content through their votes. Because policymakers decide the types of rules (or lack thereof) that platforms—and all the other actors in this model—are operating under, they affect the dynamics of misinformation and correction within those spaces. Policy can also affect other actors in the system through rules and funding structures, which we'll also describe below in context.

PROFESSIONALS

Professionals are the third category of actor: those who communicate expert knowledge to the public. There are several different ways that can happen. Sometimes, a professional may be someone with expertise on a particular topic who is directly working to explain difficult concepts to the public and correct inaccurate information. This is the role the umpire is playing in our baseball example: they have deep knowledge of the topic and personally communicate that knowledge to the public. But people with direct knowledge may not always be the best communicators; indeed, that's often not a skillset they learn concurrently with their expertise.[5] Because science is best understood as a long-term process of repeated trials, we also have more faith in accumulated (or a lot of) findings pointing in the same direction, rather than any individual scientist's perspective or a single study. As a result, much of the time professionals communicate with the public indirectly through organizations tasked with curating the aggregated knowledge on a topic and then translating sometimes opaque knowledge from experts (like umpires) in a specific domain (baseball rules) to the public. In many cases, these are professional organizations in a particular subfield: for baseball, Major League Baseball itself could put out an explainer regarding confusing rules; in health and science, this includes organizations like the US Centers for Disease Control (CDC), the National Academies of Sciences, Engineering, and Medicine (NASEM), or the global World Health Organization (WHO), all of which represent many scientists and the best available accumulated evidence. We'll hear from professionals in Chapters 8 and 9.

PRESS

Our fourth actor is the *press*. When we say "the press," we are referring to organizations that produce news —or in other words, journalists.[6] In many ways, the press shares many of the goals of professional communicators: they want to convey accurate information about a particular topic to the public.

Several things make the press distinct from other types of professionals, however. First, on average they have greater reach than most professionals. Whereas the majority of people engage with the press on a regular basis—for instance, 60% of people say they often get news on a digital device[7]—this is not the case for most professional organizations. For example, Although it's not a perfect comparison, 33% of social media users report that they follow a page or account focused on science.[8] For example, when learning about COVID-19 rates in my area throughout the pandemic, I (Emily) turned to a local journalist (David Montgomery) for these trends—even when he was often repackaging information from the CDC (a professional organization) that I could have sought out myself. Second, professionals and the press rely on different financial structures to fund their work. In general, professional organizations around science and health are not-for-profit, meaning their goal is not to make money. In contrast, most media in the US must generate a profit, while balancing that imperative with a public service interest.[9] Third, the timeline on which professionals and the press operate are different. The press are required to publish frequently, often daily or even more often. Professional organizations work on a different timeline. While they certainly have internal deadlines to meet, the frequency with which they publish is more flexible and often depends on other campaigns and world events. These features shape the kinds of content that the press and professionals create, even when they are working in the same space.

Despite these differences, professionals and the press are united by a public service orientation and a desire to offer accurate, evidence-based information to the public.[10] Additionally, norms of expert sourcing and the development of journalistic beats (or expertise) means that the press and professionals often work closely together.[11] This might explain why, as we'll see in Chapters 8 and 9, professionals and the press operate very similarly in relation to observed correction, albeit with some notable differences.

While the press overall is important in the information landscape, fact-checking journalists are of particular relevance in this space. Fact-checking journalists' work is explicitly focused on debunking, correcting, or setting the record straight.[12] Essentially, fact checkers focus on creating corrections as journalistic content, so they are more deeply embedded in and focused on monitoring the misinformation landscape. We'll hear more from fact checkers about the role of their work in observed correction in Chapters 8 and 9.

PUBLIC

The final P is *the public,* and here we refer to anyone who is acting in their capacity as a member of a society, rather than any of the roles we describe above. Most of the time, we're thinking of the public as the users of a given social media platform, and we'll discuss their experiences with observed correction throughout the book, including whether observed correction makes people more accurate (Chapter 3), when observed correction is more successful (Chapter 4), public perceptions of how often observed correction occurs (Chapter 5), how willing people are to engage in correction themselves (Chapter 6), and what we can do to motivate more people to say they are willing to correct (Chapter 7). In our baseball example, all the reddit users except for the umpire—including the person who posted the bad information, those who upvoted the umpire's correction, and those who witnessed the exchange—are members of the public. Notably, the public is not solely a passive actor in this system—they may choose to actively engage in correction themselves, or, as in our baseball example, explicitly weight a correction's value to the conversation through their endorsements (like votes, likes, retweets, or reinforcing comments, depending on what is allowed by the platform's design). Many users will choose not to do any of these things, but the point is that they have agency and autonomy to do so.

Notably, the lines between the Ps are blurry, and any given person could be thought of as a different type of actor depending on the context in which they're operating. For example, a virologist correcting someone about how diseases spread would be acting as a professional given their credentials and (presumably) knowledge on the subject, but that same virologist correcting someone about how voting machines operate would be acting as a member of the public. When we spoke with the public about their willingness to correct other people (Chapter 6), they often described being more comfortable correcting misinformation when they felt they had the expertise, either from their job or from their personal experience, to communicate authoritatively—that is, when they felt like a professional. When I (Leticia) was chatting with my friend Teri, a thermal engineer, and she overheard another of our friends sharing incorrect information about temperatures, she left our conversation to correct them, saying, "Someone just said something was colder than absolute zero, I can't let that go." Her professional expertise gave her the confidence and the willingness to correct them.

But the categorization of these actors does not just rely on objective definitions (someone does or does not have credentials in an area) or on self-identification (whether an actor sees themselves as a professional or a member of the public). The audience can also assign these roles to individuals or organizations depending on their own perceptions of their value to the system. Discrimination against women and people of color often hinder their ability to serve as professionals, despite their self-perceived and actual expertise.[13] And individual perceptions of expertise and credibility vary—while most Americans would likely agree that the CDC is a professional organization, Republicans and Democrats increasingly differ in their *trust* toward the CDC: for example, by April of 2022, only 41% of Republicans trusted the CDC to provide information about COVID-19 vaccines compared to 88% of Democrats.[14] The partisan discrepancy in trust in scientists (not just the CDC) has only grown in recent years, and shows no sign of abating.[15] To sum up, who is acting in what role can be thought of as the intersection of three forces: their actual identity or credentials, what role they see themselves as fulfilling in a given situation, and the role that *others* ascribe to them.

Additionally, the presence and prominence of these actors depends on the context in which they're operating (see the following section for more on this). In a country with a trusted news media and a long tradition of fact checking,[16] for example, the role of the press may be particularly important in efforts to correct misinformation. In countries where the press is less reliable, controlled by the state, or otherwise compromised, the public may instead turn to professionals, the government itself, or members of the public for information.[17] We also acknowledge that while we are interested in these actors for their role in misinformation mitigation—and specifically correction—these same actors can also be responsible for misinformation spread. We'll talk more about these contextual differences below.

The Audience for Observed Correction

Having identified these five categories of actors, we turn to thinking about when, whether, and how they interact within a *system* to produce the conditions for observed correction. We'll start by talking about the audience for correction—arguably the most important part of observed correction. Observed correction requires some actor to directly respond to misinformation with accurate information *publicly*, such that someone else can witness it. Whether and how these corrections are observed depends on specific ways that different social media platforms operate.

One way that scholars think about what a platform can do is through its *affordances*. This has been defined in a lot of ways, but generally it describes both what you can actually do on a platform (the technological capabilities) and what you think you can do (the imagined properties).[18] Platform choices around design and architecture affect what behaviors are permitted or encouraged from a structural standpoint,[19] making some spaces more amenable to observed correction than others. But affordances are not just what platforms encourage, facilitate, or even allow—they're also what users (which we use to refer to anyone on the platform, meaning it incorporates all 5 Ps) *think* they can or should do on each platform. If a user doesn't imagine a platform as being a place for correction, for whatever reason, they will not use it in that way, even if corrections are technically possible on the platform. Three commonly recognized affordances of social media that are particularly relevant to observed correction are visibility, persistence, and association.[20]

The *visibility* affordance is just what it sounds like: the ability to see what other people are doing on social media in a way that previously just wasn't possible. Behaviors that are invisible in other spaces (e.g., thinking I enjoyed an article I just read) are made visible on social media (e.g., I "like" this article using a button, and that "like" is shown to others). Critically, the visibility of conversations on social media is something that allows others to witness them, in a way that they usually don't in other media like email, phone, or texts. This visibility is essential for observed correction, since it requires being seen by other people.

While all social media have some degree of visibility, this is something that varies by platform—for instance, some platforms make comments (where corrections often occur) more visible than others. Platforms may hide comments by default (TikTok, YouTube, Instagram), they may prioritize comments from people in your network (Facebook, Twitter), or they may show the "best" comments (reddit, where they typically define best as most upvotes with fewest downvotes).[21] Comments can also differ in terms of their visibility relative to the misinformation: for example, comments that are smaller in size than the original (misinformation) post or that are relegated to the side of the screen are less likely to be noticed by potential audiences, even if they are technically visible (not surprisingly, it turns out this has implications for the success of observed correction, which will be the focus of Chapter 4). And video-based platforms can make it easier (TikTok) or more difficult (YouTube) to join two videos together in a way that facilitates correction (on TikTok these are often called stitches or duets).

Platforms can also alter the visibility of content through their content moderation rules.[22] If a platform judges the veracity of posted content and removes any content that has been deemed untrue, that will decrease both the amount of misinformation and the amount of correction that people see on that platform. Platform choices to curate content they hope will be most relevant to users—that is, how the algorithm decides what to make *visible* to different users[23]—can also affect the types of information that people see, creating different experiences for different people even within the same social media platform—often in a biased way.[24]

A second affordance we've found helpful to think about in the context of correction is that of *persistence*, which just means that content doesn't (generally) disappear when a user isn't actively present on the site. Because of the persistence of content, people can see conversations whenever they log in, even hours or days later. It also means that when misinformation is shared, someone who comes across it later has the opportunity not only to see it, but also to correct it. And once they do correct it, everyone *else* who comes to the conversation afterward can see both posts at the exact same time (this co-occurrence is an important feature of observed correction, as we'll discuss below).

Most but not all social media have the affordance of persistence. For instance, Snapchat deletes content as soon as all group members have opened it[25] and Instagram stories (but not posts or reels) disappear after 24 hours. Facebook Live videos have scrolling comments that appear alongside the video; these comments may be technically persistent but are no longer *visible* without substantial effort on the part of audiences. Downvoted comments on reddit are similarly present but largely invisible unless audiences are actively searching for them. In general, the less persistent content is, the less opportunity there is to correct it and for others to see that correction. But as these examples suggest, persistence and visibility may not be the same across platforms or across content within a platform. As a result, a Facebook Live video or reddit post containing misinformation may remain visible longer than any corrective comments, creating inequalities in which type of content can affect audiences' perceptions.

The third affordance of social media we want to highlight is *association,* which refers to how different elements on the platform are connected to each other. Two types of association matter most for correction: the connections between users, and the connections between pieces of content. The way that users associate with each other forms a network through which content flows, determining how misinformation and correction can happen and spread across a platform. Those networks are often very large and diverse, which enables people to see content they may not choose or seek out on their own.[26] Different platforms form networks in different ways, which affects who can see and respond to misinformation. Likewise, there are differences in how pieces of content are associated on different social media platforms. Most platforms create opportunities to directly link content, for example by commenting (Facebook, reddit, YouTube) or replying (Twitter) to the post, or resharing it in a variety of ways. Altogether, both kinds of connections allow the sharing of *visible* information, misinformation, and correction across networks of people.

Two additional features of social media platforms merit mention. The first is the way in which social media architecture flattens the media landscape.[27] Thus, a post from the *New York Times*—which aspires to quality control through a robust system of verification and a commitment to factual reporting—often looks the same, and takes up the same platform real estate, as a post from a random blog that does not have those same structures, or a post from *The Onion*, a satirical news source that mimics news formatting.[28] Information about the coronavirus from the World Health Organization, a leader in public health, has the same prominence as my (Leticia) acquaintance's ruminations on whether facemasks give you acne (answer: maybe).[29] Scholars have referred to this complicated mix of sources as context collapse.[30] And because social media companies would not exist without facilitating and encouraging the ability of ordinary users to share their own experiences, perspectives, and stories,[31] this is baked into the very architecture of the platforms—it's a feature, not a bug.[32]

This flattened architecture offers both benefits and drawbacks. Information production itself has been democratized, letting more diverse voices enter the conversation.[33] Historically marginalized groups can bypass traditional gate-keepers to enter the public sphere, as seen in the cases of Black Lives Matter,[34] #MeToo,[35] and other social movements.[36] But the information being created is not necessarily accurate, and bad information spreads at least as fast, and perhaps faster, than good information on social media.[37]

The second feature of social media is its inherent *socialness*. By making our interests and habits *visible* through our posts and likes and sharing them with our *associations* (friends, family, and other members of our online communities), social media also reinforce social norms, by which we mean perceptions of the attitudes and behaviors of respected others.[38] Because we are more likely to value and do things we think people around us value (injunctive norms) or do themselves (descriptive norms), norms often lead to related behaviors, including corrections.[39] Indeed, these social norms themselves become affordances—if we see many other people we respect correcting misinformation on our feed, we *imagine* correction is an appropriate use of social media and become more likely to correct ourselves. We'll talk more about the motivating power of social norms for correction in Chapters 5 and 7.

All these elements together may facilitate or hinder observed correction, by impacting whether, when, and how people are likely to see a correction take place on social media. That makes social media particularly interesting and important to study.

Why Correction Works

Different aspects of a correction—including the relationship between the misinformation poster and the corrector, the situation in which the information is shared, and the nature of the corrective information—will affect when, whether, and how that correction takes place, and whether it works when it does. But what do we know about why correction works in general?

Research interest in correction—and not just on social media—has been growing dramatically in the past decade.[40] In general, these studies conclude that correction does increase people's accuracy.[41] These studies do *not* say that correction is a panacea—indeed, while correction can make people's beliefs more accurate, it is much more difficult to change their broader attitudes on a topic or alter their behaviors.[42] So even if my (baseball) team suffered from what I incorrectly thought was a "wrong call," the correction may convince me that the *call* was right without changing my perceptions of the quality of the officiating for that game. For example, providing people accurate information about the number of refugees in the US or the percentage of refugees who rely on welfare made people more accurate about those specific facts, but did not change their support for refugee-friendly policies.[43]

In thinking about how correction leads to belief accuracy, it's useful to think about what motivates people when they consume information on social media. This is complicated, and requires an integrated understanding of cognitive, affective, and social factors that all contribute to information processing and belief formation.[44] To vastly oversimplify, people can be motivated by (at least) two possible goals: an accuracy goal to develop the most accurate beliefs, and a directional goal to use information to support one's existing worldviews and identities.[45]

These two goals sometimes come into conflict. For instance, I (Leticia) live in a neighborhood with bus service but no subway access. The Washington Metro Area Transit Authority's data shows that bus ridership is down since the pandemic, and they're trying to cut bus service to my neighborhood as a result.[46] But because I feel a strong identity with my neighborhood, my directional goal to support that identity (and therefore oppose cuts to bus service) butts up against my accuracy goal to believe the credible data produced by an authoritative organization (if I ignore the data that ridership is down, there's no reason to cut service). More generally, when someone's attitude on a topic becomes strongly associated with their identity, information that undermines that attitude may lead them to engage in motivated reasoning and discredit the information, and a lot of research has focused on this tendency.[47]

But despite the attention to—and the importance of—these directional goals, there are several reasons we should not expect them to dominate how people respond to correction. First, people are "cognitive misers,"[48] reluctant to expend unnecessary effort and willing to reach a satisfactory rather than an optimal decision.[49] Motivated reasoning takes a lot of mental work,[50] so in many cases, it may simply not be worth the effort to defend a specific belief in the face of accurate information. So being a cognitive miser can cut both ways: while many beliefs in misinformation are driven by inattention or laziness,[51] that same lazy thinking may lead people to accept corrections.

Second, often people don't even *have* directional goals to drive their information processing. For many topics, people are neither informed nor misinformed—they just aren't thinking about that topic at all.[52] Without any strong link to a deeply held identity, there is no need for directionally based processing. In these cases, people have no reason to reject high-quality information over lower quality information, so they might as well accept corrections. If the correction about the baseball rule isn't about the Astros I (Leticia – yes, I know they cheated. Identities aren't logical), probably don't care enough to reject it (and Emily doesn't care about baseball at all, so she would likely be willing to accept any baseball-related correction). In those cases, directional goals are just not salient.

Third, even when people *are* driven by directional goals, they do not entirely overwhelm accuracy motivations. They still want to maintain an "illusion of objectivity" to justify their conclusions,[53] and even motivated reasoning has a tipping point when someone can no longer resist incoming information without changing their mind.[54] This can explain why encouraging people to be critical thinkers, to act like a fact checker, or even just to think about accuracy can reduce belief in and sharing of misinformation.[55] A correction could create some of these same pressures, encouraging people to slow down and motivating them to consider the accuracy of the information before allowing it to inform their beliefs—or, if they are behaving as critical thinkers, to accept the correction and reject the misinformation.

Why Observed Correction Works

The distinction between accuracy and directional motivations is useful in thinking about why corrections in general might lead people to become more accurate. But observed correction is more specific than correction, so what are some of the unique features that make observed correction on social media powerful?

First, the experience of observed correction is passive and incidental. People witnessing others corrected on social media are not seeking out that experience; they are probably on social media to learn what is happening with friends and family or to watch cute turtle videos (or is that just me?). This incidental experience has two main benefits: it broadens the number of people who can see correction (because it can happen to anyone, not just people actively looking for it), and it makes people more receptive to such corrections when they see them.

On the first point, we know relatively few people deliberately consume information from fact-checking organizations or health experts.[56] For instance, in 2021, only 44% in the United States, 31% in Canada, 27% in the United Kingdom, and 21% of people in France said they visited the website or social media page of a fact-checking organization at least rarely.[57] This problem of limited audience is something the fact checkers we spoke with were quite aware of and are actively trying to improve (see Chapters 8–9). But even though many people are not getting information directly from the source, they can still see that content if other people in their network use this information in their corrections. Of course this is still not a perfect system, as research suggests that networks can and do still share fact checks in biased or partisan ways.[58]

On the second point, attention is directed toward *social* experiences online—that is, we use social media for social purposes.[59] It's right there in the name! Remember, humans are lazy and try to minimize the effort we spend on things we don't care that much about. This means on social media our attention is therefore drawn toward social and entertainment content and we aren't as quick to activate the directional goals that cause motivated reasoning. In other words, when people encounter news incidentally on social media, in the midst of cat videos and baby pictures, it reduces barriers that would interfere with acceptance of such information.[60] This should be true for corrections as well. Because observed correction happens when people are not prepared for mental battle, the path of least resistance may be to just accept the correction and keep scrolling, making such corrections more effective.

A second element unique to observed correction is that when someone observes it, exposure to both the correction and the misinformation are occurring at the same point in time. Research suggests that misinformation has a "continued influence effect"—that is, it can continue to affect beliefs even after being corrected—in part because the misinformation is encoded first in memory and thus is easier to retrieve.[61] But coactivation—or directly linking misinformation and correction—makes correction more effective.[62] The affordances of social media (can) do exactly that, explicitly linking corrections as direct rebuttals to misinformation, reducing the inherent advantage for the misinformation and making corrections more effective. Obviously some people will still see misinformation before it is corrected, but once the correction happens, it should be explicitly linked to the misinformation.

Third, observed correction makes the potential reputational cost of sharing misinformation visible. Research shows that sharing misinformation can hurt one's reputation,[63] and the fear of such reputational cost can inhibit sharing false information.[64] As we'll describe in Chapter 6, people also perceive a social cost to offering a correction on social media, but are more likely to correct when they feel certain on the topic. So when they do correct, they are communicating not just their own confidence in the accurate information, but also creating or reinforcing social norms around what the community believes and values—both in terms of the content itself (what is true and what is false) as well as the behavior (correction and truth are valued, see more on this in Chapter 5). Putting a visible cost on misinformation sharing (and implicitly, misinformation belief) should encourage bystanders to adjust their attitudes to avoid having to face any such penalty in the future.

Fourth, observed correction can come in a variety of forms and formats that (ideally) can be tailored toward the intended audience and the specific manifestation of a misinformation claim. Would-be correctors can and should consider the kinds of correction that will be most effective, especially thinking about the broader secondary audience who witnesses the correction. In some cases, this may mean offering a factual correction, describing the best available evidence on the topic.[65] In others, it could be describing the logical fallacies of the misinformation and how it misleads people.[66] Another approach would be to offer a personal narrative that serves as a rebuttal to the misinformation; such personal narratives can be quite convincing,[67] especially when they tap into the identities that misinformation preys on.[68]

Additionally, observed correction can (but does not always) come from personal connections, and they may carry a level of trust that other sources do not. Such trust makes corrections more effective, even more so than expertise.[69] In one example of direct public corrections on Twitter, corrections that came from friends were accepted roughly 79% of the time, whereas corrections from strangers were only accepted 39% of the time.[70] Finally, when social support bolsters the correction—either through additional comments reinforcing the correction or through likes or favorites—it can speak to social norms in favor of the correction, rather than the misinformation, although there is mixed evidence about whether such endorsements make corrections more effective.[71]

The Context for Observed Correction

Lots of things will affect how likely correction is to occur, what it looks like, and how persuasive it is. But all of these things are contingent on the context, including the broader built environment,[72] in which corrections occur. Context can manifest in lots of different ways, but we'll highlight a few aspects that we think are key for understanding how and when observed correction happens and the extent to which it's effective. Context is determined by the same actors we've already discussed—platforms, policymakers, professionals, the press, and the public. Considering the broader context in which correction happens may also be useful for thinking about when, whether, and how corrections happen in the contexts outside the one our data focus on (health and political correction in the US).

The first layer of context comes from the social media *platforms* on which observed correction can occur. As we described above, platforms have different affordances and make different choices about their design and rules. These choices inform the context in which correction may or may not happen and may or may not be seen on any given social media platform. Platform rules reflect decisions on what information is allowed in the first place—often described as "community guidelines" or "terms of service" more broadly—and what actions are taken if those standards are violated.[73] But they also include choices that may not seem directly related to misinformation on their face. For instance, platform policies about hate speech can affect the fears people have about engaging in correction (see Chapter 6)—if you know people can harass you without the platform restricting or punishing them, you may be less likely to engage in any behavior that feels like it may provoke that kind of harassment, like correction. Platforms that allow anonymity may empower people to correct, whereas those that require real names may add to the perception that engaging with others could result in real personal harm.[74] On the other hand, anonymity can lead to a toxic disinhibition effect, where people are more willing to engage in hate and abuse because they feel protected hiding behind their anonymous screenname.[75] Platforms also make choices about their design, including choices about color, size, placement, and interactivity, as well as the affordances we've already discussed, like how visible, persistent, and connected the content is. All of those choices can combine in unique ways to affect the prevalence, type, and nature of corrections, as well as how they are perceived by users.

These affordances may not just differ across platforms but also across countries. The *policy* context can determine which platforms operate at all in a particular place, like when China banned access to Facebook, Instagram, Twitter, Google, and other platforms for its citizens,[76] or when the US "banned" TikTok.[77] It can place constraints on platforms through regulations—for example, regulations in the European Union and Australia (but not the United States) require removal of dangerous or abusive content,[78] and require certain types of information disclosure from platforms.[79] And policy can create rules about how misinformation is treated in general, and on social media specifically.

A society's political, media, and economic systems will play a similar role in setting the stage for misinformation and correction. Edda Humprecht and her colleagues proposed a model that suggests disinformation resilience around the world depends on elements of the political context (polarization, populist communication), media system (trust in news, public service media, audience fragmentation), and economic environment (ad revenue, social media use).[80] As a result, they argue that media-supportive and consensual societies like many European democracies and Canada are likely to have more disinformation resilience, whereas low-trust, polarized, and fragmented societies like the US are most susceptible to disinformation. Similarly, the expectations around speech, as defined by the political, legal, and media systems will determine to what extent people are allowed or willing to speak up, and on what issues.[81] As just one example, some countries have tons of fact-checking organizations—the United States has 78, for instance, and India has 27—whereas others—like Algeria, Vietnam, and Iceland—have zero.[82] Similarly, an authoritarian country with state-controlled media will have a different supply of and trust in information compared to a democratic country with privately controlled media outlets.[83]

These features not only affect the existence of reliable information in each country, but also the general sense that the society cares about facts over other motivations.

This also extends to investing resources in public health and other civic institutions that can affect public knowledge, attitudes, and resilience. For instance, in the Netherlands, 71.4% of people have "adequate" or "excellent" general health literacy (i.e., people's ability to use health information to make good decisions), as compared to 41.7% of people in Spain.[84] How official health information is produced, vetted, and communicated, and especially how people *perceive* the quality of that information will also affect how the public makes sense of the information they encounter on social media. For instance, while 97% of people in Australia and New Zealand trust medical advice from medical workers, only 57% of people in Cameroon, Chad, Republic of the Congo, and Gabon do.[85] That culture of trust or distrust is often rooted in years of experiences with the health authorities in those contexts, making differences in trust both totally understandable and also difficult to change quickly.[86] This context of health literacy and trust in health institutions is key to understanding whether, when, and how corrections happen, and how they are perceived when they do.

Major world, national, and local events also matter in thinking about context.[87] Perhaps most notably for the purposes of this book, COVID-19 emerged as a global pandemic shortly after we started writing it in 2020. As of spring 2025, at least 775,000,000 people have been infected around the world, and tragically over 7,000,000 have lost their lives.[88] This context necessarily informs the book, as well as the conclusions we draw throughout. While much (but not all) of our experimental data collection took place before COVID-19 emerged, our survey and interview data were entirely collected after the pandemic began in 2020. The participants' lived experiences that are reflected in those data were very strongly colored by the context of the pandemic, although of course even collective events like the pandemic are experienced in very different ways.

Finally, this context also includes the ways in which an individual's identity shapes the ways in which they can and cannot participate in the information system. Part of this impact comes from personal experiences that are unique to each person, and color the way we think about things. But it is also important to note how specific racial and gender identities play a role. Disinformation campaigns sometimes target women and racial minorities in the US,[89] and recommendation systems that are key to surfacing information and misinformation also treat these groups differently.[90] These groups also face additional barriers in their ability to be correctors, not least among them the continued oppression of structural racism.[91] And they've often been ignored or left out of social science research.[92] Given all this history, they are likely to interpret information and expertise—and misinformation and correction—in different ways as well.

It's also worth noting that, temporally, we live in a unique time, when information is truly abundant in a way it never has been before. Indeed, for many people around the globe, the entirety of knowledge is contained in a device they keep in their pocket. Of course information is not the only element needed, given that knowledge resistance is multifaceted and widespread,[93] but it highlights the importance of information quality, not just quantity.

All of these contexts interact to produce complicated circumstances in which observed correction may happen. This book, focused on a single context, will necessarily represent only a tiny slice of what observed correction might look like in the world.

Conclusion

The modern information ecosystem is complicated, and observed correction constitutes only a small part of the communication that happens within that system. Understanding the key actors that operate in this space as well as how they interact and under what circumstances will provide useful context for understanding how we think about observed correction throughout the rest of the book. This better understanding of the actors and the broader system will help us clarify when and how observed correction happens and why it makes people more accurate.

TL; DR

- Five types of actors—the public, platforms, policymakers, the press, and professionals—shape the context in which observed correction occurs.
- Observed correction works because it is indirect, occurs incidentally, highlights the social costs of sharing misinformation, and happens at the same time as misinformation exposure.
- Observed correction happens within broader contexts, which meaningfully affect whether, when, and how correction occurs.

Chapter 3

Observed Correction Increases Accuracy

Having established why and how observed correction should work in Chapter 2, we turn to the empirical evidence supporting observed correction. That is, does observed correction make people more accurate? The short answer is yes. Using a series of experimental tests, we demonstrate that observed correction consistently and modestly increases accuracy among the community witnessing that correction across a range of health topics, sources of correction, and social media platforms. We also find that the effectiveness of observed correction does not noticeably differ across many individual characteristics, including age, education, and political orientations. As such, observed correction is a robust approach to increasing accuracy, applicable for different kinds of people across a broad range of contexts.

Answering This Question

Most of our work over the past decade has been dedicated to answering the question of whether and under what conditions observed correction is most effective. In this chapter, we analyze data from eight experiments we conducted between 2014 and 2020 related to the effectiveness of observed correction. Each experiment contains observed correction: someone directly responding to misinformation with accurate information and doing so where others can see it. In every case the misinformation clearly contradicts the expert consensus on the topic.[1] We vary the features of observed correction both across and within each experiment, including what the misinformation is about, on what platform the correction occurs, and the source, tone, or number of corrections. Because each of these correction features may impact the effectiveness of the correction, we'll test each individual correction—24 experimental comparisons across those

Observed Correction. Leticia Bode and Emily K. Vraga, Oxford University Press.
© Leticia Bode and Emily K. Vraga (2025). DOI: 10.1093/oso/9780197565896.003.0003

eight data collections—separately. We briefly describe each experiment and its conditions in Table 3.1, but you can learn more about each in detail in our online appendix. Four of these experiments were collected with our excellent coauthor, Melissa Tully of the University of Iowa.[2]

The protocol is similar across the experiments. People are invited to participate in an online survey, where they answer some questions before they are asked to scroll through a simulated social media feed as if it were their own (see Figure 3.1 for an example).[3] Most of the posts on the feed are on innocuous topics, but our experimental conditions included a single post (usually as the second or third post) where someone shares misinformation (point 1 in Figure 3.1), and then some person or organization directly replies to them sharing corrective information (point 2 in Figure 3.1). This is observed correction because the participant in the experiment sees the interaction without being an active participant (they are neither the person who posted the misinformation nor the person who engaged in correction), and the same would be true of any people who came across this exchange on their social media feed in the real world. The control condition is identical except without any mention of the misinformation topic(s) we are interested in. After viewing the simulated feed and answering questions about their experience, participants are debriefed about the purposes of the experiment. As part of these debriefings, we always carefully explained the nature of the misinformation and the scientific consensus regarding the topic to reinforce accurate information for all participants.[4]

To illustrate, we'll show you an experiment that used this approach. In Figure 3.1, you see a simulated Twitter feed.[5] On the feed, there are several posts that do not relate to the topic of the experiment (in this case, the safety of GMO foods) but mimic the experience of social media, where a range of posts compete for our attention. Having these posts offers two advantages. First, it makes the experiment feel more like a real social media feed, hopefully encouraging people to process the information like they would if they were really on social media (rather than viewing the posts as part of an experiment). Second, we also hope to make the post we are most interested in—the GMO misinformation—blend in, so people are less likely to figure out what we're trying to test. In this example, the misinformation comes from a Twitter user named Tyler[6] sharing a meme claiming that scientists know GMO foods aren't safe to eat, labeled with "1" in the figure. We show the Pew Research Center—a (real) nonpartisan think tank that collects and shares public opinion data—directly and publicly responds to Tyler with a correction (labeled with "2"), offering evidence from their (actual) survey that 88% of scientists say GMO foods are safe to eat.[7] Pew's post includes a figure and a link to their website to visualize and reinforce their point: the scientific consensus is that GMOs are safe. In the other correction conditions, we varied the number of "likes" for Pew's correction or added a second

Table 3.1 **Brief Description of Experiments**

Topic	Misinformation Claim	Year	Platform(s)	Corrections
Zika	Zika is caused by GMO mosquitoes	2016 (Spring)	Facebook, Twitter	1) Two users on Twitter, no sources
				2) Two users on Twitter, links to expert sources
				3) Two users on Facebook, no sources
				4) Two users on Facebook, links to expert sources
				5) Two related stories on Facebook
Zika	Zika is caused by GMO mosquitoes	2016 (Fall)	Twitter	1) Single user, discredit language
				2) Single user, consensus language
				3) Single expert, discredit language
				4) Single expert, consensus language
				5) User discredit + expert consensus
				6) User consensus + expert discredit
				7) Expert discredit + user consensus
				8) Expert consensus + user discredit
Fluoride	Fluoride in drinking water reduces IQ	2017–2018	Facebook	1) Two users with links

Continued

Table 3.1 Continued

Topic	Misinformation Claim	Year	Platform(s)	Corrections
GMO	Scientists know GMO foods are unsafe to eat	2017–2018	Twitter	1) Expert correction, low engagement 2) Expert correction, high engagement 3) User + expert correction
Flu	The flu vaccine causes the flu	2018	Twitter	1) Expert correction
Raw milk	Raw milk is more nutritious than pasteurized milk	2018	Twitter	1) Two users use factual language with links 2) Two users use affirmative language with links 3) Two users use uncivil language with links
Sunscreen	Sunscreen use causes cancer, damages DNA	2019	Facebook Live	1) Two users with links
COVID-19	COVID-19 can be prevented by a hot bath	2020	Facebook	1) Expert bot with graphic 2) User with same graphic

Notes: Please see our online appendix (https://bode.vraga.org/) for additional information regarding each study, including sample size and population, precise wording for the misinformation claim, and accuracy measures.

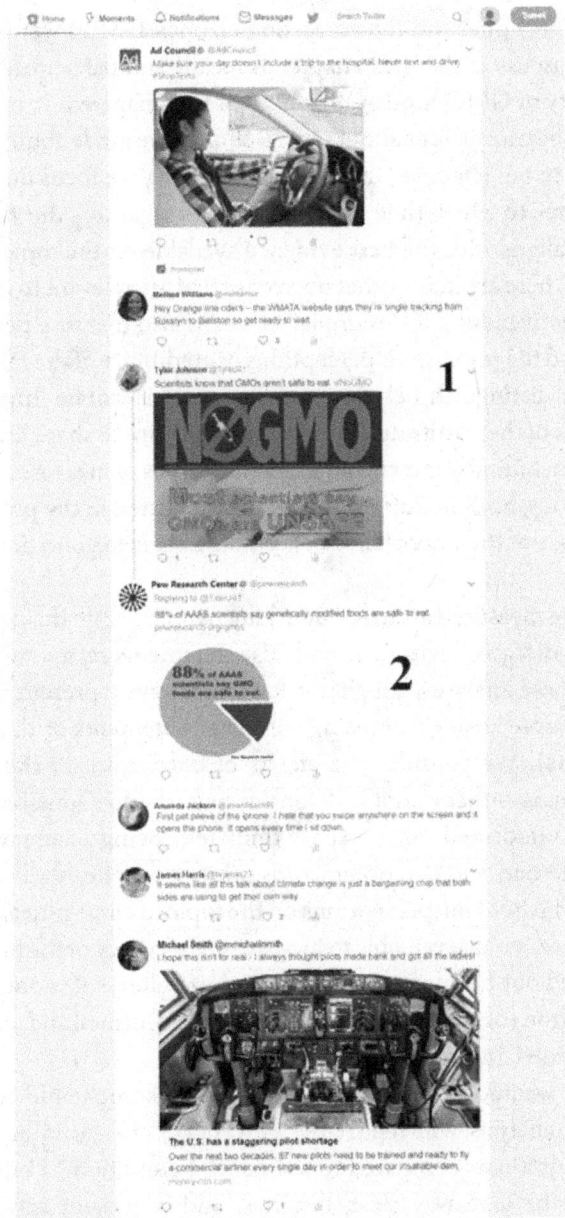

Figure 3.1   An example of an experimental feed on Twitter. Credit: Leticia Bode, 2024.

correction from another social media user (named Drew). In the control condition, participants saw the same non–GMO posts, but the post about GMO foods was replaced with a news article about a noncontroversial science-related story (about planets), with no misinformation attached. After reading the simulated feed, we asked people about their experiences. Questions included whether the original GMO post and the correction claimed GMOs were safe or unsafe (which we'll discuss in the next chapter as recall) and participants' own beliefs about the safety of GMO foods—the focus of this chapter.

We want to be transparent about several choices we made about what it means for correction to be "effective" in these studies. First, we focus on people's *accuracy*—the degree to which their expressed beliefs regarding the misinformation being studied aligns with the best evidence available on the topic (i.e., accurate information). There are many other outcomes that are relevant to the question of correction effectiveness—for example, we could also measure people's broader attitudes toward the topic, their perceptions of credibility of the misinformation, their ability to distinguish between accurate and inaccurate information, how certain they are of their attitudes, or how likely they are to share the information. Lots of work, including our own, has used these types of measures. We choose to focus on accuracy, both because it is directly implicated in the process of *correction*, and because of the importance of accurate beliefs to good decision-making and to society.

Typically, we measured accuracy by asking people to rate the degree to which they agreed or disagreed with true and false statements related to the misinformation.[8] For these analyses, a higher value will always represent more accurate attitudes (i.e., more strongly agreeing with true statements or disagreeing with false statements). We consider the effects of correction on the full range of possible responses—that is, not just considering whether someone "flips" from misinformed to informed—because we think improving accuracy is important no matter where one starts. In other words, while it may be especially important to help those who hold misperceptions on the topic to come into alignment with the best evidence, it's also valuable to increase the accuracy of the beliefs of someone who started out believing the true thing but believes it more strongly after seeing a correction (or someone who starts out misinformed and after correction is still misinformed, but less so).

Second, we wanted changes in accuracy to be comparable across studies. Therefore, our analysis will report the percentage change in accuracy in the correction condition as compared to the control condition.[9] Using percentage change makes the takeaway clear, intuitive, and consistent across the different ways we measured accuracy—for example, on five-point versus seven-point scales. Additionally, focusing on percentage change helps us account for the fact that some beliefs are easier to adjust than others. For example, when not that many people believe the misinformation to start with, there is less opportunity to make people more accurate. This is the case with misperceptions regarding the link between the MMR (measles, mumps, and rubella) vaccine and autism. While this is an enduring topic that is the focus of a lot of academic research[10] and of course has huge practical implications, relatively few people are vaccine hesitant and most people know that the MMR vaccine does not cause autism,[11] so there's a limit to how much we can improve accuracy. Statisticians sometimes call this a ceiling effect, because you cannot move attitudes (or in this case accuracy) any higher than they already are. But when accuracy is low, there is much more opportunity to change someone's mind when seeing a correction—and indeed, we'll see some of those differences by topic play out in our analyses below.

Finally, we had to decide what the relevant comparison would be—that is, observed correction is effective compared to *what*? We define a successful correction as one that increases accuracy as compared to a control condition where people see no information (neither the misinformation nor the correction) on the topic at all.[12] We can think of that control condition, where people see no relevant information, as essentially capturing baseline public accuracy on the topic. Therefore, our results represent whether people are more accurate after seeing *both* misinformation and correction as compared to seeing nothing on the topic. We examine all 24 experimental conditions we've tested since 2014 (when we began this research) that meet these three requirements: they 1) examine observed correction, 2) measure post-test accuracy, and 3) include the relevant control condition.

Observed Correction Increases Accuracy

The results of our analysis across these 24 experimental comparisons are convincing: observed correction is broadly effective across a range of topics, platforms, and correction types. In Figure 3.2 we represent these findings: each black diamond represents our best estimate of the change in accuracy between the control and correction conditions, with estimates to the right indicating improved accuracy. The dashed horizontal lines provide the confidence interval (range of likely values) for each estimate. The further the diamond is from the dotted vertical line, the stronger the effect is, but when the dashed horizontal lines cross the vertical line, we cannot be confident that there is a meaningful (i.e., statistically significant) change in accuracy for that specific correction.

We see descriptive increases in accuracy in 22 of the 24 experimental comparisons, with a median[13] increase of accuracy of 4.1% across all comparisons. This may seem like a relatively modest effect, but it can be quite meaningful.[14] For example, if my temperature is 4% higher than usual, I would be running a fever of 102.5 degrees Fahrenheit—certainly enough to make me feel quite lousy. We also consider this a lower bound of the effectiveness of observed correction. In Chapter 4, we'll show that once we account for whether or not people recall what the correction said, the adjusted effect is substantially larger, producing almost a 12% median increase in accuracy.

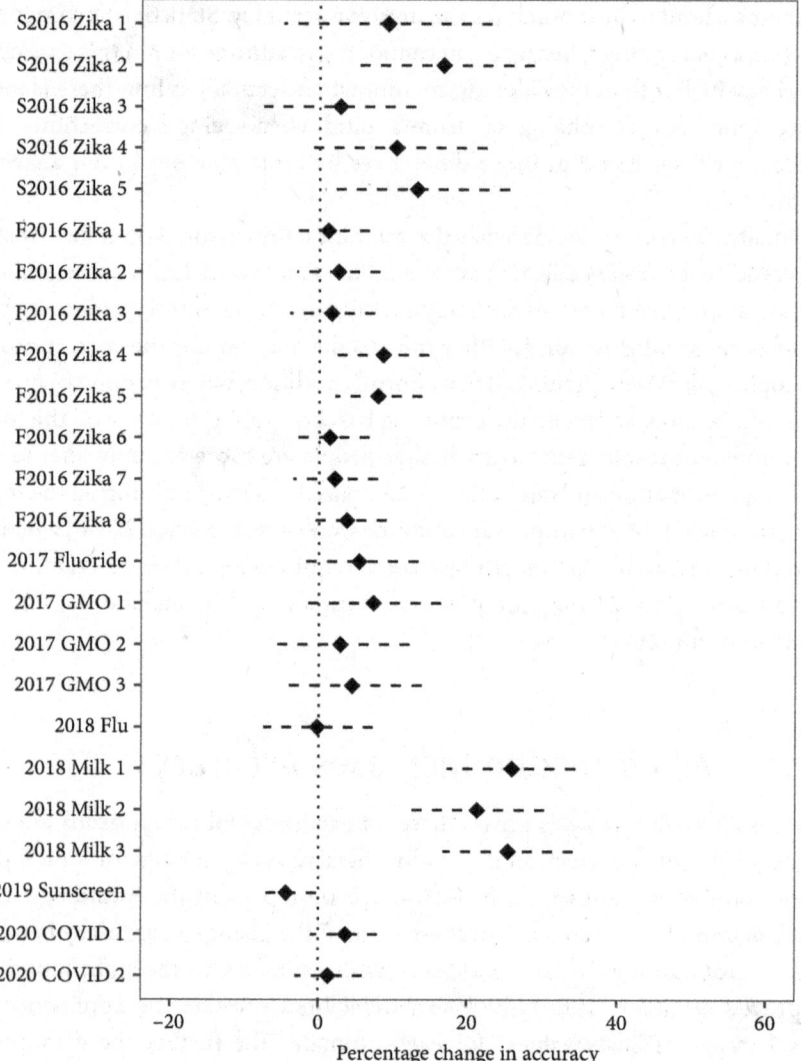

Figure 3.2   Changes in accuracy across experimental conditions. *Notes:* We list the different studies by year, topic, and correction number (reflecting which condition it is) on the y-axis (please see Table 3.1 for more information about each study, and the data are included in our online appendix). The x-axis represents the percentage change in accuracy between each correction and the control condition. Results to the right of the vertical dotted line represent increased accuracy and those to the left represent decreased accuracy. The diamonds represent the average percentage change, and the horizontal dashed line represents the 95% confidence interval for this difference. Values further from the vertical dotted line indicate stronger effects. When the confidence interval crosses the vertical dotted line, the relationship is not statistically significant.

However, in many of these cases the confidence intervals (the dashed horizontal lines) cross the "0" point on the scale (indicated by the vertical dotted line), meaning we cannot be confident that these are real effects. To demonstrate not only the consistency of our results across studies (22 out of 24 is pretty consistent!) but our confidence that these effects are real, we analyze the trend of our studies through a small-scale meta-analysis (sometimes called a "mini meta"). A meta-analysis tests the effects of an intervention across multiple studies, to ensure that the results are significant and to give a more precise estimate of the size of the effect by taking into account the idiosyncrasies of each study.[15] When we apply this approach to our eight studies,[16] the results $(d=.15)$ confirm that observed correction produces a statistically significant positive impact on accuracy.[17]

Reflecting on when observed correction works particularly well, one study stands out: the correction of misinformation regarding raw milk's nutritional value. Each of the three corrections in this study comes from two social media users linking to expert sources (the difference between the three is the tone of their corrections), and each increases accuracy by 20%–25%. We suspect these larger effects are due to several elements. First, only 34% of participants hold accurate beliefs[18] about the nutritional value of raw milk in the control condition, offering substantial opportunity to improve accuracy. Put simply, people don't know that much about raw milk. For comparison, the percentage of people holding accurate beliefs in the control condition was 86% for our sunscreen study, 67% for our COVID-19 study, and 44% in our fluoride study. Research shows that correction tends to work best where fewer people are starting off accurate,[19] which is why we and many others advocate for responding quickly when misinformation begins to spread.[20] Second, while misinformation surrounding raw milk may not be new, it is also a topic on which people are unlikely to have strong feelings or resistance to correction. With the possible exception of dairy farmers, your thoughts about raw milk are less likely to be related to salient aspects of your identity like your partisanship,[21] your general worldview, or your core values, and therefore the personal costs of accepting a correction are low. Topics—like raw milk—where people hold inaccurate beliefs but also don't feel strongly about the topic are likely especially amenable to correction.

Although raw milk looks like an outlier in our data, we do not think that these large effects are rare. While discourse about misinformation and related interventions often focuses on socially divisive issues like vaccination, infectious diseases, elections, or smoking,[22] a lot of misinformation being shared on social media is on topics people don't know or care much about. For instance, out of the top 10 untrue articles with the most Facebook engagement in 2017, only two ("President Trump Orders the Execution of Five Turkeys Pardoned by Obama" and "Female Legislators Unveil 'Male Ejaculation Bill' Forbidding the Disposal of Unused Semen") were remotely political in nature, and those on health topics all involved genitals, rather than core public health topics like GMOs or vaccination (e.g., "Babysitter Transported to Hospital After Inserting a Baby Into her Vagina," "FBI Seizes Over 3.000 Penises During Raid at Morgue Employee's Home").[23] In our own work, observed correction appears to perform best for those topics where attitudes were unlikely to be set in stone: when the Zika pandemic was first unfolding in spring of 2016 (when only 23% held accurate attitudes in the control condition) and the ongoing but low-level controversy surrounding the nutritional value of raw milk. As such, corrections to circulating misinformation may be especially important—and best targeted—in these understudied spaces, where the public may be more willing to listen.

Beyond topic, our analyses suggest that increases in accuracy occur across several platforms and sources. Looking first at platform, only in one study did we explicitly compare the exact same misinformation and user correction on two platforms—Facebook and Twitter. In that study, we found no substantial differences in the effectiveness of peer correction in increasing accuracy. When looking across a range of studies, we find further evidence for this idea: observed correction produces a median increase of accuracy of 4.5% on both Facebook and Twitter. Although we've only done enough studies on Twitter and Facebook to analyze these differences, initial evidence suggests observed correction functions similarly on a variety of other platforms, including Instagram,[24] Facebook Live,[25] WhatsApp,[26] and TikTok.[27]

We argued in Chapter 2 that corrections could hypothetically come from a wide variety of actors—including the press, a platform, a professional, or members of the public (i.e., users). But we are especially interested in user corrections[28] because observed correction becomes most scalable when we can get a lot of people engaged in the practices, and most corrections do come from members of the public, not professionals.[29] Our analyses suggest that user corrections produced a median increase in accuracy of 7.3%, confirming their value.[30]

While we've so far highlighted the cases where observed correction is particularly good at increasing accuracy, it's also instructive to dig into the cases where observed correction *doesn't* work well. This is most noticeable for the topic of sunscreen misinformation, where we see a 4.4% *decrease* in accuracy as compared to the control where people did not see any misinformation on the topic of sunscreens. However, this study shared video misinformation from a purported professional on the topic (i.e., a doctor), and we know that this tactic of "fake experts" is an effective (and common) disinformation tactic.[31] This persuasive misinformation is combined with corrections from two users in the form of scrolling "live" comments alongside this video (see Figure 3.3). While these users follow best practices with multiple people responding to the misinformation and providing links to expert health organizations, the relative brevity of their comments as compared to the video misinformation, the less persuasive medium of text as compared to video,[32] and the less visible relegation of the comments to the side of the screen, where attention is not generally directed[33] — which we'll discuss more in the next chapter—likely all reduced their effectiveness.

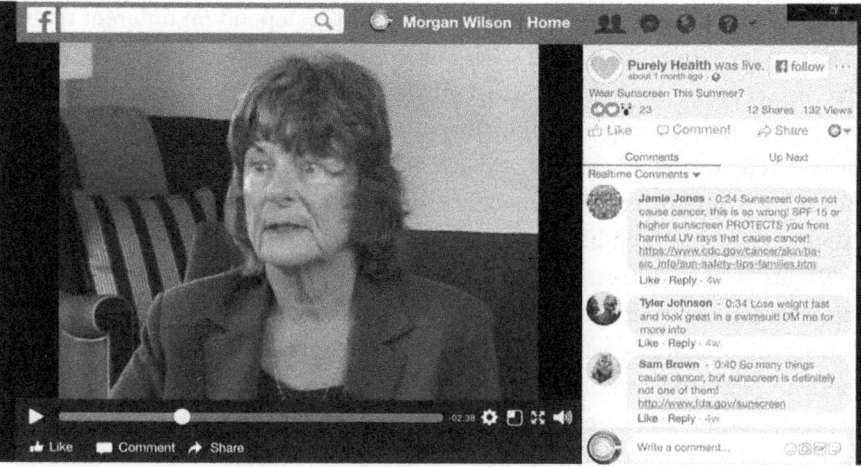

Figure 3.3   Observed correction on Facebook Live.

Moreover, our existing research found that the video misinformation proved quite persuasive in this case and the corrections partially (but not completely) restored attitudes to their baseline.[34] Where misinformation is especially persuasive, corrections face a more difficult task in not just *restoring* accuracy but *improving* it.

The second case where observed correction has no effect is a single correction from the American Medical Association (AMA) in response to a tweet falsely claiming that the flu shot causes the flu. We see several possible explanations for this. Perhaps people did not recognize or trust the AMA as an expert organization providing the correction, and so were less persuaded by it. Another possibility is the relatively entrenched nature of the misinformation—the myth that a flu shot can cause the flu is well-established,[35] and we (and others) have found vaccination myths more difficult to correct.[36] It's also worth noting that our previous research on this topic shows that observed correction was effective in making those who initially held more inaccurate beliefs more accurate (i.e., believed the flu shot causes the flu)[37] — it just didn't have that effect for everyone, which is what we examined here.

Individual Differences in Observed Correction Effectiveness

Our previous analysis suggests that observed correction works to increase accuracy for the general community for a range of health topics, platforms, and sources. The next step is to ensure that observed correction increases accuracy across many groups in society. We know that people tend to be embedded in different information environments, where they may be exposed to more or less misinformation and correction.[38] Likewise, people depend on different trusted sources—so a correction from what one group deems a highly credible expert may be seen as a biased or untrustworthy agent by another group.[39] As one example, think about party affiliation in the US: Republicans tend to report lower levels of trust in science and scientists,[40] health experts,[41] and the news media.[42] As our corrections generally rely on expert sources and scientific data (often seen as less credible among Republicans) to refute misinformation, Republicans may therefore be less accepting of the correction.[43] Therefore, we explore whether observed correction increases accuracy equally for six different individual characteristics that we measured across studies: age,[44] education,[45] gender,[46] race,[47] party affiliation,[48] and partisan strength.[49]

Ideally, observed correction will make everyone more accurate, and we may have reason to believe that's the case—increasingly research suggests that treatment effects in the social sciences tend to be felt across the board: in other words, everyone is impacted by experiments roughly equally.[50] But even if observed correction only works for some people—for example, younger adults or men—we could still think about ways to strategically target the groups for whom observed correction is most effective. In either case, knowing for whom observed correction works is important for maximizing its effectiveness.

Observed Correction Makes Everyone More Accurate

Looking at the same 24 experimental comparisons, we explore whether correction is equally effective in increasing accuracy (as compared to the same pure control group we considered above) depending on each of these individual characteristics. We present these results in Figure 3.4, which represents the relationship between each of the independent variables (on the y-axis) and the outcome (in this case, changes in accuracy compared to the control) averaged across the 24 correction types from Table 3.1.[51] Like Figure 3.2, we cannot be confident the relationship is meaningful when the confidence interval (horizontal lines) crosses the dotted vertical line.

These results provide little evidence of systematic differences in how various groups respond to correction. Specifically, when looking at the average effect of the interaction between each characteristic and exposure to correction across the (up to)[52] 24 experimental conditions, each of the estimates is close to zero and the confidence intervals always include "0," which means that none of the characteristics or attributes we measured consistently affect how people receive corrections (see the supplemental appendix for more information on these analyses).[53]

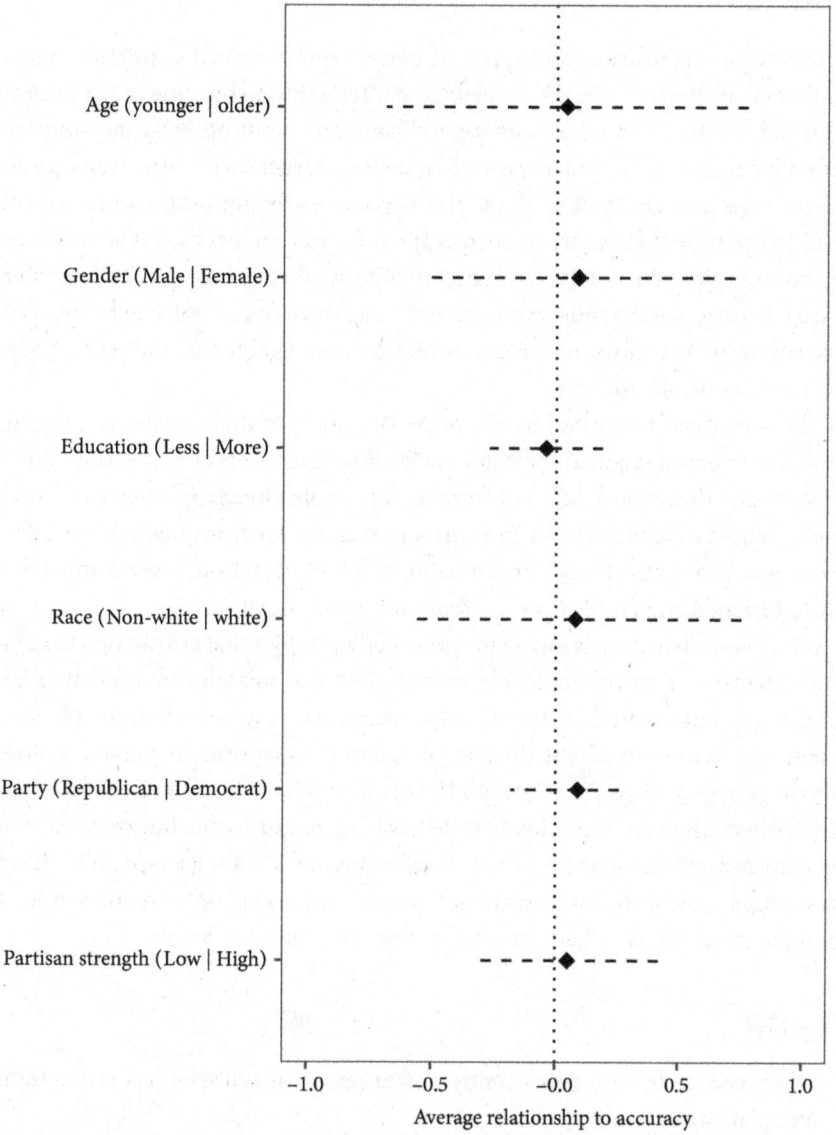

Figure 3.4 Average interaction effect between participant characteristics and correction.
Notes: We list the independent variables on the y-axis and include their low and high values within the parentheses. The x-axis represents how each independent variable is related to change in accuracy (between those who see a correction and those who see no information in the control condition) using linear regression, averaged across all 20 comparisons (see Table 3.1). Results to the right of the vertical dotted line represent a stronger relationship between the right-hand characteristic (i.e., older age) and increased accuracy, whereas those to the left represent a relationship between the left-hand characteristic (i.e., younger age) and increased accuracy. The diamonds represent the average percentage change, and the horizontal dashed line represents the 95% confidence interval. Values further from the vertical dotted line indicate stronger effects. When the confidence interval crosses the vertical dotted line, the relationship is not statistically significant.

Conclusion

Across topics, platforms, and types of correction, observed correction consistently and modestly helps those seeing the interaction to become more accurate. Men and women, Democrats and Republicans, and many other social groups update their accuracy in similar ways when seeing corrections. Corrections are also effective from a variety of sources. This is particularly important when we consider the potential for users to correct misinformation, because it is only when the community gets involved—when many members of the public are willing to do correction—that observed correction achieves its promise of being a scalable solution. Therefore, observed correction is an egalitarian and participatory solution to misinformation.

These studies are limited by the artificial nature of the experiences, because we can't use people's actual social media feeds to test observed correction. But we do not think they are so different from many people's lived experiences on social media, where misinformation and correction can come from anyone. The effects of observed correction may be even stronger if the corrections were coming from trusted friends and family,[54] rather than unknown users.

Observed correction is especially powerful for topics that are not tied to someone's identity or worldview. This matters because misinformation often isn't particularly entrenched or well-known; frequently it arises when people share something inaccurate about their local community, sports, or popular culture. Where people are less familiar with the topic and have fewer reasons to defend their beliefs, they are more likely to be swayed, either by misinformation if left uncorrected or by observed correction if someone is willing to weigh in. It is in these spaces—where attitudes are not entrenched and people are more open to changing their mind—that observed correction is most valuable.

TL; DR

- Observed correction consistently makes people more accurate across topics and platforms.
- Users are effective sources of observed correction.
- Observed correction increases accuracy for everyone, including across political orientations, education, age, and gender.
- Observed correction is particularly effective for topics where people have less entrenched beliefs, like emerging issues.

Chapter 4

Recall Is Everything

Our previous chapter shows that observed correction increases accuracy and does so equally for many different groups of people. The way we thought about effectiveness in Chapter 3 is important to understand, as it most closely reflects how people use social media—all different kinds of people, some of whom are paying more attention to the feed or to the correction than others. We know, however, that lots of people *aren't* paying that much attention when they're scrolling through social media, and even those who are paying attention still may not remember what they've seen. But does that matter? To find out, we ask: do people who recall the corrections show greater improvements in accuracy?

In this chapter, we use a couple of different approaches to get at whether people can recall what they saw in the feed we showed them, and what impact that recall has on accuracy. In doing so, we better understand the *promise* of observed correction—what it would look like if we could help people remember the corrections they see—even if we cannot always achieve that promise.

When we consider only those who can tell us what a correction said (i.e., that it offered accurate information), observed correction looks substantially more effective. In contrast to the modest 4.1% median increase in accuracy we saw in Chapter 3, we see a much larger 11.9% median increase in accuracy (see Figure 4.1) among those who recall the correction.[1] When people *don't* remember what a correction said, though, they often become less accurate. We might think of this new analysis as more of an *aspirational* effectiveness of observed correction, that can be achieved if we can increase recall for corrective responses.

We'll talk more about what can be done to make corrections more easily recalled later in the chapter. But first, let's convince you that recall matters for effective corrections.

Observed Correction. Leticia Bode and Emily K. Vraga, Oxford University Press.
© Leticia Bode and Emily K. Vraga (2025). DOI: 10.1093/oso/9780197565896.003.0004

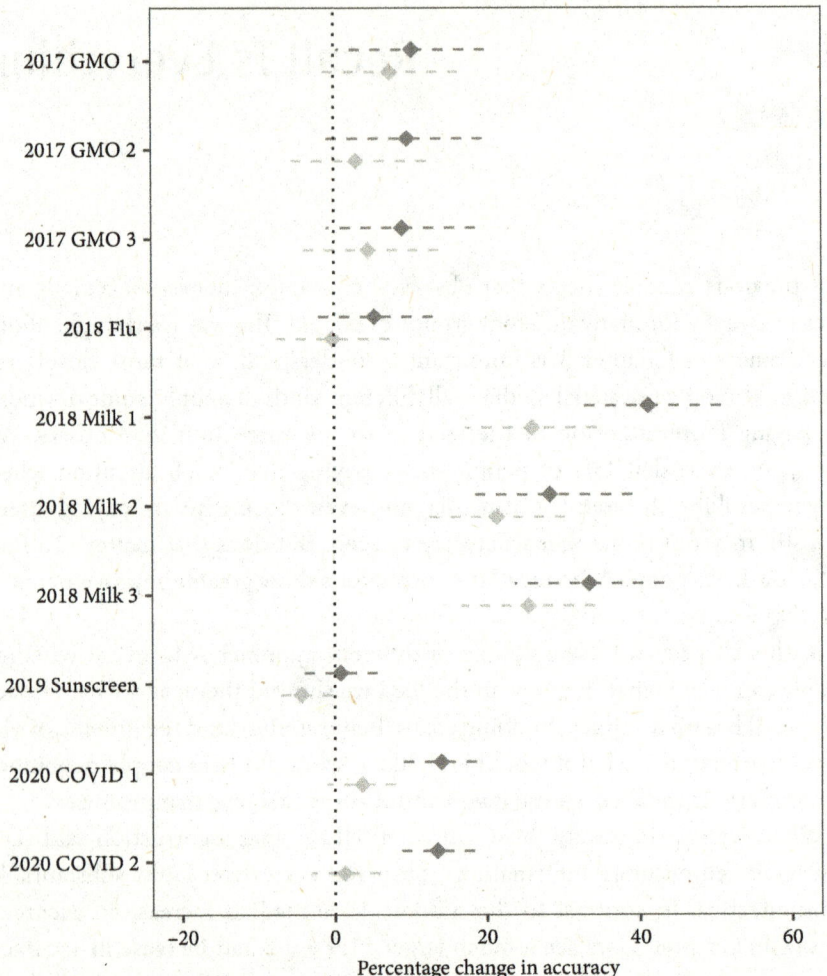

Figure 4.1 A revised look at changes in accuracy, accounting for correction recall. *Notes:* We list the different studies by year, topic, and correction number (reflecting which condition it is) on the y-axis (please see Table 3.1 for more information about each study, and the data are included in our online appendix). The x-axis represents percentage change in accuracy between each correction and the control condition. Results to the right of the vertical dotted line represent increased accuracy and those to the left represent decreased accuracy. The diamonds represent the average percentage change, and the horizontal dashed line represents the 95% confidence interval for this difference. Different color diamonds are assigned for those who recall the correction (dark gray) and for everyone in that condition (light gray). Values further from the vertical dotted line indicate stronger effects. When the confidence interval crosses the vertical dotted line, the relationship is not statistically significant.

Testing Recall

To measure recall, people answered two questions immediately after viewing the simulated social media feed. First, we asked them what the original (misinformation) post said. We gave them a series of options: the post shared misinformation (the right answer—it did), it shared accurate information, it shared some other kind of information, or they didn't know. For example, on the GMO topic, people were asked what comes closest to the position of the original tweet about the safety of GMO foods: 1) most scientists believe GMO foods are *not* safe to eat (the right answer, as this is what the misinformation post said), 2) most scientists believe GMO foods are safe to eat, 3) scientists are uncertain about whether GMO foods are safe to eat, or 4) don't know. We'll call this misinformation recall.

We did basically the same thing to measure correction recall. Immediately after the question about the original (misinformation) post, we asked people what the *response* to that post said, offering the same options. In this case, correction recall occurred when people correctly selected that the reply shared accurate information (in this case, that most scientists believe GMO foods are safe to eat). Our analyses are limited to the five (out of eight) datasets (that include 10 experimental comparisons) where we asked about recall in this manner.

Next, we ran the exact same analyses as in the previous chapter to explore the change in accuracy between the correction conditions and the control conditions, but *only* among those people who correctly said that the reply posts offered corrective information. When we do so, we find a much larger increase in accuracy (see Figure 4.1; the dark grey diamonds are updated estimates accounting for recall. The light grey diamonds are estimates for everyone, as in chapter 3.). On average across the 10 cases we can test, accuracy increases by 11.9% compared to the control group. And for our most effective corrections (about the nutritional value of raw milk), we see a quite large 28%–41% increase in accuracy. In addition, corrections to misinformation about COVID-19 also improve substantially when only considering their effects among those who recall the correction, producing a roughly 13% increase in accuracy (compared to increases of 1% and 4% when not accounting for recall). These two cases are particularly important, as they represent both topics where relatively few people were accurate (34% for raw milk), as well as topics where accuracy was already quite high (67% for hot baths prevent COVID-19) among the public (i.e., the control group). Moreover, both are topics where we might expect observed correction to be quite powerful, although for different reasons. In the case of raw milk, very few people deeply care about the topic, so attitudes are less resistant to correction. In the case of COVID-19, people cared deeply but we were looking at misinformation just as it began to circulate (in the spring of 2020), so attitudes were likely not (yet) set on the topic, allowing corrections to work quickly to debunk misinformation before it was widely believed.

To verify these results are not due to chance, we repeat the mini-meta analysis from the previous chapter among those with recall for the correction message. This analysis confirms that corrections significantly increase accuracy across our studies among those with accurate recall. Once we account for correction recall, we find an average effect size of $d=.43$,[2] which approaches a medium effect size,[3] and is notably larger than the mini-meta effect size from the previous chapter ($d=.15$). This general finding, that recalling corrections matters for their effectiveness, is consistent with other research showing that memory of corrections and their effectiveness are intrinsically linked.[4]

It's worth taking a moment to consider what it means to account for correction recall. What can these new analyses really tell us? Experiments work because of random assignment. This means that each group is theoretically identical when they begin the study, so any differences between the groups (in our case, the control versus correction conditions) after exposure to a manipulation (the correction) must result from that manipulation. But recall itself can be influenced both by the experimental manipulations themselves (some types of corrections are easier to recall) and by people's initial characteristics (people with accurate beliefs are more likely to recall the corrections). This raises a limitation of our approach to studying recall: the differences between the control and correction groups that we observe result from complicated intersections of forces, rather than being purely a result of being exposed to the correction.

One way to think of this would be differences between the *exposed* population (everyone, Chapter 3) versus among the *treated* population (those who experienced the manipulation as intended—in our case, by recalling the corrections, Chapter 4). This echoes the distinction in clinical trials between analyzing on the basis of intent-to-treat (all people assigned to a specific regimen—including those who stopped taking the treatment or didn't take it as directed—turns out people are bad at following directions) versus per-protocol (those who received and stuck with the treatments as intended, sometimes also called "treatment on the treated").[5] This second approach (what we'll show in this chapter) based on recall gives us more of an understanding of what the effects of observed correction *could be* if people could recall it, whereas the first approach (what we showed in the last chapter) gives a more conservative understanding of the effects that likely better approximates how they function in the real world of limited attention.

This is also a space where there is substantial disagreement about the degree to which comparing these groups is problematic. While many researchers use these types of analyses regularly,[6] others are strongly opposed to considering downstream effects of any variables that could be impacted by the treatment itself. This is often referred to as "conditioning on posttreatment variables"—that is, variables that are measured after the experimental treatment—because it can introduce unknown biases into the estimates of the effects in question.[7] In the analysis we present here, we are doing just that—the measure of recall we use is taken *after* participants are exposed to treatment or control conditions (as it would have to be—you can't recall something you haven't yet seen), so it is impacted by the treatment itself. It's more complicated to know what estimates of recall effects mean because we lose some of the benefits of random assignment—so if there are inherent differences that cause people to recall more or less, we could be measuring those differences rather than the impact of recall itself.[8] This makes us less confident in the specific estimates of the effects we present below. We mitigate that reduced confidence by looking for consistency across multiple datasets and methods. Ultimately, we believe the value of considering how information recall affects observed correction is important enough to outweigh the drawbacks of this approach.

What We Mean By Recall

These analyses suggest that recall greatly enhances the power of observed correction to increase accuracy. Given that, we need to take a step back and describe what we mean by *recall*. To do so, we offer a very brief overview of an extensive academic literature on information processing, which we summarize in four steps (see Figure 4.2).

The first step in information processing is *exposure*, by which we mean whether or not people have the opportunity to see the information. Kjerstin Thorson and Chris Wells describe the complicated process of what people see on

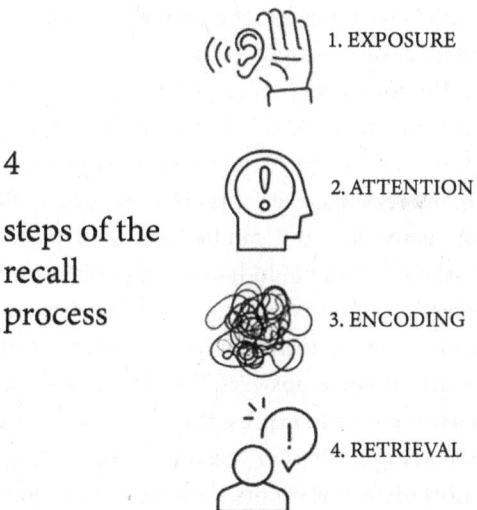

4

steps of the recall process

1. EXPOSURE

2. ATTENTION

3. ENCODING

4. RETRIEVAL

Figure 4.2   The four steps of the recall process. Credit: Dhriti Gupta, 2024

social media as resulting from "curated flows,"[9] determined by a number of factors including what networks you join, what your friends like, what algorithms predict you want to see, and what advertisements are inserted into the content. But no matter where it comes from, when content shows up on your feed, and you open your social media app, you are exposed to that content. In our experiments, we know exactly what content people were exposed to because we show it to them. So this first step is held constant.

The second step is *attention*, formally defined as information that enters our visual stream.[10] When people come across information (i.e., are *exposed* to information) on a social media feed or elsewhere, several conscious and unconscious processes direct attention. Sometimes, attention is quite deliberate, with people choosing what they wish to pay attention to from the available options,[11] typically based on their interest in particular topics, by their pre-existing beliefs, or by their goals.[12] Other times, these processes are relatively involuntary, when attention is unconsciously drawn to some kinds of stimuli over others. Accidental (or incidental) attention is often driven by design or content features—for example, vivid colors or images.[13] Yes, we really are drawn to shiny objects.

The third step is *encoding*, which is essentially dedicating brain space to the message.[14] Like attention, encoding can also be conscious or unconscious, and we can attend to something without ever encoding it[15]—if you've ever driven home from an event and realized after getting home you can't quite remember the drive itself, you've experienced attention but not (deep) encoding. Even in this initial stage, encoding can be inaccurate or incomplete: if someone misunderstands a message, they will encode the wrong thing (and thus can never recall the right thing). Think of the children's game of telephone, where messages get mangled from one person to another—in that case, the kids later in the game never have the opportunity to encode the (original) accurate message and will instead encode an inaccurate message.

Finally, we get to the fourth step of *retrieval:* being able to tell others about the encoded information when asked.[16] In our studies, this happened when we asked people to report on what the correction post said using survey questions. Recall can fail for many reasons, even if there is exposure, attention, and (correct) encoding. One reason is that it can be hard to map our experiences onto how questions are asked.[17] This could happen if people remembered the misinformation (or correction) post as saying something else entirely (for example, that it said GMO foods are more nutritious), so they don't know how to align that with the options we give them as answers. People can also choose to intentionally misreport their experiences to express their support for an identity or group, often called "expressive responding" or "partisan cheerleading,"[18] although there are questions as to how often this occurs.[19] Finally, common experiences can be difficult to separate in memory from other similar experiences and thus harder to recall.[20] In these cases, people tend to offer their best guess about an experience, rather than remembering a concrete example.[21] For example, if you asked me (Emily) how often I made chicken for dinner last week, I would have a hard time answering. I make dinner a lot and chicken is often on the menu, so trying to specifically remember what I made last week is a lost cause. To answer your question, I would instead estimate based on the kinds of meals I often make, rather than counting the number of times I actually made chicken last week.[22] This process is likely similar for estimates of social media use, which tends to be a habitual or background experience.[23] So when someone is asked about what they saw on social media in one particular case (even quite recently), they may confuse that instance with another time they saw something like it on social media.

Our measure of recall taps into all these processes. We can say with confidence whether someone was *exposed* to the misinformation or correction stimuli, as it either did or did not appear on their screens. But we do not know the extent to which they *paid attention* to that correction, what they *encoded* as a result of that attention, or how easily they could *retrieve* that information when asked about it. Therefore, we don't know whether people with inaccurate recall didn't pay attention to the messages, failed to encode them into memory, or are misreporting what they saw, either accidentally or for strategic reasons. We'll use the term "recall" as a shorthand way of referring to this entire process of attention, encoding, and reporting, and we'll test the relationship between recall and accuracy several different ways to attempt to sort out these different processes.

Types of Recall: Misinformation and Correction Recall

The results we presented at the start of this chapter (see Figure 4.1) showed that when people accurately report what a correction post says, they become more accurate. Given what we know about how recall works, we also wanted to know which types of recall were most important for successful correction. In Figure 4.3, we explore different combinations of people remembering either what the misinformation post said, what the correction post said, neither, or both. Like our analyses from Chapter 3, positive values (to the right) indicate that accuracy is improved as compared to the pure control condition, reported as a percentage increase.

In all cases, observed correction increases accuracy when people can report what both the original misinformation post and the corrective reply posts said, which we'll call "perfect recall." We suspect these might be the people who are paying the most attention to the feed, enabling them to report what the various actors in the exchange surrounding the misinformation all said. Importantly, we also find that accuracy increased in six out of the 10 cases when people recall

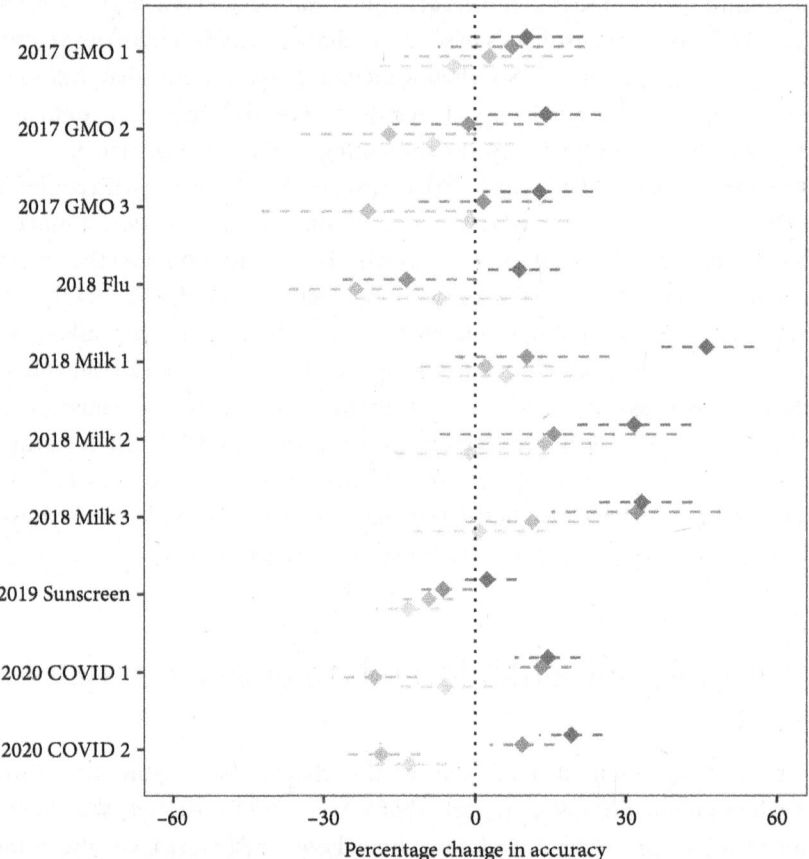

Figure 4.3 Change in accuracy depending on misinformation and correction recall.
Notes: We list the different studies by year, topic, and correction number (reflecting which condition it is) on the y-axis (please see Table 3.1 for more information about each study, and the data are included in our online appendix). The x-axis represents the percentage change in accuracy between the correction and control condition, where results to the right of the vertical dotted line represent increased accuracy and those to the left represent decreased accuracy. The diamonds represent the average percentage change and the horizontal dashed line represents the 95% confidence interval for this difference. Different color diamonds are assigned depending on the type of recall and paired to facilitate comparison. Values further from the dashed line indicate stronger effects, while those whose confidence interval cross the vertical dotted line are not statistically significant.

the corrective replies but not the misinformation post itself. In total, this means that in 16 of the 20 cases where people accurately report what the corrections said, they become more accurate (compared to people who weren't exposed to a correction). Conversely, when people cannot recall the correction, accuracy decreases in 13 of the 20 cases, evenly spread across whether they can or cannot recall what the misinformation said. Together, these analyses suggest that recall for the correction message is required for observed correction to increase accuracy, while recall for the misinformation post is helpful but not necessary.

Levels of Recall

Having established that correction recall likely matters for observed correction, we wondered how often and under what conditions people actually recall what the correction said. We think about this in two ways. First, we consider the general level of recall across our five different studies (see Figure 4.4) to explore possible differences among topics, platforms, and correction types, and second, we test whether different types of people are more or less likely to recall a correction.

When looking across our five studies, on average 64% of people recall what the correction said. Recall for the correction message is relatively stable (ranging between about 60–80%) across nine of the 10 comparisons, with no major differences in terms of the source of the correction (users versus experts), the topic (GMO foods, flu vaccines, raw milk, COVID), or the platform (Twitter versus Facebook). The one major exception is the sunscreen study on Facebook Live. In this case, the corrections appeared as textual comments scrolling alongside a video containing misinformation, and correction recall suffered considerably. Only 40% of people correctly recalled what those corrections said in the sunscreen study, and a separate survey question found that only 52% of people said they saw the comments at all. This example demonstrates the importance of platform affordances in displaying comments, encouraging us to think more critically about ways to increase visibility and recall for corrective content—something we'll dig into theoretically and practically below.

Platform affordances—especially comment visibility—matter for correction recall, but so too might individual characteristics. When we test the impact of individual characteristics (see online appendix), we find that (much like the previous chapter) there are no consistent individual differences associated with correction recall. In other words, men and women, Democrats and Republicans, and those with different levels of education (to name a few) have similar levels of recall for what the correction message said.[24]

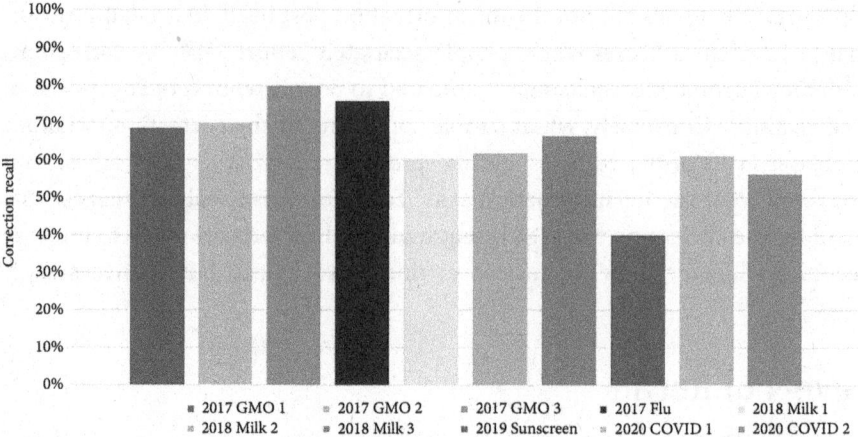

Figure 4.4   Levels of correction recall across studies. *Notes:* We list the different studies by year, topic, and correction number (reflecting which condition it is) beneath the figure (please see Table 3.1 for more information about each study, and the data are included in our online appendix) and assign each a different color to represent the levels of correction recall in each correction condition.

These analyses are limited to the individual characteristics that we measured across all five studies. Another element that might be important is pre-existing belief accuracy. We have two reasons to think that people's initial beliefs on the topic should matter in explaining recall. First, people's beliefs may motivate them to pay more (or less) attention to the stimuli depending on their beliefs. This can cut both ways—people tend to seek out information on topics they care about or that agree with their beliefs,[25] but also pay more attention when confronted with information that runs against their beliefs in order to counter-argue against it.[26] This additional attention (regardless of its motivation) may lead to greater encoding of the correction and thus higher recall. Second, the retrieval process can be compromised by strategic misreporting,[27] which could lead those with low initial accuracy to demonstrate *lower* recall if they don't want to report what the post said when it disagrees with their beliefs.

We explore whether correction recall differs for people who start out with higher or lower accuracy in the only two studies where we measured accuracy before the experiment and also measured recall after: the GMO and the flu studies. When we replicated the analysis above, adding a question asking people about their attitudes on the topic when they enter the study (i.e., before they see the simulated feed), we find that those who were initially more accurate also had higher correction recall.[28] We visualize this relationship in Figure 4.5, comparing those who are misinformed when entering the study (i.e., think that GMO foods are not safe to eat or believe the flu vaccine will cause the flu), those who are accurate, or those who are neutral. For both

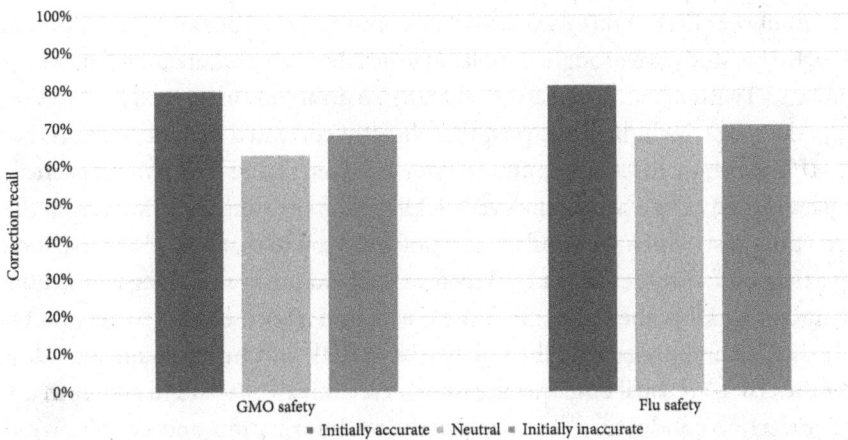

Figure 4.5   Correction recall based on pre-existing accuracy. *Notes:* This figure describes data from two studies, which are grouped along the x-axis. Different color lines indicate whether participants held reported accurate, neutral, or inaccurate in the pre-test of each study, collapsed across all the control and correction conditions.

topics, correction recall is higher among those with accurate beliefs than among the misinformed. Recall is lowest among those who are neutral (or ambivalent) on the topic, who may be the least motivated to pay attention to the topic.

Overall, these results suggest that few demographic characteristics systematically bias correction recall, but recall is instead shaped by motivational characteristics—in particular, pre-existing beliefs. However, we cannot tell whether those people for whom the correction is disagreeable are paying less attention to the correction, not encoding it properly, or failing to retrieve and report on its content, either accidentally or strategically. Our next set of analyses uses eye-tracking technology to start to disentangle these results by allowing us to consider attention separately from the encoding/retrieval process.

Isolating Attention to the Correction

Eye tracking works by flashing a laser beam at a participant's eye every 8 milliseconds to detect what part of a screen or other stimulus they're looking at (cool, right?). There are 1,000 milliseconds in a second, so that means we get 125 separate measurements of what a participant is looking at every second. For our purposes, this means we can very precisely time how long people are looking at corrections. This helps us better understand whether differences in correction recall are driven by attention (time spent looking at a correction), or other parts of the memory process (i.e., encoding or retrieval).

I (Emily) collected this next set of data with Sojung Kim and John Cook in 2019. In this study, we brought people into the laboratory, where they looked at a simulated Twitter feed. To measure what they paid attention to, each post was on a separate page, including one post that directly corrected misinformation that the HPV vaccine causes autoimmune disorders (see Figure 4.6). We are particularly interested in one part of the eye-tracking data: the time spent looking at the correction post, which is a good measure of attention to that post.[29] We also look at participants' attitudes about HPV before they did the eye-tracking task (initial accuracy), whether they remember the correction after the task (correction recall), and accuracy regarding the link between HPV and autoimmune disorders after the task (our usual outcome measure). We limit all analyses to people in the two correction conditions,[30] as people in the misinformation-only condition did not see the correction and thus could not spend any time looking at it.

We find that two features predict accurate correction recall. First, people who pay more attention to (i.e., spend longer looking at) the correction post show higher recall for what that correction post said.[31] On average, people with inaccurate correction recall spent about 10 seconds looking at the correction tweet, while those with accurate correction recall spent nearly 15 seconds looking at the correction tweet. In other words, people who recalled what the correction tweet said spent nearly 50% longer looking at it than people with inaccurate recall, a sizeable difference[32] given that attention is at a premium on social media.[33]

Second, pre-existing accuracy also contributes to recall. Specifically, recall was 60% for those with HPV misperceptions (note: this is only six people, so we have to be very cautious in our interpretation) versus 94% for those with accurate beliefs (18 people) and 82% for those who were neutral (37 people), in

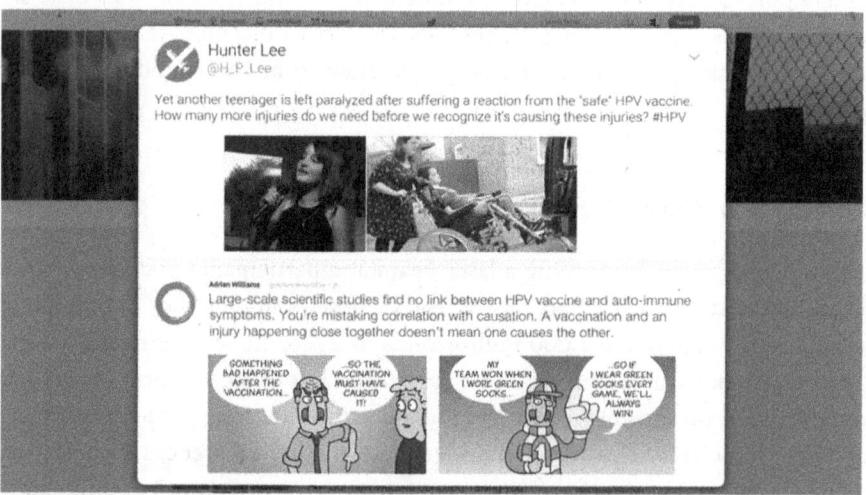

Figure 4.6 Misinformation and correction stimuli in the eye-tracking experiment.
Credit: John Cook, 2019.

line with what we reported above. Part of this relationship could be due to differences in attention to the correction posts. Those with initial HPV misperceptions spent about 10 seconds looking at the correction post, while those who were neutral or accurate spent about 15 seconds, suggesting those with misperceptions may have skipped over content they are uninterested in or disagree with.[34] Thus, both motivations (initial accuracy) and attention contribute to correction recall.[35]

Finally, we consider whether attention and recall predict *change* in accuracy after exposure to the correction. To do so, we look at people's change in accuracy from before the study (between 1–7 days before seeing the feed on average) to after exposure to the simulated feed. Our results suggest that spending longer looking at the correction did *not* make people more accurate,[36] but people who recalled the correction improved their accuracy substantially more (13%) than those who did not recall the correction (5%, see Figure 4.7).

This eye-tracking data allows us to unpack the attention element of correction recall. Both attention to a correction, as well as the motivation to accurately report its message (i.e., by aligning with what someone already believes on a topic), contribute to correction recall. This correction recall is then associated with a larger boost in accuracy after seeing a correction (in line with our other results). Importantly, it is recall, rather than attention itself, that explains these changes in accuracy.[37] Thus, getting people to pay attention to the correction—especially people who are not inclined to believe it already—is only one step in producing the *recall* for the correction that is of critical importance for changing people's beliefs.

Why It's Hard to Remember Social Media Content

These results suggest that correction recall is important for observed correction to increase accuracy. But if correction works best when people recall the corrections, we need to think about ways to ensure that recall occurs. Before offering specific recommendations for how to make corrections more memorable (i.e., more easily recalled), we need to discuss the context in which corrections are happening. Consider an example of what correction on Facebook looks like, that I (Leticia) saw on my feed back in 2019 (Figure 4.8).

In this case, multiple comments repeat essentially the same argument (that the source may not be credible), which should boost their collective effectiveness, increasing the accuracy of people who see the post and comments. And those corrective posts occur almost immediately (within 15 minutes) after the misinformation post, so few people likely saw the misinformation absent the corrections. But the misinformation in the original post is quite large, taking up over twice the area of the correction that comes in the comments below and thus likely

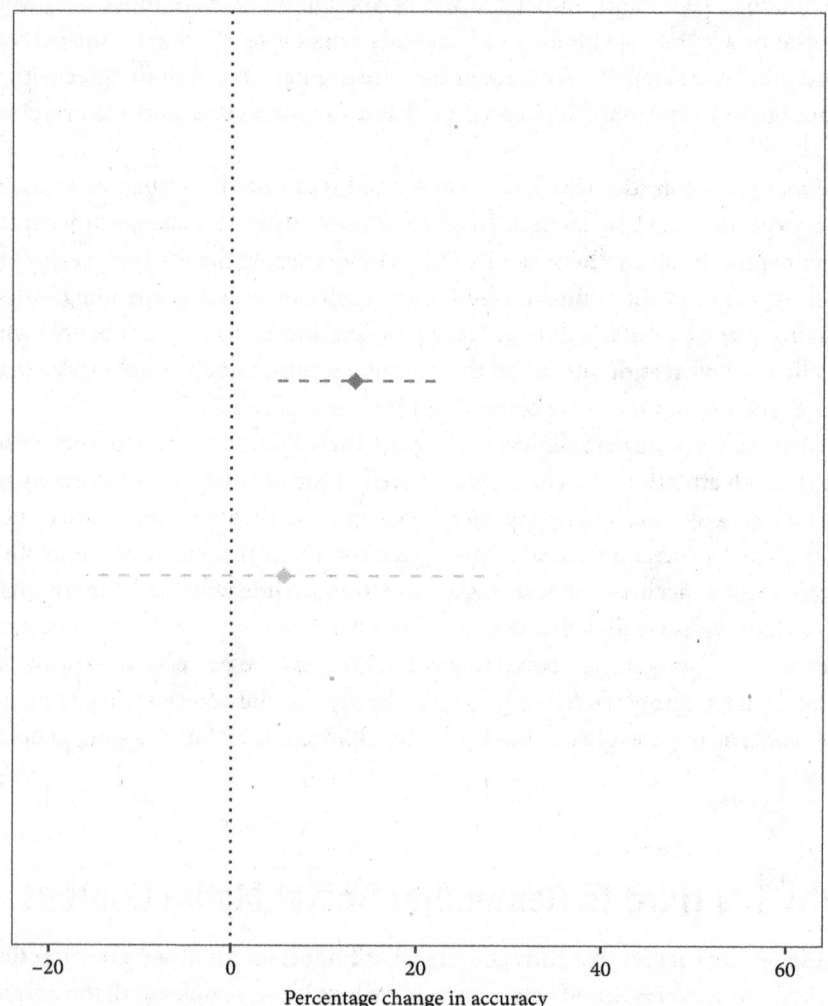

Figure 4.7 Change in accuracy, depending on correction recall. *Notes:* The results in this figure rely on a single study, which used eye tracking to explore corrections to HPV misinformation. The x-axis represents the percentage change in accuracy between the pre-test (i.e., before seeing the stimuli) versus the post-test (after seeing the HPV misinformation and correction), collapsed across both correction types. Results to the right of the vertical dotted line represent increased accuracy and those to the left represent decreased accuracy. The diamonds represent the average percentage change, and the horizontal dashed line represents the 95% confidence interval for this difference. Values further from the vertical dotted line indicate stronger effects. When the confidence interval crosses the vertical dotted line, the relationship is not statistically significant.

Figure 4.8 A real-world example of correction on Facebook.

to draw more attention.[38] The misinformation is also brightly colored and includes a clearly recognizable political figure—all things likely to make it more memorable.[39] In contrast, the first comment criticizes the credibility of the link from the misinformation post by linking to its home page, but the comment (and associated link) lacks contrast, bright colors, or other elements of vividness that might help it stand out. The second comment reinforces the point of the first but contains only a wall of text. And this is by design! It's not that social media platforms want to give less real estate or fewer memorable attributes to correction; it's that they are thinking about the value of showing a post versus showing a comment. As one social media employee (who we'll call Erin, see Table 8.3 for more information) reminded us, platforms are trying to moderate content in lots of different ways to make the content that people see on their feeds maximally relevant and interesting to them:

> I think, though, that the public underestimates, though, how bad and spammy and low-quality content is if there's no type of content moderation at all. Everybody who talks about, "Oh, stop with the algorithm, stop with the content moderation, just give me a reverse chronological feed," it's just going to be garbage. . . . I think that people underestimate how crappy social media would be without any content moderation.

Most people would probably rather see posts than their associated comments, which are less likely to be interesting or relevant to them. Indeed, some platforms hide comments by default (TikTok) or place them such that a user has to scroll to see them (YouTube). These are all probably the "right" choice for platforms to optimize for the best user experience, but it means that comments that are correcting misinformation are less likely to be seen—and therefore less likely to help people become more accurate.

So this is a way that platforms can be very consequential, incorporating design features[40] that make corrections (or responses likely to be corrections) salient and vivid, or failing to do so, and offering fewer opportunities for successful correction to occur on that platform. One of the reasons platforms haven't amplified corrections is because they are worried about getting things wrong. As Pablo (social media) described,

> There's often [a concern] that we might be wrong, or a vague feeling that maybe . . . this is the wrong comment to make it more visible.

This is particularly true because of the automation required to make these sorts of decisions about what to do with misinformation at scale. Doing so requires training machine learning algorithms to identify relevant content that needs to be addressed, which is an imperfect science, as Gabrielle (social media) describes:

> It's a very imprecise classifier. So that signal, it's only telling you this vague shadow of what it is trying to be. It's still trying to measure the weather from putting your finger out the window. You're like, "My finger says it's cold."

Ideally, platforms could identify misinformation and demote it, and identify correction and amplify it, but it can be very difficult (or even functionally impossible) to identify with confidence what is misinformation and what is a correction quickly or at scale.[41]

Platforms are also keenly aware of how design choices relate to what types of information and misinformation get traction. As Sebastien (social media) put it, "So there's a lot of things in product design that not obviously prevent misinformation, because that's an impossible task, but to prevent quite the same level of spread of misinformation." It's worth noting that when platforms do choose to label content with corrective information (generally from third-party fact checkers), they often recognize the value of memorability associated with images and put an "interstitial" (e.g., dulling or covering) over post images to mitigate this effect (Facebook, Instagram, Twitter). Academic research has demonstrated that such warnings and interstitials can reduce the perceived credibility of the misinformation[42] and reduce post-sharing,[43] with one review highlighting that "label effectiveness increases with visibility".[44] You can see an example of this in Figure 4.9.

In addition, the nature of social media is not one that encourages deep attention to and processing of its content. In contrast, platforms aim to keep people engaged on their platform so they can sell their consumers' attention to advertisers, who are willing to pay a premium to reach targeted audiences.[45] This overarching aim frequently leads platforms to implement addictive design features, like infinite scrolling (continually producing more content no matter how far you scroll down), variable rewards (usually implemented through intermittent push notifications), social reciprocity (creating incentives to regularly interact with social connections), and gamification (small rewards to generate a sense of achievement).[46] Addictive design features have been criticized for promoting prolonged time spent on the platform, sometimes at the cost of other outcomes.[47] Within the context of these design features, users may effectively zone out, entering a state where they no longer absorb information.[48] Obviously, this could also make them less likely to recall the content to which they are exposed.

While platforms have a lot of control over the affordances of their platform, that is not to say that users (members of the public, the press, or professionals) are powerless. While our experiments weren't designed to test how message features affect recall, there is a wealth of research on memorability that offers suggestions of how to make content easier to remember. In this research, effectiveness and memorability are essentially synonymous.[49] Memorability of an image is a stable and intrinsic property,[50] meaning that it's consistent across time and people. Anything that makes an image more vivid— adding color[51] (red is the most memorable hue),[52] "visual embellishments,"[53]

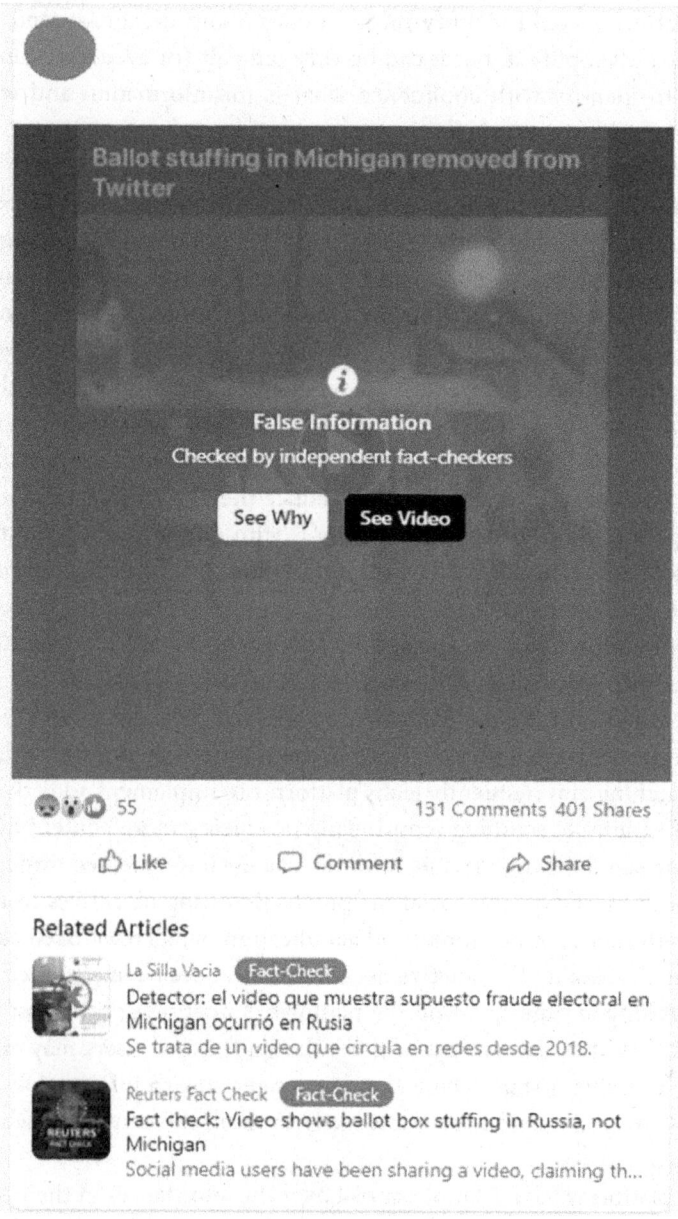

Figure 4.9 Example of interstitial intervention on false information.

or humans,[54] or increasing contrast, saturation, or brightness[55]—also makes it easier to recall. From a design perspective, making something stand out is a way to make information clearer and easier to recall.[56] Part of this is just making things visual in the first place—most often this means including an image or replacing text with images—because text is inherently less memorable than pictures.

This has also been studied at least to some extent in the context of misinformation and correction. For example, my (Emily) work with Sojung Kim and John Cook found that humorous corrections tended to garner more attention on social media, and this attention indirectly reduced HPV misperceptions.[57] Adding images to corrections may also be an effective strategy to capture attention (and thus theoretically, recall and effectiveness) on social media.[58] One test of adding "truth scale" visuals to correction posts found adding these scales made nonpolitical health corrections more effective,[59] although later research found the impact of adding visual features (including graphical representations) to be minimal or nonexistent.[60] And some research has even shown that when participants are encouraged to pay extra close attention to content, it produces more biased processing – that is, they resist corrections that disagree with them.[61]

Given competing findings in this area, we join existing calls for more attention to be paid to making corrections memorable,[62] and we urge all actors—platforms as well as members of the public, the press, or professionals—to think about what aspects of their corrections will make them vivid, relevant, salient, and therefore able to overcome the challenges to correction memorability that are built in to social media platforms.

Conclusion

Our findings suggest that the effectiveness of observed correction hinges on recall—effective correction is highly concentrated in those who accurately recall what the correction said. The takeaway is clearly to carefully consider how to make memorable corrections, but we also need much more research to offer concrete guidelines about which features of correction are most important for memorability and effectiveness.

Maximizing the memorability of corrections is also a space where platforms can be consequential, incorporating design features that make corrections (or responses likely to be corrections) salient and vivid, or making posts that are tagged as misinformation less visually appealing. This could include highlighting corrective information by making it bigger, bolder, or brighter. Platforms that do not do this—for example, Facebook Live's reliance on scrolling comments alongside a video—offer fewer opportunities for successful observed correction to occur on that platform.

Correctors—including professionals, the press, and the public—can also work to make their responses memorable. One effective way to do so might be creating visual and memorable accessible curated evidence (ACE) that users can apply in their own corrections (see Chapter 9). Across the board, memorability should be top of mind when engaging in correction.

TL; DR

- Recalling what a correction said improves the effectiveness of observed correction.
- Just over half of people recall what the correction said, but recall depends on platform affordances.
- Correctors should think about how to make their corrections more memorable.

Chapter 5

Perceptions of Correction

In our previous two chapters, we showed that when people witness corrections on social media (and especially when they recall them), they adjust their beliefs and become more accurate as a result. But this doesn't answer the question: what do people think about observed correction and its value on social media? In this chapter, we use survey data to show that many people (around 40%) tell us that they correct misinformation when they see it on social media. Even more people say they witness such corrections happening (i.e., experience observed correction) in their own social media feeds (around 50%). We think both numbers are an overestimate of how many people actually perform and see correction, but the reported prevalence speaks to potentially powerful social norms surrounding correction. People tend to overreport behaviors they think are valued by society,[1] so when people tell us that they are correcting misinformation and seeing others do the same, it partly means correction is something they think they *should* be doing. However, some people are more likely to say they see and perform correction than others, suggesting that effort is needed to encourage broad uptake of this norm. Observed correction is valued, but not consistently and not for everyone.

Measuring Perceived Correction Experiences

To understand the public's perceived experiences with correction on social media, we use surveys to ask people whether they have personally seen correction on social media and whether they have performed correction themselves. In general, we'll show you data from four datasets: two surveys collected in October 2020 (one about politics and one about COVID-19) and two collected in April 2021 (one about politics and one about COVID-19). A summary of the four datasets is provided in Table 5.1, and full details on our methodology and

Observed Correction. Leticia Bode and Emily K. Vraga, Oxford University Press.
© Leticia Bode and Emily K. Vraga (2025). DOI: 10.1093/oso/9780197565896.003.0005

Table 5.1 **Descriptions of Survey Data**

Date	Topic	Total Sample	Passed Attention Check
October 2020	COVID-19	1,907	1,616
October 2020	Politics	1,832	1,631
April 2021	COVID-19	1,674	1,488
April 2021	Politics	1,690	1,501

Notes: Please see our online appendix (https://bode.vraga.org/) for additional information regarding the data collections.

question wording are available in the online appendix.[2] These surveys allow us to understand how people are thinking about their experiences of correction, but in doing so also reflect the social norms surrounding behaviors (because we say we do things we think others value) and the difficulties in trying to recall concrete experiences among routine habits (like social media use).

What People Say About Performing Correction

There are lots of ways people can respond to misinformation on social media: while some may choose to correct it, others may instead contribute their own falsehoods, interject hate speech into the conversation, flood the space with irrelevant information, privately verify that the information is false but not share that information with the network, or, most likely, just ignore the content entirely.[3] We asked people in our surveys how often they had corrected someone else on social media in the past week and considered someone a "corrector" if they said they had done so at least "sometimes" in the past week (as compared to "rarely" or "never").[4] In these surveys, many people told us they had corrected someone else on social media, with roughly 40% of people saying they had done so in the past week (Figure 5.1). However, self-reports of performed correction can vary widely depending on the year, the country, the topic of misinformation, the social media platform studied (if specified), and the question wording.[5]

In any case, we are quite certain that fewer than 40% of Americans corrected someone else on social media (at least using our definition of a direct response to misinformation with correct information) in the past week. Attempts to study correction directly on social media have shown that public corrections do happen with some regularity across social media platforms for both health and political topics—for example, two analyses of COVID-19 misinformation tweets found that between 1–3% of all misinformation tweets studied had corrective responses[6]—but much less often than what these survey responses would suggest.

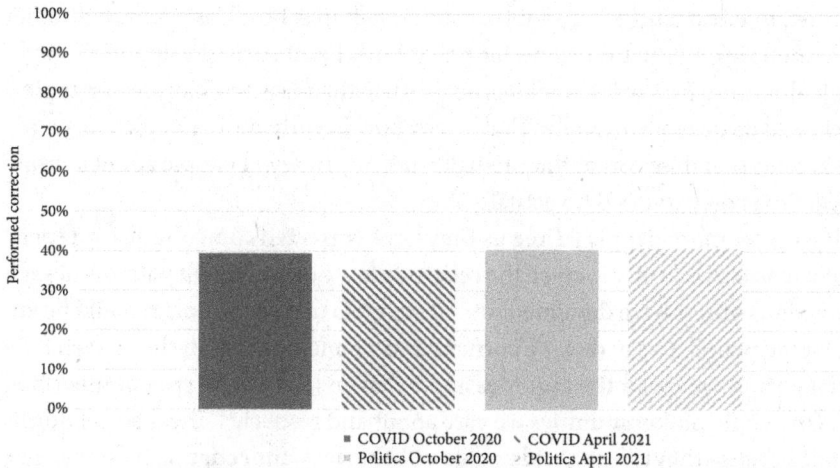

Figure 5.1 Performing correction in the US across topics and time. *Notes:* We list the different studies by year and topic beneath the figure (please see Table 5.1 for more information about each study, and the data are included in our online appendix). We assign a different color to the different correction topics (i.e., black for COVID and gray for politics) and use shading to indicate when the data was collected (e.g., solid fill represents October 2020 and dashed fill indicates April 2021) to facilitate comparison. The bars represent the percentage who report that experience in the previous week on social media along the y-axis.

So why the difference between what we observe on social media and what people tell us they do? First, there are all the issues with people's ability to recall what they've seen that we talked about in the previous chapter—especially their ability to pinpoint exactly when they had a particular experience. Even though we both (Leticia and Emily) have corrected people on social media, it would be very hard for either of us to tell you precisely when it occurred. As a result, we might tell you we sometimes corrected misinformation in the past week because we know we have done it but just can't quite tell you when. We might even know that it didn't happen in the past week, but still want to get credit for being a sometimes-corrector. Therefore, our answer reflects our habits rather than our specific experiences in the last week. It's also possible people who say they are doing correction are doing something else that falls outside of our definition, including engaging in debates with people on social media or simply sharing high-quality information on a contentious topic. Because we rely entirely on what people tell us, it's possible that some of the people who say they are performing corrections may in fact be sharing what we would call misinformation on the topic (i.e., it counters the best available evidence)—but call it a correction because they think it's true.

Even more importantly in this context, survey responses are often aspirational, especially when they invoke a socially desirable behavior.[7] When someone asks me (both of us in this case!) if I worked out in the past week, I might feel tempted to cheat a little—count that short walk that I took as a workout rather than admitting I didn't do something that both I and society value. Or I might think about my *best* week working out, rather than last week or even a typical week, and answer accordingly. This is why consistently more people tell survey researchers that they voted[8] than actually did, or why fewer people admit to using illegal drugs on surveys than actually do.[9]

If we have more people telling us they have corrected someone else on social media than seems realistic given the relatively low but consistent patterns of such corrections others have documented,[10] it suggests that social norms could be encouraging people to say they've corrected someone even when they haven't. By social norms, we mean the attitudes and behaviors, or other types of unwritten rules of people or communities we care about and respect.[11] These social norms matter because they affect a wide range of behaviors. Indeed, social norms are a fundamental component of several models that try to explain why people change their behaviors (like quitting smoking[12] or drinking less[13]). These include the theory of planned behavior, which is foundational to communication research[14] and strategic science communication,[15] and has more recently been applied to explaining correction behaviors.[16] Consistent with these theories, if correction is seen as normatively valuable, people are going to be motivated to tell you they did it, even when they didn't.[17]

Our survey data provide evidence suggesting that corrections are seen as socially desirable. Consistent with previous research,[18] about 50% of people said they *like* it when people correct others on social media in our survey data, whereas only about 15% disagree (see Figure 5.2A). Moreover, they also saw corrections to be part of the public's *duty*, agreeing that people should respond when they see misinformation on social media and that it's everyone's responsibility (see Figures 5.2B and 5.2C).[19] These twin pressures—saying that they value (or like) correction and that they see it as a public responsibility—contribute to why people would also tell us they had corrected misinformation personally in the past week, even if the best estimates based on observations on social media suggest such behaviors are not as common as our self-reported data implies.

But while these self-reported behaviors are aspirational, they matter because we can think of the people who say they corrected misinformation on social media as a pool of *potential* correctors. So even if we don't believe this many people performed correction in the past week (or perhaps even at all), these are people who want to think of themselves as correctors. As such, they represent people who we may be able to mobilize, given the right set of circumstances or motivations, to correct in the future. This pair of questions—how people decide whether to correct and how we can shift those motivations—will be the focus of the next two chapters.

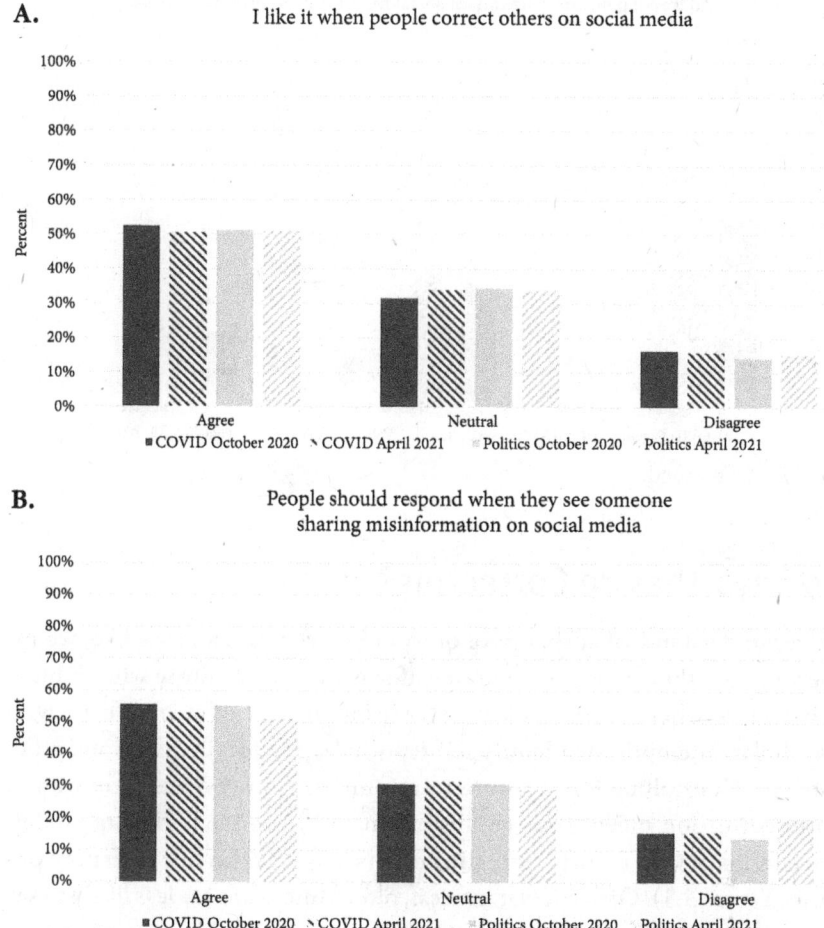

A. I like it when people correct others on social media

B. People should respond when they see someone sharing misinformation on social media

Figure 5.2 Perceptions of correction. *Notes:* We list the different studies by year and topic beneath the figure (please see Table 5.1 for more information about each study, and the data are included in our online appendix). We assign a different color to the different correction topics (i.e., black for COVID and gray for politics) and use shading to indicate when the data was collected (e.g., solid fill represents October 2020 and dashed fill indicates April 2021) to facilitate comparison. We categorize and group participants by whether they somewhat to strongly agree with the statement, whether they are neutral on the statement, or whether they somewhat to strongly disagree with the statement. The y-axis represents the percentage of participants who fall into each of these categories (agree, neutral, disagree) for each study. Panel A represents agreement with the statement "I like it when people correct others on social media," Panel B represents agreement with the statement "People should respond when they see someone sharing misinformation on social media," and Panel C represents agreement with the statement "Addressing misinformation on social media is everyone's responsibility."

C.   Addressing misinformation on social media is everyone's responsibility

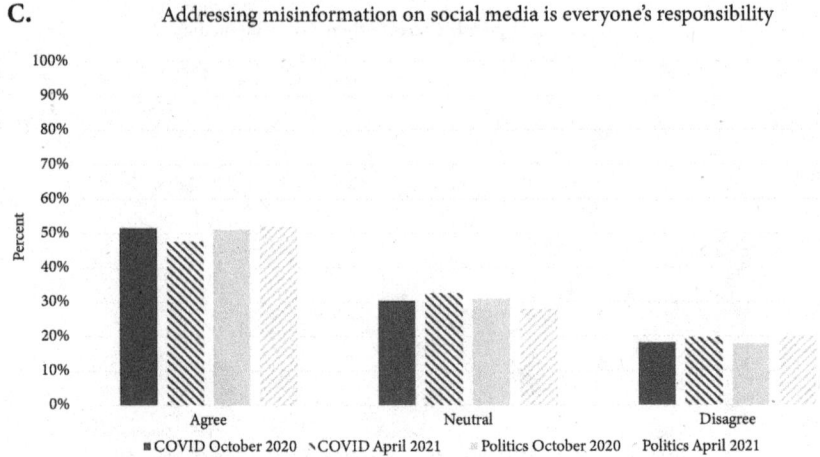

Figure 5.2 Continued.

Who Says They're Correcting?

To better understand what that pool of would-be correctors looks like, we examine who says they have corrected misinformation versus those who did not. This is a place where there has been increasing interest in recent years, with many scholars attempting to identify self-reported correctors in the US and other countries.[20] Controlling for exposure to misinformation (because you cannot perform correction unless you see misinformation), we see fairly large differences in terms of who reports correcting others in the US (in line with previous research, Figure 5.3). Of particular interest, older Americans are less likely to say they are correcting misinformation—which is especially problematic given they are also more likely to share and see misinformation on social media.[21] Likewise, women are less likely to say they corrected misinformation (especially on political topics), consistent with previous research about correction,[22] as well as research that shows women are less willing to engage with politics online.[23]

Turning to political orientations, it is noteworthy that roughly equal numbers of Democrats and Republicans said they had corrected someone on social media in the past week for both political topics and for COVID-19. Given the importance of trusted sources for effective observed correction,[24] it is good news that we have potential correctors on both sides of the political aisle. What is less ideal is that stronger partisans (from both sides of the aisle) are more likely to say they correct. This could imply that the large middle between the polar extremes is less likely to get involved in correcting misinformation, which might make corrections themselves less moderate.[25]

Overall, the most important conclusion from this analysis is that correction behaviors (real and aspirational) are not equally distributed among the population. We must think carefully about how to make correction more egalitarian to fulfill its normative potential.

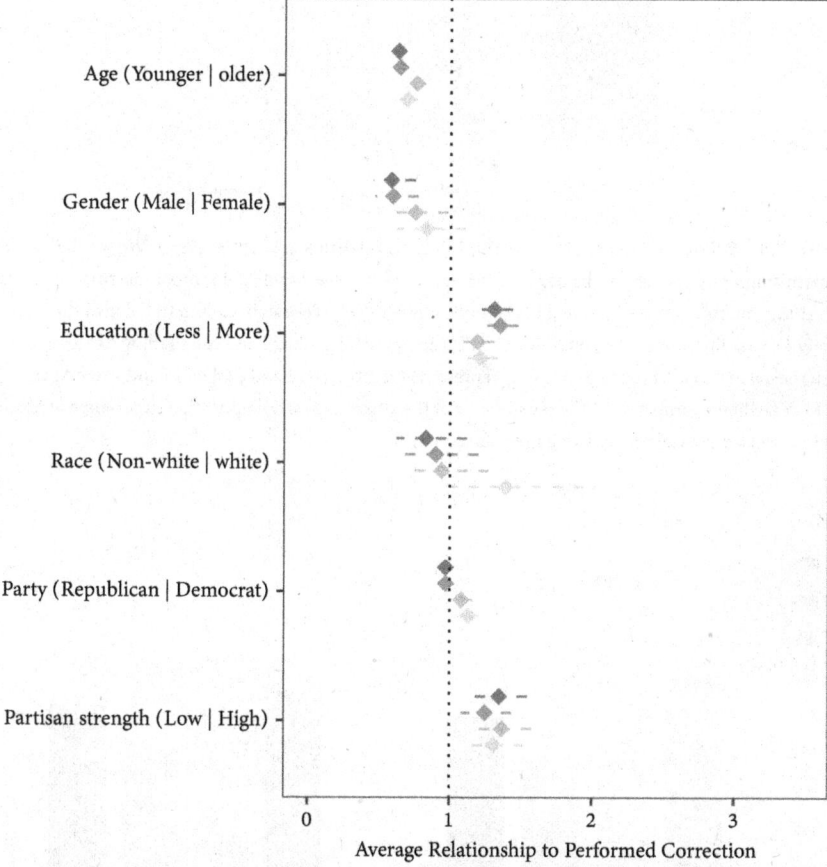

Figure 5.3 Predicting performed correction. *Notes:* We list the independent variables on the y-axis and include their endpoints within the parentheses. The x-axis represents how each independent variable is related to self-reported performed correction using logistic regression. We use different color diamonds to represent each data collection (four in total). Results to the right of the vertical dotted line represent a stronger relationship between the right-hand characteristic (i.e., older age) and performed correction whereas those to the left represent a relationship between the left-hand characteristic (i.e., younger age) and performed correction. The diamonds represent the average relationship, and the horizontal dashed line represents the 95% confidence interval. Values further from the dotted line indicate stronger effects. When the confidence interval crosses the vertical dotted line, the relationship is not statistically significant. We do not include seeing misinformation in the figure because they are the single largest predictors of performing correction and their coefficients dramatically exceed the other estimates in the figure. Please see the online appendix for the full regression results.

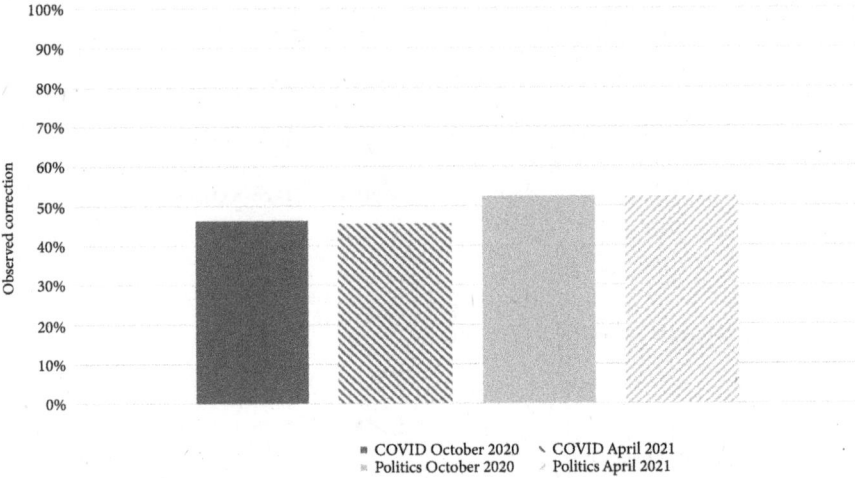

Figure 5.4 Observed correction in the US across topics and time. *Notes:* We list the different studies by year and topic beneath the figure (please see Table 5.1 for more information about each study, and the data are included in our online appendix). We assign a different color to the different correction topics (i.e., black for COVID and gray for politics) and use shading to indicate when the data was collected (e.g., solid fill represents October 2020 and dashed fill indicates April 2021) to facilitate comparison. The bars represent the percentage who report that experience in the previous week on social media along the y-axis.

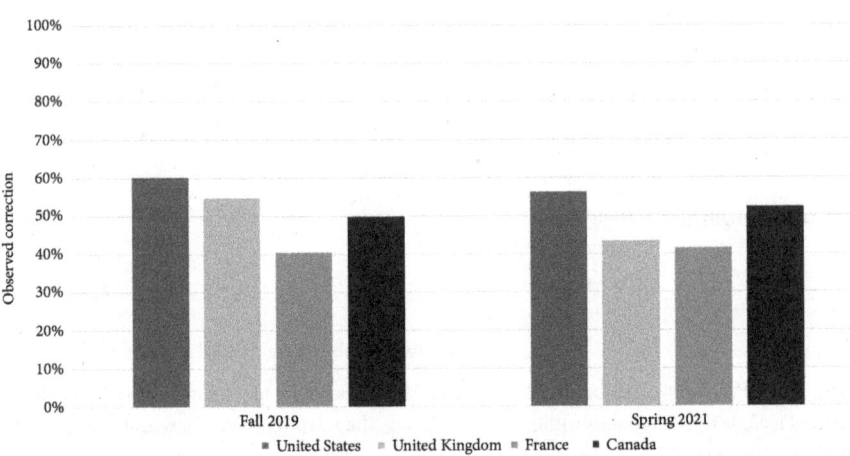

Figure 5.5 Observed correction by country. *Notes:* We list the different studies by country beneath the figure and assign a different color to each study to represent the percentage who report observing correction of misinformation on social media in the previous month along the y-axis. These results are grouped by the time of the data collection along the x-axis.

Perceptions of Observed Correction

We have established that many people tell us they correct misinformation on social media, but we would expect even more people to say they *witness* such corrections. After all, one reason that observed correction on social media holds promise is that a single correction can be seen by many people. This pattern is seen in other types of behaviors as well. Some people contribute a lot of content online, whereas others merely "lurk"—they observe and consume content, but don't create any of their own.[26] And more people tend to be lurkers in online communities than participate across a whole range of behaviors: research generally finds a 90–9–1 rule for online communities, where 90% of users lurk, 9% contribute some, and 1% account for most online activity.[27] We would expect this to also be true of correction on social media, where a few people do a lot of the correcting that other people can then observe.

- Consistent with those expectations, our survey data show a strong sense among the public that observed correction happens regularly on social media, and more often than people report engaging in correction themselves. Like before, we look at those who say they had seen someone else being corrected on social media in the past week at least sometimes. Roughly half of our participants say they have seen someone else being corrected on social media in the past week (Figure 5.4). The percentage of people who say they see these corrections is somewhat higher for political topics (~52%) as compared to COVID-19 (~46%), but the percentage of people who report seeing corrections is quite stable on both topics from fall of 2020 to the spring of 2021. More recently, our colleagues at the University of Wisconsin-Madison collected nationally representative survey using similar measures of observed correction. Sijia Yang and Liwei Shen were kind enough to share their data with us. These data, from November 2022, present a similar picture: 41% of Americans reported witnessing someone else being corrected on social media. Additionally, data from the United States, the United Kingdom, France, and Canada in fall of 2019 and again in early 2021 (shared with us by the very generous Shelley Boulianne) suggests that people report experiencing observed correction fairly often across all four countries (Figure 5.5).[28]

Much like with performed correction, we do not necessarily think that half of people in the US or elsewhere witnessed observed correction on social media in the past week. Unlike with performing corrections, wherein social norms likely encourage people to say they've corrected even when they haven't, here it is likely more about the inherent difficulty people have in reporting on the information they consume accurately. For example, research shows that people are pretty terrible at remembering what news and information they've consumed—although patterns of reported TV news consumption mirror Nielsen ratings, they are inflated by about 300%.[29] And while some of this is about social norms (we want to say we're responsible news consumers), this overreporting may be less about social desirability and more about sheer inability to estimate the amount of news watched (p. 138). As we discussed in Chapter 4, common experiences tend to be particularly difficult to report accurately (it's hard to remember

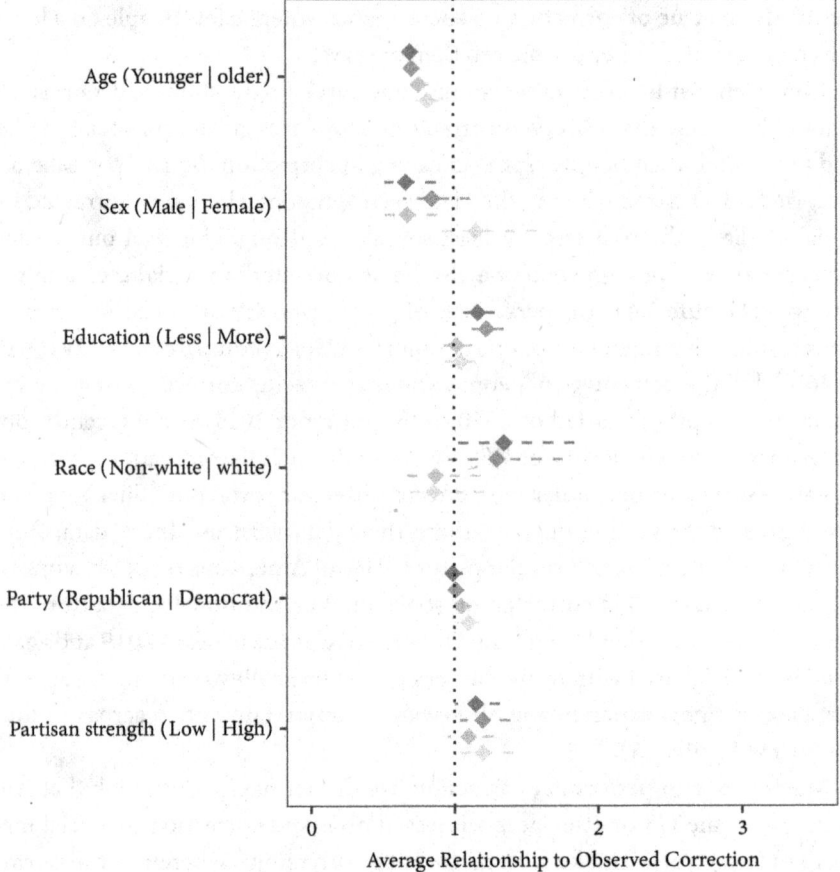

Figure 5.6 Predicting observed correction. *Notes:* We list the independent variables on the y-axis and include their endpoints within the parentheses. The x-axis represents how each independent variable is related to observed correction using logistic regression. We use different color diamonds to represent each data collection (four in total). Results to the right of the vertical dotted line represent a stronger relationship between the right-hand characteristic (i.e., older age) and observed correction whereas those to the left represent a relationship between the left-hand characteristic (i.e., younger age) and observed correction. The diamonds represent the average relationship, and the horizontal dashed line represents the 95% confidence interval. Values further from the dotted line indicate stronger effects. When the confidence interval crosses the vertical dotted line, the relationship is not statistically significant. While it is included in the model, we do not include seeing misinformation in the figure because it is the single largest predictor of observed correction and its coefficient dramatically exceeds the other estimates in the figure. Please see the online appendix for the full regression results.

what happened when)—and can be even further skewed when people are reporting on something that is especially vivid in memory (a correction) as part of a routine experience (social media use generally).[30]

This is something that also came up in our qualitative interviews with social media users when we asked about corrections. For example, when asked about seeing correction on social media, Vince (user) told us in the same comment both that "I know there's so many" but also that "I hardly ever see correction." The opposite can also occur—Earl (user) told us that he had seen a correction on social media in the past week in a survey question, but then when asked about it during our conversation, wanted to share a vivid example from "probably three years ago." But again, it demonstrates that there is a sense that corrections are occurring on social media, ingraining them in our collective imagined affordances of what social media allows or encourages.

Who Says They Have Experienced Observed Correction?

Observed correction is perceived to be happening across different topics, time, and countries. The next question is whether some people are more likely to report seeing these corrections. Each person's experience on social media is very much *individualized*, shaped by their own previous engagements, their social network and its choices, strategic actors, and the algorithms that use all of these inputs to create environments designed to keep each individual engaged.[31] Some individuals will have networks filled with people who share misinformation, others may have networks filled with correctors, and yet others may not see either. Likewise, my own willingness to engage with (i.e., like, share, or comment upon) some types of content rather than others may signal to the algorithm that I want to see more fact checks, or more misinformation, in a way that other users may not.[32] Indeed, the platform employees we spoke with confirmed the idea that algorithms are trained to give more content deemed to be similar to what people have already engaged with. As Pablo (social media) put it:

> So there's liking something. There's viewing the article, there's reacting, there's commenting, there's sharing. And commenting particularly if you use more than four words, it's one of like the strongest signals of positive engagement.

All these forms of interaction create a positive reinforcement for the algorithm that decides what content to show next. So even people who start out with the same set of characteristics and preferences will eventually get different content depending on how they and others in their network engage with posts in different ways.

We also know there are systematic differences in terms of who shares and believes misinformation[33] as well as in who says they perform correction,[34] but little research has explored these potential differences in who reports they *see* correction across a number of topics and time periods.[35]

Therefore, we look at the individual predictors that may influence who reports seeing correction (that is, who is experiencing observed correction). We again control for whether someone reported seeing misinformation on the topic in the previous week, and find systematic differences in who is reporting observed correction (see Figure 5.6). The largest and most consistent demographic predictor is again age. Much like with performed correction, older adults were less likely to report having experienced observed correction across both topics (COVID-19 and politics) and time periods (October 2020 and April 2021, and consistent with data from March 2020)[36] suggesting that observed correction is leaving out a particularly vulnerable audience.[37] Similarly, women are less likely to say they see (as well as perform) correction on political topics than their male counterparts. More educated participants were also more likely to report seeing correction at least in some cases. The similarities we see in who says they correct and who says they see correction collectively underline the importance of motivating a variety of trusted messengers to be willing to correct others online, so as to reach more people (which we'll work on in Chapter 7).

But equally important is where we still don't see meaningful differences: in party affiliation. There is no consistent pattern of differences between Democrats and Republicans in terms of who says they are exposed to observed correction. This is quite important, given that we know differences occur among these groups in terms of their social media information environments more broadly.[38] Given the difficulty in finding misinformation mitigation approaches that reach across party lines during these polarized times—something that plagues other misinformation mitigation strategies, like platform-based content moderation[39]—observed correction may offer a unique bipartisan opportunity.

We do note that those with stronger affiliations with *either* the Democratic or Republican party report more exposure to observed correction (mimicking the relationship with partisan strength and correcting). It makes sense that strong partisans may be the ones most likely to see the kinds of contentious spaces where correction may be occurring most regularly (refer back to Figure 5.4, which shows corrections happen more often about politics than about COVID-19). It may also reflect that less partisan individuals are less interested in political or politicized topics and thus are seeing any political content—including correction—less often.[40]

Conclusion

This chapter provides evidence that lots of people *say* that they see and do correction on social media, although it is hard to get a very clear picture of just how often that happens. Fewer people say they correct than say they see correction, and these numbers are almost certainly aspirational. But we think measuring the number of people who *want* to tell us they corrected misinformation is quite important as well. This represents a potential wellspring of correctors. If we can understand and effectively address the barriers that prevent them from correcting, perhaps they could be motivated to carry out the behaviors they already say they're doing.

But not everyone is equally likely to say they see or perform correction, indicating that we still have a long way to go in making observed correction equitable. If performing and seeing correction remains limited to younger, educated, partisan men—as our surveys suggest—it is not including everyone, which makes it a less powerful democratic tool. Therefore, the next step is finding ways to get more people involved in correction, while still respecting their reasons for not doing so. We'll start this task in the next chapter by talking to social media users to learn about some of the common barriers to correction, as well as what leads people to correct despite their concerns, and continue it in Chapter 7, where we consider ways to get more people to correct.

TL; DR

- Lots of people say they correct misinformation on social media, and even more report seeing others do so.
- These perceptions likely speak to social norms in support of correction.
- Witnessing and performing correction are not equally distributed among the population.

Chapter 6

Conflicted Correctors

Our previous chapter suggests that many people value corrections on social media, claim to engage in corrections themselves, and report seeing others correct as well. In this chapter, we turn our attention to how people navigate their own choice to engage in correction. That is, what leads some people to correct misinformation on social media, and what explains why others don't?

By and large, the members of the public we spoke with were *conflicted correctors* (see Figure 6.1). Many endorsed the value of correction in the abstract but were hesitant to engage in it themselves except in a few select cases. Those who were most in favor of correction were thinking about the audiences who could be harmed by misinformation, and felt a responsibility to respond. Even with those motivations, they would still only correct when they felt confident and that at least some people would listen.

But the costs of correction were also very salient to the users we spoke with. Their foremost concerns included a perception that corrections wouldn't do any good, would damage important relationships, would provoke toxic responses, and were quite costly, both in terms of time and emotional investment. When added together, these motivations and concerns produced *conflicted correctors*: they sometimes wanted to correct, but often felt the cost of doing so was too great to bear.

How We Approached This Research

To understand how members of the public are thinking about whether they would correct misinformation on social media, we talked to 32 social media users identified from an online panel. We recruited participants for interviews based on their answers to survey questions about their correction

Observed Correction. Leticia Bode and Emily K. Vraga, Oxford University Press. © Leticia Bode and Emily K. Vraga (2025). DOI: 10.1093/oso/9780197565896.003.0006

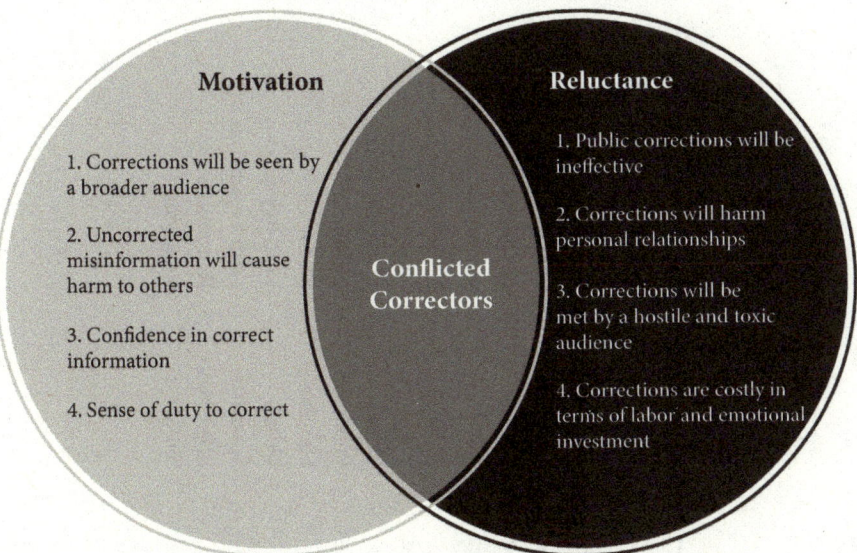

Motivation

1. Corrections will be seen by a broader audience

2. Uncorrected misinformation will cause harm to others

3. Confidence in correct information

4. Sense of duty to correct

Conflicted Correctors

Reluctance

1. Public corrections will be ineffective

2. Corrections will harm personal relationships

3. Corrections will be met by a hostile and toxic audience

4. Corrections are costly in terms of labor and emotional investment

Figure 6.1   Conflicted correctors Credit: Meghan Landsberg, 2024.

experiences, and to ensure a diverse sample of participants based on gender, race, age, geography, political party, and education (see Table 6.1). We paid participants to speak with us for up to an hour about their encounters with misinformation on social media and how they decide whether or not to engage with it. These interviews took place during the spring and summer of 2022, over Zoom or other online platforms, and were conducted by the amazing research assistant, Rowan McMullen Cheng. For more information about these interviews, the participants, and the questions we asked, see our online appendix. All participants were given pseudonyms, which we'll use throughout the chapter. All quotes in this chapter are from these users unless otherwise noted.

For these interviews, we wanted to identify and speak with what we thought would be two groups of people—correctors and noncorrectors. To do so, we first tried asking people how often they had corrected someone else on social media in the past week (using the same survey questions as the previous chapter). But our first set of interviews suggested that many people who had said in the survey that they had corrected someone in the past week were unable to tell us about actually doing so, or vice versa—people who reported in the survey they hadn't corrected someone in the past week told us about cases where they had or would correct.

As just one example, in the survey Philippe told us he had never corrected someone on social media, which was echoed in what he initially told us in the interview: "Oh, I never, I never do that . . . I just don't, I don't engage with it." But as he continued to speak, it came out that he was willing to correct if

Table 6.1 **Members of the Public We Spoke With**

Pseudonym	Gender	Age	Race/Ethnicity	Education	Geography	Party Affiliation
Colin	Male	Old	Black	Some college	Urban	Democrat
Alex	Nonbinary	Young	Hispanic	Bachelor's degree	Suburban	Strong Democrat
Bonnie	Female	Young	White	Bachelor's degree	Urban	Democrat
Danielle	Female	Young	Hispanic	Bachelor's degree	Urban	Democrat
Fiona	Female	Middle	White	Associate's degree	Rural	Strong Democrat
Earl	Male	Young	White	Some college	Rural	Independent
Gaston	Male	Middle	White	Bachelor's degree	Rural	Lean Republican
Ian	Male	Middle	White	Graduate degree	Urban	Strong Democrat
Karl	Male	Middle	White	Bachelor's degree	Suburban	Democrat
Martin	Male	Middle	White	Some college	Suburban	Strong Democrat
Owen	Male	Middle	White	Come college	Urban	Lean Republican
Hermine	Female	Old	White	Graduate degree	Suburban	Lean Republican
Julia	Female	Middle	White	Graduate degree	Suburban	Republican
Lisa	Female	Old	White	Bachelor's degree	Suburban	Republican

Name	Gender	Age	Race	Education	Location	Politics
Richard	Male	Middle	Asian	Bachelor's degree	Suburban	Democrat
Nicole	Female	Old	Black	Some college	Urban	Lean Democrat
Tobias	Male	Old	Mixed Race	Graduate degree	Urban	Lean Republican
Walter	Male	Old	White	Bachelor's degree	Urban	Independent
Bret	Male	Old	Hispanic	Bachelor's degree	Suburban	Democrat
Don	Male	Middle	White	Bachelor's degree	Urban	Republican
Paula	Female	Middle	Black	Graduate degree	Urban	Democrat
Franklin	Male	Middle	Asian	Graduate degree	Suburban	Independent
Harold	Male	Middle	White	Bachelor's degree	Suburban	Democrat
Jose	Male	Middle	White	Bachelor's degree	Suburban	Strong Republican
Lee	Male	Middle	Asian	Some college	Suburban	Independent
Shary	Female	Old	White	Some college	Suburban	Democrat
Nigel	Male	Young	Asian	Bachelor's degree	Urban	Democrat
Philippe	Male	Middle	White	Associate's degree	Urban	Independent
Sean	Male	Middle	White	High school/ GED	Suburban	Lean Republican
Vince	Male	Middle	White	Bachelor's degree	Urban	Lean Democrat
Alberto	Male	Middle	White	High school/ GED	Urban	Strong Republican
Chris	Male	Young	Mixed Race	Bachelor's degree	Suburban	Democrat

"it's something I know for an absolute fact." Similarly, Earl told us in the survey he had engaged in correction in the past week and started the conversation talking about a decision-making process of responding to misinformation, suggesting that sometimes "something inside me might be like, 'No, that's wrong.' And . . . just sometimes you get that nerve that just strikes." But as the conversation continued, he displayed a strong reluctance to correct, saying that when he sees misinformation, "I ignore a lot of it" because he doesn't think corrections work.

In response to this challenge, we changed our approach, fielding a second survey to try to identify people who said they *always* or *never* corrected misinformation on social media. But we found the same thing. No matter what participants told us on the survey, most of the people we talked to ended up being *conflicted correctors*: people who are sometimes willing to correct under the right circumstances but have a lot of reasons to feel reluctant to do so generally.

Reluctance and Self-Censorship

The concept of reluctance comes up in a lot of research, generally describing hesitation, unwillingness, or lack of intention to perform some task.[1] By describing participants as reluctant, we mean that the people we spoke with were mostly hesitant to personally engage in correction on social media. They also expressed a general approval of correction and reasons why it was valuable, reflecting the social norms we discussed in the last chapter. Because their reluctance pushed them away from correcting, but other motivations pushed them toward it, we think *conflicted* is the best way to describe them. While these conflicted correctors by and large refrain from engaging with posters of misinformation in a systematic or routine way, sometimes they do so when the right set of circumstances align.

The idea that people are often reluctant to express their opinion is by no means new. People are habitually attuned to considering what others think of them, and an innate desire to engage in impression management—that is, trying to control how other people see them—can be readily triggered in social situations.[2] Given these impression management motives, people often engage in self-censorship—that is, they keep quiet so that others won't think badly of them. This is the same kind of reluctance to communicate that the interview participants described to us.

Online spaces exacerbate many people's desires to think about how they are presenting themselves, including deciding to self-censor. Writing before the rise of social media platforms, Joseph Walther argued that asynchronous (doesn't happen in real time) communication and limited number of social cues (that is, people don't really know who you are or how you're responding to content) means that computer-mediated communication (which he was largely thinking about in terms of chatrooms and bulletin boards) would generally allow people more opportunities to engage in strategic self-presentation. The key affordance of visibility (as we discussed in Chapter 2) also contributes, creating large imagined audiences and thus reinforcing desires to deliberately curate one's personal image. Thus, it is not surprising that strategic self-presentation occurs in these online social spaces like social media,[3] allowing people to create idealized versions of themselves.[4]

The desire to present our best selves on social media further intersects with the affordances and norms of these platforms to deter engaging in controversial topics. For example, people often avoid posting about contentious issues, especially political topics, on social media. Therefore, it is hardly surprising that in the context of correction, people are generally quite reluctant to correct about issues they perceive as "contentious."[5]

How can we square these general pressures—the ways in which social media make us want to put our best foot forward and heighten the reasons we might be reluctant to correct—with the fact so many people in the previous chapter told us they did correct? We'll start with the reasons people think correction is valuable or why they would engage in it (at least theoretically), before turning to the concrete roadblocks that often prevent these normative desires to correct from turning into action.

Why Correct: The Imagined Audience for Correction

Among people who say they correct misinformation on social media, four main reasons stand out: a recognition of a broader audience who might see their correction, concerns about the potential harm that uncorrected misinformation could cause to that audience, general confidence in the knowledge needed to correct, and a sense of duty to correct. Recognizing these reasons to correct and their resonance across groups suggests they may be powerful motivators in getting even more people to perform corrections (stay tuned for the next chapter).

BROADER AUDIENCES

One of the primary arguments of this book is that public correction on social media can be powerful and scalable because of the size of the audience: many people could have the opportunity to see any given correction, increasing the chances they will hold accurate attitudes on the topic. Encouragingly, many of our correctors recognized that fact, picturing a large, imagined audience for corrections that includes many people who are open to being corrected (perhaps even more than the person being corrected, a source of reluctance we'll return to below). Colin told us about a time he offered a public correction "because it's for others who might see this post," which Fiona echoed when describing "maybe a more reasonable person" who will see her corrections. This imagined audience can be generic (the public), but others imagined specific loved ones seeing their correction (or seeing uncorrected misinformation), as Alex describes:

> I think it's the public. Just anyone that I think could stumble upon, maybe someone that's younger and more susceptible to being deceived or that sort of thing. But in general I think when I correct misinformation, I think of all of my friends, my family, people close to me.

But the important point uniting these perspectives is the idea that there are lots of people on social media who will benefit from seeing the corrections that social media users might offer.

HARM

Second, people told us they corrected because of the *harm* misinformation can cause. For example, Fiona, Alex, Lisa, and Richard all made clear they were more willing to correct when they thought the misinformation in question might hurt someone who saw it, reinforcing that correctors are thinking about the audience for misinformation and correction. Richard told us that when someone is likely to believe misinformation and it can harm them, "then yeah, I do decide to act upon it." Fiona said she was generally reluctant to correct but that "if the misinformation is really, really bad, I will march myself to that person and try to correct them as soon as possible." Harm also motivated Alex when he corrected COVID-19 vaccine misinformation that his uncle had shared on Twitter:

> If I just ignored it . . . I could potentially put not only my family in harm's way, but other people . . . So, I felt just the fact that there's a sort of urgency that if I don't act. . . . I felt like that there was a lot of people that could be harmed.

For other users, lack of harm served as a deterrent to correction, leading them to ignore *less* harmful misinformation. Or as Lisa put it,

> I don't know, some things I know not to be true and I don't really care . . . if people think that whatever all-natural product they're using is better than Windex, I don't care, just let them think that.

This concern about the potential for harm to others resonates with what we know from the third-person effect literature in general: that people see *others* as more vulnerable to negative media effects (like misinformation) than themselves, often leading them to support action to protect those vulnerable others. New research confirms what we saw in our interviews, that stronger perceptions of the vulnerability of others as compared to oneself to harmful misinformation tends to motivate correction.[6]

HARM 2.0: PLATFORM PERSPECTIVES ON HARM

Notably, multiple people who had worked on misinformation policy at social media platforms also highlighted the perceived harmful impact of misinformation as being a key consideration in whether and how to take action. For instance, Erin (social media)[7] said the platform she worked for focused on misinformation with "a real-world harm attached to it," and Jerry (search) highlighted that the platform he worked for was "centering around user harm [as] the way to differentiate where to intervene versus where not to." Importantly, different platforms thought about harm in different ways. Often this was a very narrow perception of harm—specifically misinformation that had been clearly linked to a specific negative and serious physical outcome, like drinking bleach to cure COVID-19 (Erin). But some platforms thought more broadly about harm, including topics like "planetary destruction" (Jerry), which manifested as misinformation about climate change.

Platforms are also often framing harm as being related to the size of the audience (often called "reach") likely to see a piece of content. As Dexter (other) puts it:

> We largely thought about bad content in terms of impressions. Like the volume of people that look at a piece of [content that violates platform rules] is like the thing that drives harm. The existence of that is actually not something that drives harm, it's that it is shared, that it is viewed, that it is disseminated.

This focus on impressions was echoed by Erin (social media) who highlighted that reach is a key way of thinking about harmfulness of misinformation. It's also present in a 2022 tweet by Yoel Roth, then the head of Trust and Safety at Twitter (Figure 6.2), considering the reach of harmful content (in this case, racial slurs).

Notably, though, some platform employees saw this emphasis on harm as being merely an effort by the platforms to avoid negative publicity and engage in corporate impression management. As Gabrielle (social media) put it "It was not like, 'Gabrielle's responsible for making this work better for people.' It was,

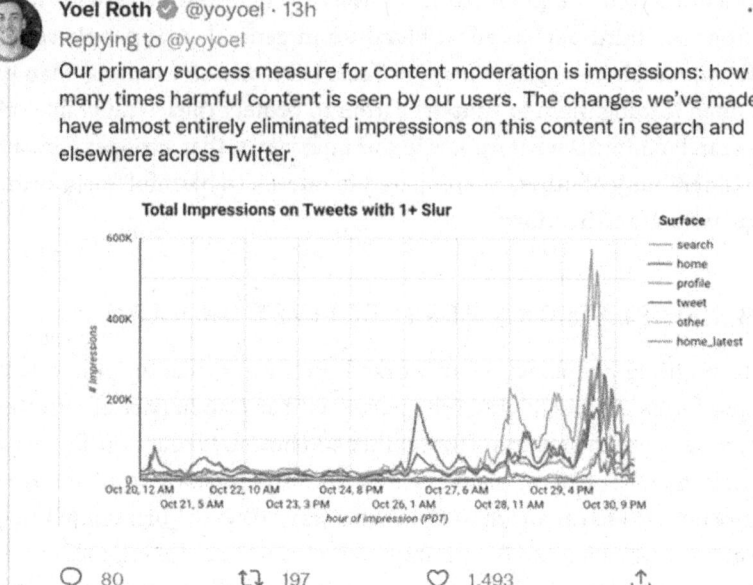

Yoel Roth ✔ @yoyoel · 13h   •••
Replying to @yoyoel

Our primary success measure for content moderation is impressions: how many times harmful content is seen by our users. The changes we've made have almost entirely eliminated impressions on this content in search and elsewhere across Twitter.

Figure 6.2   Tweet from Yoel Roth, then the head of trust and safety at Twitter

'Gabrielle's responsible for preventing it from harming people and getting [the platform] into trouble.'"

Some of the people we spoke with also perceived that platforms sometimes used harm to *avoid* engaging with misinformation. Because it is often "implausibly hard to . . . directly connect one piece of information to the offline harm or online harm" (Jerry, search), the platforms essentially have plausible deniability—they believe they cannot reasonably be held responsible if we can't be sure that some misinformation on their platform caused an offline harm. In addition, Erin (social media) pointed out that the idea of deciding what was harmful and what wasn't was

> incredibly paternalistic. I think the platforms are very uncomfortable with that reality because it means determining, what is the information that people should see or should not see? It means determining, this is the type of information that causes real-world harm, that doesn't. This is the type of information that's going to cause you to hurt yourself physically. So it's like, "Okay, bleach. Don't drink bleach." Cool, we're good with that. But no need for masks anymore? . . . Does a [platform] actually want to take a role?

But in general, when misinformation is seen as harmful, platforms and the public agree that responding to and correcting that misinformation becomes more important.

CONFIDENCE

The first two themes dealt with the perceived audience for correction: that there is an audience receptive to correction and that they might be harmed in the absence of corrections. The second two themes relate more to an individual's personal sense that *they* should be the one to respond, rather than some other social media user: that they have the confidence or experience that enables them to respond, and that it may even be their *duty* to do so.

Many people said they would only consider correcting when they were very confident both that the misinformation was wrong and that their response would definitely be right. For example, Philippe explained, "I generally do not correct people, unless it's something I know for an absolute fact that I can back it up with showing them." When offering a percentage for their certainty, the lowest percentage any of the participants offered was 80% (Colin), and several people said they had to have 100% confidence before they would correct (Richard, Bret). This also fits with what we know about self-censorship: people who care deeply about an issue and who are confident in their views are generally more willing to speak out.[8] In the case of our potential correctors this can be a motivating force, encouraging them to dive into the fray and offer the correct information in response to misinformation. But it also means that there are cases in which a vocal and confident minority engages in outspoken conversations on social media, skewing perceptions of public opinion and sometimes even spreading misinformation.[9]

People tended to feel most confident and committed to correcting when the misinformation spoke directly to their personal experience or perceived expertise. As a result, many people said they were more likely to correct when it came to misinformation related to their job. Gaston spoke about a painful failed public correction about cancer drugs where he weighed in because "I actually work in a pharmaceutical company," while Walter told us "the type of work I do . . . specifically about the company I work for that, [when I see something] I know to be wrong, I'm going to correct it." Hermine, a small business owner, spoke about her duty to correct for "business related items," despite a bad experience with trying to correct a (now former) friend:

> I'm hesitant and I think twice before correcting somebody. But if they really don't know, you know what? I will still let them know because a lot of people have never owned their own business so they have no concept of how things work. A lot of people out there just have not had a lot of the life experiences I have.

Parenting was another space users described having the confidence to correct. Lisa (a parent) said she "wouldn't mind correcting somebody or putting my two cents in" for parenting issues, while Fiona (also a parent) describes her willingness to correct misinformation about breastfeeding because of her comfort and confidence on the topic overall:

> Areas where I'm comfortable and it's been an interest for a long time and I've done some research on it in the past, I am definitely more likely to correct on those type of topics.

This emphasis on confidence also reflects our earlier conversation in Chapter 2 about the blurred distinction among the different actors in the misinformation and correction system. When would-be correctors speak about their willingness to correct only for those topics in which they feel like they have expertise, they are essentially describing the circumstances in which they feel more like a *professional* with specialized knowledge than like a member of the *public*. It also speaks to the uniquely important role that members of the public can play as correctors: in addition to factual information, they can also share personal experience as part of their corrections. And research suggests corrections that incorporating personal narratives and perspectives is not only able to increase accuracy on the topic[11] but may also offer benefits in terms of fostering respect across "moral divides."[12] That many of our correctors recognize and wish to speak up when they have personal experiences to offer may make their corrections even more valuable for democratic societies.

DUTY

To sum up these forces, many people ultimately spoke of a sense of obligation or *duty* to respond to misinformation that is being shared on social media. This echoes what we heard in the previous chapter—people want to say they are doing something that is valued by society and that they feel they should be doing. Duty is a classic motivator across a wide range of behaviors. For instance, a sense of duty has been shown to give people enough satisfaction from voting that it can overwhelm the costs and seeming ineffectiveness of it.[13] It's also been associated with pro-environmental behaviors[14] and vaccination intentions.[15]

So it's not surprising that duty can motivate people to act against misinformation as well. As Bret says, "the public is responsible for stopping misinformation." Franklin describes it as "the right thing to do," and Harold expresses a deep commitment to "reality," above all else:

> It was just a now or never kind of moment where . . . I just felt compelled, I felt like reality itself was being contested in our town . . . and I wanted to fight for the version of reality that I think is the truth.

Interestingly, as these quotes suggest, some people distinguish between their personal duty to respond versus a broadly held mandate that *the public* should respond (for the latter, refer back to Figure 5.2 in the previous chapter). For some topics or for particular cases, people (Harold, Hermine, Gaston) feel a personal responsibility to correct a specific piece of misinformation. But others (Franklin, Bret) are describing a general sense that the public (and thus themselves at least theoretically) should be engaging in this task. This difference between a sense that correction should happen, versus whether one personally feels the need to correct, will also be reflected when we try to motivate correction in the next chapter.

Sources of Reluctance

The previous section suggests that correction is often something that happens on a case-by-case basis: when the right mix of features come together to create a recognition of a broader audience who could benefit from correction (or be harmed if correction doesn't happen), where people feel they have the personal experience and/or expertise to respond, and thus ultimately feel that they have a *duty* to do so. This shouldn't obscure the main point that most people are generally unwilling to correct, even with our optimistic estimates in the previous chapter. In our interviews, we found that even those who said they had engaged or were still engaging in correction did so with hesitation, with caveats, and with real concerns. We identified four major sources of reluctance, which we summarize in Figure 6.1.

(IN)EFFECTIVENESS

Many people said they don't correct misinformation because they just don't believe it would be effective. Social media users alternately described correcting as "wasting your time" (Earl, Richard, Karl, Julia), "pointless" (Paula, Philippe), or "shouting into the void, if you don't think it's actually going to make any impact or not even be seen" (Danielle). In other words, they report feeling hopeless— many want to help address the problem of misinformation, but just don't feel like correcting misinformation will make a difference.

Other users take this one step further: they expressed the concern that correction would actually make things worse. Users worried that a correction would "make people more set on their viewpoint" (Bonnie) or "doubl[e] down" (Alex, Harold) on their original beliefs, "dig their heels in harder to the point that they were trying to make before" (Fiona). Despite these commonly expressed concerns, however, scholarship has found this type of backfire effect (when correction reinforces misperceptions rather than reducing them) is quite rare.

The vast majority of the time, giving someone accurate information makes them more accurate about the topic.[16] This offers an opportunity: communicating research showing that corrections are effective should motivate more people to correct (spoiler: doing this seems to work, as we show in the next chapter).

This belief that correction won't work also ties into a broader literature in political science, communication, and psychology on efficacy. Research describes three kinds of efficacy that are linked to behaviors: self-efficacy (Can I perform the behavior? Do I have the skills, capacity, and resources to do the behavior?), external efficacy (Will others listen to me? If I do this, will anyone else pay attention?) and response efficacy (If they do listen, will they take action? And will those actions make a difference?).[17] Each type of efficacy can motivate behaviors in different ways. As we note above, people with low self-efficacy are more likely to engage in self-censorship,[18] while those with high self-efficacy are more likely to engage in politics and other civic engagement.[19] External efficacy and response efficacy are also important in motivating behaviors, especially when the desired outcome is communal, meaning it depends on people besides just you.[20] This of course makes sense—if you don't think your action will have any impact, then why bother? In the context of correcting misinformation on social media, we think all three levels of efficacy are relevant, making low *correction efficacy* (combining all three types) a major barrier to correcting.

Interestingly, while we saw that thinking about an imagined audience can motivate people to correct, many people are also often thinking about the imagined audience for corrections when explaining why they think corrections won't work. But unlike would-be correctors imagining a receptive audience for their corrections, those who shy away from correcting instead imagine an audience that is part of a self-reinforcing community that will defend each other no matter what. Danielle connects this idea to the nature of social networks, saying,

> there is also a large toxic community on social media . . . some people are very, very rooted in their beliefs and they don't like to be challenged on it.

Users see these communities as one reason why corrections won't work, because "people have friends that only think just like them . . . all these people are not going to believe me and . . . they all stay with their own little group" (Lisa). Or as Ian puts it, correcting someone online "seems to be futile. When you see a lot of these posts, there's this little echo chamber." This can certainly be the case—humans rely on social support to maintain belief systems,[21] manage stress,[22] and even mitigate physical pain[23]—and that social support extends to supportive communication online. But many users recognize the downsides of social support, in that they can contribute to maintaining *false* beliefs.[24]

Ian's use of the term "echo chamber" is likely not incidental. The discussion of whether social media facilitates echo chambers—communities where everyone agrees with one another—is one that has drawn a lot of public interest. But what the scholarly research has broadly found is contrary to Ian's experience. While echo chambers certainly can and do exist on social media for some topics,[25] research has found little evidence of widespread echo chambers.[26] Indeed, in many cases social media is more diverse than offline social connections,[27] especially as increased partisan sorting offline means we are less and less likely to live near or connect with people who are different from us politically.[28] None of this invalidates the existence of echo chambers online,[29] completely addresses Ian's concerns, or questions his lived experience, but instead makes social media notable as one of the few remaining spaces where we can see so many different perspectives in the same space. The very fact that people are reporting that they see *other people's* echo chambers—even if it makes them hesitant to correct—is evidence that the online spaces they describe are actually quite porous.

A final reason that corrections were seen as ineffective considers not just the social network of the person being corrected but the social network and workings of the platform itself. Specifically, some users expressed concerns that the algorithm (that determines what content is shown to any given user) would interpret any comment (including those containing a correction) as a sign of interest in content, and therefore boost the signal of the original misinformation on social media to a broader audience than it originally reached, making things worse rather than better. We hear this from Shary, who, "understand[s] how these algorithms work, the more that you have conversations on these posts, the more likely they're going to show up on other people's feeds," and from Earl's sense that any kind of correction would result in the "algorithm's going to pick [the misinformation] up and start spreading it around." The sense of what algorithms may or may not do is sometimes referred to as the "algorithmic imaginary"—an unknown and unknowable sense of what algorithms amplify or demote on social media.[30]

This represents an important potential criticism of observed correction, that responding to misinformation—even to correct it—can send an engagement signal to social media algorithms,[31] which would then increase the number of people who see the misinformation post. So this was a question we posed specifically to the platform employees we spoke with. The impact of commenting in general was clear to the platform employees. As Pablo (social media) put it, "if you comment on an article, it's going to get a lot more distribution." But it was less clear the impact that commenting *to say something is false* would have. Pablo described the concern well—that the models platforms train to identify and surface relevant content to users would lead to more people seeing misinformation, even beyond the post that gets corrected:

> Due to the machine learning and the way [the platform] works, if you share an article and I say, "This is wrong," it doesn't just boost it in your share of that article, it boosts it in everyone's share of that article and articles like it . . . [The platform] will think this is great content and show it to more people.

But corrective comments can have a positive impact as well. Both Pablo and Erin (social media) pointed out that the platforms they had worked for use corrective comments as important signals for content moderation. As Erin described,

> You can definitely see people saying, "False, not true, this isn't true," and those utterances and the comments are part of what underlies the machine learning model for detecting misinformation.

In other words, platforms have algorithms that are trained to identify misinformation, and the comments that say something is not true are a useful information source for those algorithms to help them know what is likely to be misinformation so that they can apply other interventions (covering it up, removing it, reducing its reach, etc; although platforms have largely moved away from such interventions, as we'll discuss in Chapter 10) in accordance with their terms of service. Despite Pablo's concerns about amplification, he also highlighted the importance of such comments for flagging content that might be misinformation. When asked directly whether he would recommend someone commenting with a correction, he said "I don't know where it ends up in the wash right now. It's varied."

All of this highlights the complexity of the issue. No one—not even the platforms themselves, let alone researchers like us—have solid data on whether and how often correction even happens (as Sebastien, social media, said, "I don't have a quantitative or anything close to a quantitative answer on that for you"), let alone whether it helps or hurts the distribution of misinformation. All of this suggests that we need more partnerships and collaboration between technology platforms and researchers, to share knowledge, methods, and tradeoffs that come with navigating a complicated issue.[32]

BROKEN RELATIONSHIPS

A second source of reluctance comes from perceptions of what might happen after a correction. The first way people worried about post-correction reactions was the concern that correcting someone would damage valued personal relationships.

The fear of broken relationships for our members of the public is quite real. Many of the social media users we spoke with told us about specific instances where a correction had ended a friendship, making them hesitant to correct online in the future. After Gaston corrected (but failed to persuade) a friend of 12 years who had shared misinformation, Gaston's friend cut off all contact. Hermine also lost a friend after correcting them, and Bret estimates he has lost "maybe 25% of my friends" from Facebook corrections and as a result "I don't comment. . . . Because at the very end, I'm going to lose your friendship if I correct or say that you are wrong." Or as Richard puts it, "I don't want to break my relationship just to do some fact check." This can (once again) lead to self-censorship—staying quiet to avoid saying the wrong thing.

These lived experiences may be increasingly common. For instance, research around the 2012 recall of controversial Wisconsin governor Scott Walker shows that about a third of Wisconsin residents (32%) stopped talking about politics with someone over disagreements about Walker's policies.[33] 44% of people[34] also report blocking or unfriending people on social media for political reasons— a number that has risen in recent years.[35] Both practices speak to the intensely felt polarization currently dominating US politics and creeping into American culture as a whole. Vince sums up many interviewees' beliefs:

> I'm not getting involved. I learned not to get involved. It doesn't matter what my opinion is. I will not get involved. I will not voice my opinion on social media just because I remain neutral. I haven't lost a single friend during any of these tough times because I don't post anything good. Any of my opinions on any matter.

It's important to acknowledge that as painful as each of these experiences are, they remain focused on the relationship between the person doing the correction and the person being corrected. These users did not speak about—and may not have known—whether their corrections were effective for the broader community who saw the interaction. We can imagine that Gaston's willingness to respond to misinformation regarding false cancer cures with his personal experiences—both as a grandson and as someone who works in the pharmaceutical industry (in his words, "First of all, I actually work in a pharmaceutical company. If I could get access to that [miracle cure], my grandma will still be here")—may be quite persuasive to people a step removed from the interaction. But it can be hard to think about these second-order benefits when facing the reality of a lost friendship.

TOXIC REACTIONS

The second way post-correction reactions were a topic of concern manifested in the idea that corrections can create a community backlash, where correctors would face responses that not only disagree with the correction, as described in the discussion of echo chambers above, but also might contain threats or hate speech.

Several users described the fear that they might face personal retaliation or violence if they try to correct someone on social media. For many, this translates into a sense that online correction is dangerous: Sean describes responses to correction as "savage," Walter reports being a "digital punching bag," Hermine doesn't want to "start the war," Karl says he wants to avoid being (metaphorically) "stabbed," Bonnie called it "fighting" or "getting ugly," Lisa feels like she's "being attacked," and Nicole described her one attempt to correct someone else as an "all-out war scene." This sense of diffuse fear of retaliation echoes feelings voiced by minority groups, and long theorized by the so-called spiral of silence,[36] which suggests that people worry they may hold a minority view and therefore stay quiet to avoid conflict with others (that's right, more self-censorship). And we know that spirals of silence operate in today's society—recent research among Democrats in rural Texas found many were worried that speaking out against a majority could create economic or personal danger, even if they had not experienced such retaliation themselves.[37] These spirals of silence can also operate on social media, especially for contentious social issues like debates over same-sex marriage.[38]

For some, the sense that they could be attacked on social media goes beyond simple arguments or fighting to feeling a real sense of personal threat. For example, Danielle told us she doesn't correct online not only because it wouldn't do any good, but because "there is also a large toxic community on social media . . . And there's things like doxing and . . . threats or reporting your account." For Tobias, some topics (specifically the January 6 insurrection) felt too dangerous to engage with, because "100% of the time turns into, what's your address, I want to come over and—turn this into violence."

As a result, some people came up with alternative ways to correct misinformation that lowered these risks. Despite our argument that social media offers spaces for observed correction, where semipublic corrections can reach large audiences, there was not necessarily agreement among users that *public* corrections are the most appropriate way to respond to misinformation. In fact, consistent with previous research,[39] several people indicated that if they saw misinformation on social media, they would correct the person offline rather than online. Indeed, some of the users who were most committed to not correcting online were quite willing to do so offline, or as Gaston put it, "It makes you think, you can't do this online. It has to be in person." There were two main reasons they offered for this—both related to preserving relationships.

First, moving corrections offline helps correctors avoid embarrassing the person sharing misinformation. As Sean puts it, "Privately. No people. I don't want to humiliate them," or as Fiona says, "I don't really want to publicly embarrass anybody." And for many, they don't see it as a temporary or fleeting feeling of embarrassment, but something deep and profound. Tobias makes the blanket declaration that "They're embarrassed by that. Everyone is. No one wants to be and no one likes to be wrong." And this is also borne out among those who told us they had been corrected on social media. Nicole spoke about her experience sharing something inaccurate on social media and that when she found out, she felt "embarrassed, ashamed, regretful, sad, like kicking myself." These feelings lasted, and she said that she still did not want to share much of anything on social media as a result.

A second, related reason that people told us correcting offline was preferable was to avoid conflict. For many, doing correction offline fits into norms of politeness (this is consistent with research asking young adults in India why they don't correct their elders in WhatsApp groups).[40] Tobias says private correction is "common courtesy" or "human 101," and Vince suggests that to correct online through comments is to "attack the person and point fingers." These comments suggest that people perceive correction as inherently confrontational and impolite. Thus, it should be done offline where the conflict and the resulting (impolite) disagreement is not aired in public. Additionally, the affordances of text-based social media platforms don't facilitate conveying empathy and explanation, as Hermine explains:

> Social media is very impersonal in that respect because you're just posting something, you're giving additional information but the words that you use can come across the wrong way to that person [because] social media doesn't give you those same [nonverbal] tools or abilities.

Or as Julia puts it, correcting online is not consistent with her "conflict style," perceiving it as more conflictual than a similar exchange that takes place offline:

> I typically don't try to debate them online, that's not really my conflict style. . . . I would probably talk to them outside of the confines of Facebook, Twitter, wherever I saw it and kind of ask them questions. But I probably would not engage in a thread by replying and talking to people there.

Concerns about both personal backlash and broader toxic environments serve to deter many people from publicly correcting. Sometimes, these concerns lead people to still correct but in private ways, which may be powerful (sometimes even more so) for the person sharing the misinformation, but unlikely to help the broader audience who could be misled by the uncorrected misinformation. Other times, such concerns turn people off from correcting altogether.

COSTS

A final theme was the recognition that engaging in correction can be a costly activity. This is hardly surprising; people need lots of different *resources,* like skills, time, or money, to participate in virtually any political or social activity.[41] This is part of the internal efficacy we discussed above—I have to believe I can correct, and the more resources I think it takes, the lower my resulting internal self-efficacy will be. In thinking about resources, people often spoke about correction as being "time-consuming" (Sean) or "not worth my time" (Nigel, Bret), and Colin put it bluntly: "I can't stay up 24 hours 24/7 answering someone's comment." Julia sums up the general sense among social media users: "I just have more important things to do. I have work, I have to pay my bills. I can't engage in a 500 comment deep thread."

The perceived cost of correcting is not just a matter of time but also emotional labor. This can be specific to the toxic environments that people fear online (as we just described), but also even more generally when corrections are not met with anger but with apathy: "I get way too emotionally invested when I try to correct people or structure arguments, and then just get a text back" (Fiona). The desire to make things better in combination with the feeling that what they're trying to do is not working is emotionally fraught for many users. But while the emotional labor component is one that is hard to alleviate, the other costs—of time, of effort, of research—are ones that can potentially be offset, and we'll discuss the important ways in which accessible curated evidence (ACE) can help do so in Chapter 9.

Conclusion

This chapter showcases the ways in which people build symbolic folk theories— essentially stories they make up to help understand the world—to make sense of their media experiences,[42] and how they apply these theories to decide whether to correct misinformation on social media. This manifests in various ways, including believing that correction will make people less accurate and that most online communities are little more than echo chambers, even though we have little evidence to support these beliefs. People's salient experiences, described throughout this chapter, likely contribute to the development of such folk theories in an effort to make sense of a complicated and sometimes intentionally opaque media environment.

In addition, respondents described engaging in a cost-benefit analysis of how important or worthwhile they thought it was to engage with misinformation, and how much mental bandwidth, time to do research, or other capacity they had available. The downside of this calculation is that for most people, most of the time, it probably does not make sense to engage—it takes time, effort, and emotional resilience that most of us don't have on a day-to-day basis.

The upside, on the other hand, is these concerns offer a roadmap of concrete things we can do to encourage people to correct more often. We can lower some of the costs, by making corrective information easier to find and use (Chapter 9). We can also show people how effective correction is, encourage them to think about the broader audience that might see a correction, and tell them that people value correction and say they do it themselves. We'll try several of these approaches in the next chapter in an attempt to motivate people to correct.

TL; DR

- Most people are conflicted correctors, deciding whether to correct on a case-by-case basis.
- In general, correctors think about the broader audience they are reaching and describe a sense of duty to correct.
- In specific cases, the perceived harm of the misinformation and personal confidence about the topic can motivate people to correct.
- People are reluctant to correct because they see corrections as ineffective, worry about damaging personal relationships, anticipate a toxic response, and view correction as costly.

Chapter 7

Motivating Correction

In the previous chapter, we described our conversations with social media users about their experiences with and perceptions of correction on social media. By and large, people are *conflicted correctors*: they agree that something needs to be done about misinformation and describe specific cases in which they would correct, but they mostly emphasize the reasons they do not publicly correct. In this chapter, we ask: what we can do to motivate more people to correct?

We focus on a few key reasons people told us they don't correct: concerns that correction doesn't work, that people wouldn't see it, that people don't like it, or that people would respond badly. In the pages that follow, we'll investigate how common these concerns are among the American public, which concerns are most closely related to someone's willingness to correct misinformation, and whether we can encourage more people to say they would correct by addressing these concerns.

We find much of what we heard in our interviews reflects a broader sense among the American public about the risks and benefits of correction. Two beliefs stand out in explaining reported correction behaviors: whether people believe corrections will help a broader audience become more accurate (thinking about the *observers* of corrections), and whether they think other people like and perform corrections (the *social norms* we keep talking about). We follow this up with an experiment that informs people about many of the key points of this book. We find that telling people that public corrections make audiences more accurate, that people like corrections, and that other people engage in correction each encourage people to express a greater willingness to respond to specific cases of misinformation but do little to change their general willingness to correct misinformation more broadly.

Observed Correction. Leticia Bode and Emily K. Vraga, Oxford University Press. © Leticia Bode and Emily K. Vraga (2025). DOI: 10.1093/oso/9780197565896.003.0007

Common Correction Concerns

Our first question was whether the concerns that were voiced by participants in the interviews we conducted were also represented among Americans more broadly. While interviews are great for getting detailed and nuanced information from a small group of people, they're not meant to generalize to a broader population—that is, we can't be sure the concerns they told us about are also concerns shared by a larger group of people. To answer this, we surveyed 800 people in the spring of 2023 about their attitudes regarding correction and its effects.[1] To tap into the concrete concerns people raised in our interviews, we asked each of our participants what they thought would happen if they corrected someone on social media. Separately, we also asked people more generally about their perceptions of the social norms surrounding correction: whether people like and perform corrections.

Our survey data reinforces the themes that came out of our qualitative interviews (see Figure 7.1).[2] These themes are shortened in our figures, but the full question wording for each is included in Table 7.1.

First, we find an interesting distinction when it comes to people's perceptions of how effective corrections are at changing beliefs. Despite research suggesting that corrections can increase accuracy for the person sharing the misinformation,[3] very few people (17%) perceive they will be effective in that case. A

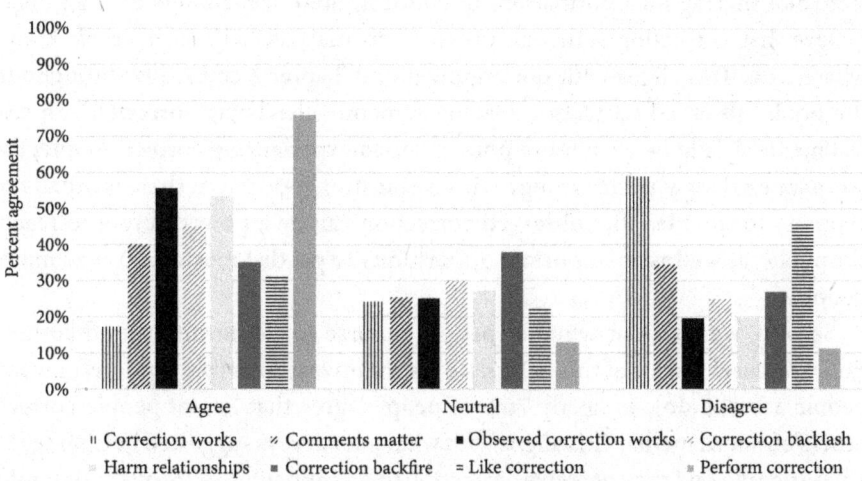

Figure 7.1 Key themes about correction among the American public. *Notes:* We list brief descriptions of the different statements beneath the figure (see Table 7.1 for the full statements) and assign a different color or texture to each statement. We group participants by whether they somewhat to strongly agree with the statement, whether they are neutral on the statement, or whether they somewhat to strongly disagree with the statement. The y-axis represents the percentage of participants who fall into each of these categories (agree, neutral, disagree) for each statement.

Table 7.1 **Question Wording and Description**

Label	Question wording
If I correct someone sharing misinformation on social media . . .	
Correction works	The person I correct will become more accurate in their beliefs
Comments matter	Many people will pay attention to the correction
Observed correction works	It will help other people know what's true
Correction backlash	People will respond harshly to my correction
Harms relationships	It will harm my relationship with the person I corrected
Corrections backfire	The person sharing the misinformation will be even more convinced it's true
Please rate your level of agreement with each of the following statements:	
Like corrections	People often like corrections on social media
Perform corrections	Lots of people correct others on social media

substantial minority (27%) believe these corrections will actually backfire for this person, making them even more convinced of their wrong beliefs, despite the academic evidence about the rareness of backfire effects.[4] This echoes what we heard in the previous chapter—people just aren't convinced that corrections can work, at least when they are thinking about changing the mind of someone sharing misinformation. In contrast, 56% of members of the public believe that correcting someone on social media will help *other people* know what's true. This aligns with our argument in Chapter 2 and really throughout the book: observed correction (seeing someone else being corrected) on social media should be even more powerful than experiencing correction directly (someone saying you are wrong). This is (mostly) good news: there is broad receptivity to the idea that observed correction can be a powerful tool to reach the public, as well as an important opportunity to get that message to even more people.

Second, we consider whether people endorse social norms around correction. We see evidence of this in terms of descriptive norms (perceptions of what people actually do), as nearly 76% of people agree that lots of people correct others on social media. This aligns with what our surveys suggested in Chapter 5, where people said they perceive correction to be happening quite often. But only 32% agree that people generally *like* these corrections, suggesting the injunctive norms around correction (what we think people *should* do) are mixed. This last number offers an interesting contrast to past research. At the start of the pandemic (spring 2020), we found that the majority of people *personally* said they like corrections on social media.[5] These numbers held relatively stable through

October 2020 and April 2021, as we reported in Chapter 5—around 50% of people said they (personally) liked it when people correct others on social media, and only about 15% disliked it. In this survey we asked not about personal attitudes but rather about their perceptions of *other people's* attitudes toward correction. The fact that 50% of people like corrections and only 32% believe this is the case reinforces that people are often quite bad judges of what the public believes or does on a particular topic.[6] It also underscores the gap between what we think about our own relationship with media content (e.g., I like corrections), versus other people's relationships with the same media content (e.g., but they do not).[7] It might also reflect that norms of correction on social media are still evolving (something that happens quite slowly).[8] Given the importance of these perceptions of other's beliefs,[9] this represents an important place where informing people about *actual* support for correction could reinforce these norms and change behaviors.[10]

Finally, our survey underscores how many people are concerned about the social risks of correction. In general, people said that correction would harm their relationships with the person they were attempting to correct (53%) and that others would respond harshly to their correction (45%). As we emphasized in Chapter 6, these beliefs are rooted in reality, as many of our would-be and actual correctors spoke about their experiences with wounded relationships and toxic reactions when they corrected others on social media (we'll talk more about toxic reactions in the next chapter as well when we hear from professionals, the press, and platform employees).

Identifying Potential Correctors

While it's helpful to know what concerns the American public has about correction, we still don't know which of these reasons matter most in explaining how likely someone is to say they correct misinformation.

To examine this, we first must consider how to measure whether someone is a corrector. Previous research has measured this in a variety of ways, most often by looking at whether (or the degree to which) someone says they are willing to correct misinformation on social media in the abstract.[11] These surveys typically ask people how likely they are to take a variety of actions if they see misinformation in their own social media feeds, without linking it to a concrete piece of misinformation.[12] We adopt a similar approach to measure what we term "*general willingness to correct*" by asking people to report their likelihood (on a seven-point scale) to respond in various ways if they saw misinformation on their own social media feed. We'll focus on analyzing the results for their likelihood of posting a public comment to directly respond to misinformation (which is the only response we offered that enables observed correction), but we gave them other options (such as reporting the post, ignoring it, or messaging the person privately) to reduce the social desirability pressures to say they would reply publicly. As we discussed in Chapter 5, however, we expect that this is probably an inflated estimate, serving as a way for people to signal they value correction and want to perform it, even if they may not actually do so when seeing misinformation in their feed. Using this measure, we find that 36% of people told us they would be at least somewhat likely to publicly comment in response to misinformation on social media—a number that aligns with the roughly 35–40% of people who told us they *had* corrected misinformation on social media in the past week in Chapter 5.

The second way we measure being a corrector is *specific* willingness to correct a concrete example of misinformation. This method has been used in our past research—for example, in a study focused on raw milk misinformation with Melissa Tully, we asked people how likely they would be to respond to a misinformation post claiming that raw milk is more nutritious than pasteurized milk (it's not; pasteurization doesn't affect the nutrition of milk[13]), with a follow-up question asking them what they would say if they did respond.[14] That research suggested that (much like we find here) few people say they would be likely to correct that specific piece of misinformation, but they mostly would offer accurate information if they did (hypothetically) reply.

We used a similar design in our spring 2023 survey to measure *specific* willingness to correct. We obscured our purpose by asking people about their willingness to respond to five simulated Facebook posts. Four of these posts were typically innocuous social media posts, but one was misinformation—claiming that sunscreen changes your DNA (see Figure 7.2, on the left). Each of these posts had a short line of text with an accompanying picture and were shown in random order. We asked participants to rate their likelihood of responding to each of these posts, giving them seven options that range from "very unlikely" to "very likely."

We deliberately selected the sunscreen misinformation as the topic for several reasons. First, we wanted to select a topic where the misinformation could harm people if they believe it, since people told us perceived harm was a motivating factor in deciding whether to correct (Chapter 6). If people avoid using sunscreen, they could end up with severe sunburn or even skin cancer,[15] so that's a clear harm (and a harm likely known to our participants). Second, we needed a topic where people are mostly well-informed, because you can't correct misinformation if you don't know it's false, and we aren't giving our participants an opportunity to find out what's true or not (for example, through online search, as we'll discuss in Chapter 9)—so it needs to be a topic they already know about. In our sample, 86% of people agreed that using sunscreen prevents cancer

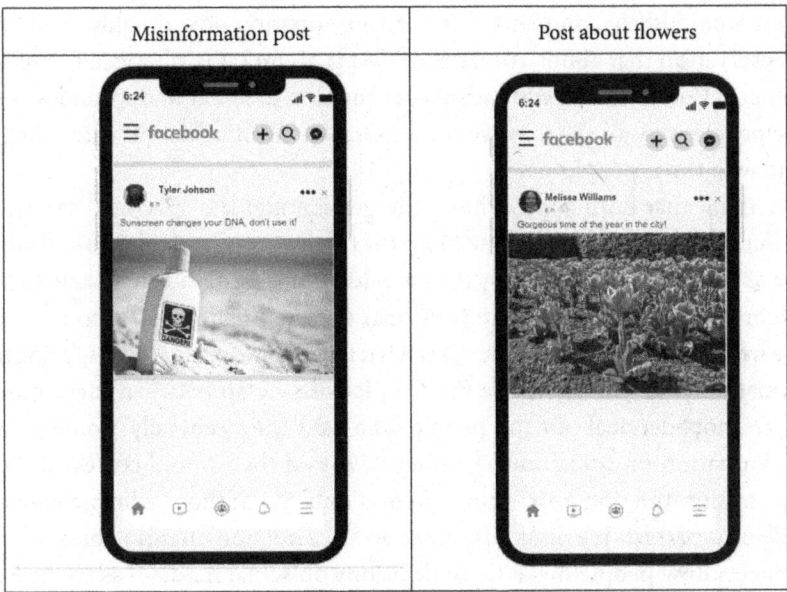

Misinformation post	Post about flowers

Figure 7.2 Examples of posts participants viewed Credit: Dhriti Gupta, 2024.

before seeing our simulated posts, suggesting it's a topic where many people have the knowledge they need to be able to correct (and recall from Chapter 6 that people needed to feel very confident about a topic to correct someone else). Third, sunscreen is not typically seen as a divisive issue and indeed has been an area for bipartisan legislation.[16] Finally, while the misinformation may seem kind of ridiculous, our previous research found a video sharing this misinformation (about sunscreen's purported impact on DNA) and other false claims about sunscreen's dangers was quite persuasive.[17] It's worth noting that this intersection—where people think misinformation is harmful for others, but also have the information they need to be able to correct it—may not be all that common. As such, we're picking in some ways an ideal case, where correction may be more likely than is the norm.

Even with this ideal case, though, most people didn't want to respond. Only 18% of people said they were at least somewhat likely to respond to the sunscreen post, as compared to the 48% who said they were somewhat likely to respond to a post about beautiful flowers (our most popular post—to be fair those are really pretty flowers, great work Georgetown University landscaping crew; see Figure 7.2, on the right). This means we're starting from a pretty low baseline (most people are not inclined to comment on a misinformation post) even in the expected best-case scenario when the misinformation could cause harm, they (likely) know it to be false, and it's unlikely to spur a partisan attack.

To be clear, these numbers still should not be thought of as perfectly accurate reflections of the likelihood of commenting. But the 18% of people who told us they would likely comment on the misinformation post roughly aligns with the observation that about 10–20% of tweets about COVID vaccines received comments.[18] And we can still use this information to better understand whether some people want to say they would respond to misinformation when they see it, and who those people are.

We think that both approaches—the general and the specific—are important but distinct ways to study willingness to correct misinformation. Roughly twice as many people (36%) say they would be at least somewhat likely to publicly comment in response to misinformation on social media as compared to those who said they were at least somewhat likely to respond to the specific misinformation post (18%). While there's a lot of overlap between these groups, they are not identical. Of the people who said they generally would correct misinformation on social media, about 37% said they would correct the sunscreen misinformation post—compared to only 5% of those who are generally *unwilling* to correct. We think that the specific correction intention measure better reflects how people make these decisions on social media—as we heard in the previous chapter, those decisions happen on a case-by-case basis depending upon the user's confidence about the topic, a sense of duty, and the potential for harm—while the general correction measure offers a sense of potential correctors who *could* be activated in the right set of circumstances (even if this specific sunscreen post doesn't reflect those circumstances for many of these would-be correctors).

Attitudes That Matter for Correction

Now that we can measure general versus specific willingness to correct, we turn to thinking about which attitudes that we outlined above seem to be acting on that willingness. That is, which attitudes seem to play the biggest role in whether people say they're willing to correct misinformation or not? When we test this, two attitudes stand out.[19] In Figure 7.3, the light grey diamonds show general willingness to correct, and the dark grey diamonds show specific willingness to correct. Results to the right of the vertical dashed line suggest that agreement with that statement is related to a greater willingness to correct, whereas those to the left indicate less willingness. Any estimates that cross the vertical line in the middle of the graph suggest there is no meaningful relationship between the belief and correction intentions.

The strongest predictor of correction intentions—both in responding to the specific sunscreen misinformation and more generally—is believing that observed correction works. People who more strongly agreed that posting a

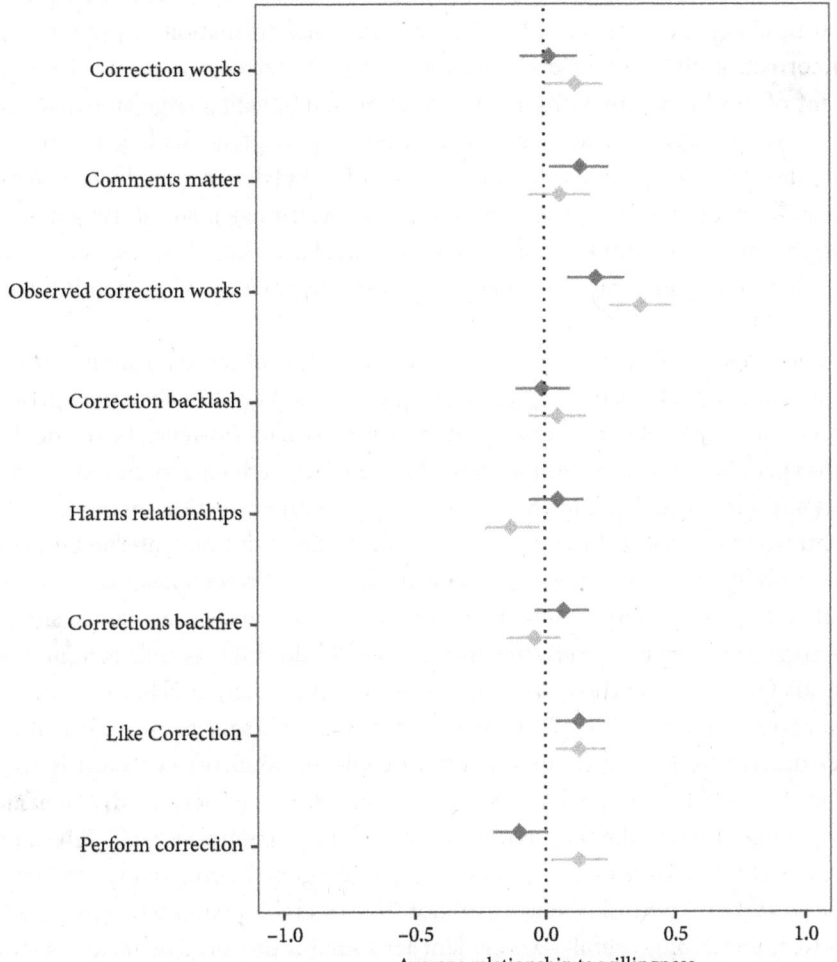

Figure 7.3 Explaining general and specific willingness to correct. *Notes:* We list the independent variables on the y-axis as agreement with a series of statements about correction in our study during the spring of 2023. The x-axis represents how each independent variable is related to self-reported willingness to correct using linear regression. We use different color diamonds to represent each dependent variable. Results to the right of the vertical dotted line mean stronger agreement with the statement on the y-axis is associated with greater willingness to correct, while results to the left of the vertical dotted line mean stronger agreement with the statement on the y-axis is associated with lower willingness to correct. The diamonds represent the averaged relationship, and the horizontal dashed line represents the 95% confidence interval for the size of this relationship. Values further from the dotted line indicate stronger effects. When the confidence interval crosses the vertical dotted line, the relationship is not statistically significant.

correction helps other people know what's true expressed higher correction intentions. In contrast, the belief that correction works to impact the person *sharing* the misinformation (and does not backfire) is not related to correction intentions. These findings are consistent with what users told us last chapter—that thinking about people who could see the misinformation motivates them to correct. It also underscores that we need to better communicate the argument of this book—that observed correction can benefit a large audience—to more people. As we also heard in the previous chapter, this larger audience for observed correction is often not top of mind when people talk about their decisions for or against correcting on social media, so efforts aimed at helping people to think of that secondary audience could be especially important in encouraging more people to become correctors (something we'll test next).

Second, we find yet more evidence about the value of social norms for correction behaviors. The belief that other people like corrections encourages greater specific and general correction intentions. Interestingly, however, believing that other people *perform* corrections has a mixed effect, reducing intentions to correct specific misinformation while boosting general correction intentions. The contrasting effects of these descriptive norms align with our interpretation of these two types of measures. General willingness to correct reflects social desirability as well as intentions—a belief that the "right" answer is that we should be correcting others. Descriptive norms (people do this), as well as injunctive norms (people value this), are quite powerful for predicting behaviors, including correction behaviors.[20] But when confronted with specific misinformation, this descriptive norm may instead offer people an opportunity to justify their nonresponse. If lots of people correct misinformation on social media, then any individual may feel like they don't have to because someone else will. Given the personal and social risks of corrections, they have good reason to hope someone else will take on the task. Concerns about "free riders"—people who rely on others to do something useful—are evident across many prosocial behaviors, so this tendency is not particularly surprising.[21]

Finally, people who believe that correcting harms personal relationships have lower general correction intentions, but that belief does not affect willingness to correct a specific piece of misinformation. This makes sense: the specific post is from an unknown other, so their nonexistent relationship of course cannot be harmed—there is no relationship in the first place. But the social costs of correction continue to loom large, making people less likely to say they would correct in general. These general corrections would presumably occur on their own personal social media feeds, where any effort to correct misinformation is more likely to involve—either directly as the target of our correction or indirectly as the audience—friends and family.

Interestingly, although we heard a lot of concern about toxicity from the online community from our interviews in Chapter 6, correction backlash does not relate to general or specific willingness to correct. It's likely that correction backlash is not as salient in an online survey as it would be when actually immersed in the social media environment.

Motivating Correction

The previous section investigated the beliefs about correction that already exist among the American public and whether these beliefs are associated with correction intentions. But as we stressed in Chapter 2, observed correction is only a scalable solution if a lot of people are doing it. The final step in our effort to understand individual correction choices, then, is to test the extent to which we can *shift* people's willingness to correct—essentially, convince more people to do it—either by emphasizing the value of correction or addressing their concerns about the risks of correction. We designed an experiment in the spring of 2023 to test exactly that.

For the experiment, we considered six beliefs that people said informed their correction decision. We used two criteria in selecting these beliefs. First, we identified themes that were common across many interviews. Second, we picked topics for which we had a lot of existing data and theory to inform our interventions to ensure we are giving people accurate information about the world. For example, a common concern raised is that performing corrections would harm interpersonal relationships, and this belief is a powerful deterrent to general correction intentions as we saw above. This is a credible fear, and one that many of our interview participants had personal experience with. We just didn't think there was a realistic intervention that could mitigate these fears.

We designed three messages to address concerns about the *effectiveness* of correction on social media for increasing accuracy. What we spent all of Chapters 3 and 4 discussing needed to be distilled down into two sentences and a graph for this experiment. Specifically, we told people that research demonstrates that correction works to increase the accuracy of the person sharing the misinformation,[22] that people pay attention to comments (where corrections often occur) on social media,[23] and that seeing corrections makes the broader public more accurate.[24] Collectively these three tap into external and response efficacy of correction—that people will see corrections and when they do, they can sway attitudes—because we know efficacy matters for behaviors.[25]

We also designed two messages to address different types of *social norms* regarding correction. Specifically, we told people that research—both in Chapters 5–6 and previously—demonstrates that people generally like corrections[26] and many people say they perform corrections on social media.[27] These messages should reinforce injunctive (liking) and descriptive (performing) norms surrounding correction that research consistently shows tends to boost people's behavioral intentions.[28]

The final message reflects the grave concerns many people (and professionals and the press as well, as we'll hear in the next chapter) expressed about the risk of public correction in terms of facing a toxic audience. Research suggests that a lot of the trolling and toxicity on social media often originates from a few bad actors.[29] If platforms were to take steps to enforce their terms of service—which by and large prohibit harassment or threats of violence[30]—it might reduce a lot of that toxicity. Indeed, one study found that a message posted to r/feminism on reddit that suggested that trolls remain a minority of community members boosted comments from new participants to the community by 20%.[31] Our last message thus suggests that platforms are taking efforts to remove repeated offenders, theoretically addressing the concerns about toxicity that our participants expressed (note that this message is the only one that isn't true; it can be thought of more as an aspirational but plausible possibility).

In our experiment, we randomly assigned 1,200 people to see one of the six different motivational messages (200 per message). Each message contained a graph meant to draw attention (because recall matters and pictures are attention-grabbing; see Chapter 4) and two sentences making the relevant claims.[32] These messages appear to come from Facebook and were shown before people saw the other simulated Facebook posts that we describe in the previous section. You can see an example of the "observed correction works" message in Figure 7.4, and the text of each of these messages in Table 7.2. We compared these people to the 800 people in our control condition (which we used for our survey analysis above;

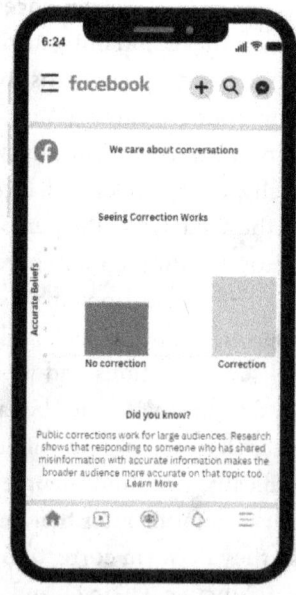

Figure 7.4 Example experimental message: observed correction works. Credit: Dhriti Gupta, 2024.

Table 7.2 **Experimental Messages to Promote Correction**

Condition	Text
Correction works	Corrections work. Research shows that responding to someone who has shared misinformation with accurate information helps them become more accurate on that topic too.
Imagined audience	Public corrections on social media reach lots of people. Research shows that people really pay attention to the comments on social media posts.
Observed correction works	Public corrections work for large audiences. Research shows that responding to someone who has shared misinformation with accurate information makes the broader audience more accurate on that topic too.
People like corrections	People like seeing corrections on social media. Research shows that most people say they like it when people respond to misinformation with accurate information on social media.
People perform corrections	Many people correct misinformation on social media. Research shows that most people say they respond to misinformation with accurate information when they see it on social media.
Platforms address trolling	Social media companies are taking steps to crack down on bad actors on social media. Repeated offenders with toxic comments are being removed from platforms, making online environments safer.

these people saw no motivating message, just a similarly formatted message about the dangers of distracted driving).

So did these messages encourage people to say they would be more likely to correct misinformation? We first examine people's willingness to respond to the specific sunscreen misinformation post in each of the experimental conditions as compared to the control condition.[33] Following our approach in Chapters 3 and 4, we report the percentage change in willingness to respond to the post as compared to the control condition.

Happily, our results suggest that addressing people's concerns can increase their willingness to correct specific misinformation (Figure 7.5). Specifically, four of the messages—that correction works for the individual sharing the misinformation, that observed correction works for the larger audience seeing the

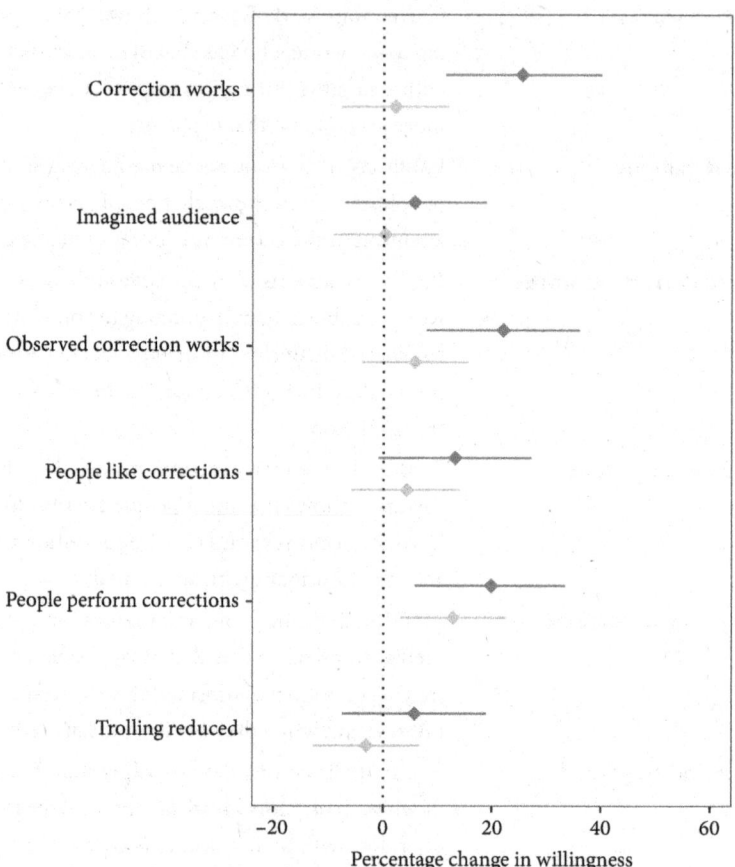

Figure 7.5 Motivating specific and general willingness to correct. *Notes:* The y-axis represents which of the six experimental messages regarding correction participants saw in a single study in the spring of 2023. The x-axis represents the percentage change in willingness to correct misinformation comparing the experimental condition to the control group. We use different color diamonds to represent each dependent variable. The x-axis represents change in willingness to correct between the correction and control condition, where results to the right of the vertical dotted line represent increased willingness to correct and those to the left represent decreased willingness to correct. The diamonds represent the averaged percentage change, and the horizontal dashed line represents the 95% confidence interval for this difference. Values further from the dotted line indicate stronger effects. When the confidence interval crosses the vertical dotted line, the relationship is not statistically significant.

interaction, that people like corrections, and that people perform corrections— each significantly boosted people's self-reported willingness to respond to the sunscreen post containing misinformation as compared to the control condition. The effects of these messages are also quite sizable, increasing willingness by between 13% (people like correction) and 26% (correction works). Part of why these effects look impressive is because we were starting from such low levels of correction willingness. Only 18% were at least somewhat willing to correct this misinformation post in the control condition, so that makes even a relatively small change in absolute willingness look impressive. Looking at this another way, the number of willing correctors increased to between 26% (people like correction) and 29% (correction works) as compared to that baseline number of 18% without any encouraging message. And because 86% of our participants said in our pre-test that sunscreen use reduces cancer risk, the vast majority of these would-be correctors should (theoretically) be offering accurate information.

This first set of results is quite encouraging—a single simple message that reinforces the benefits of correction can lead people to say they would be more likely to respond to a specific case of misinformation when they see it. The second question is whether these messages also move people in terms of their general willingness to correct misinformation publicly. Maybe they didn't want to respond to the specific sunscreen post, because they felt they lacked adequate knowledge, didn't think that post would cause harm, or just didn't feel like it. But the experimental messages still could have impacted their general ideas about correction. Unfortunately, only one message significantly affected people's general willingness to correct misinformation publicly: the descriptive norm message stating that lots of people perform corrections.[34] Admittedly, similar absolute changes in willingness would look smaller because more people in the control condition said they would address misinformation than would respond to the sunscreen post. However, this would not affect the significance of (or our confidence in) the results. But general willingness to respond is still quite low (remember, it started at 36%) so there is a lot of room for improvement, and the absolute differences between the messages and control condition remain quite small.

Instead, these results again suggest that general willingness to correct taps into perceptions about the desirability of correction as much as it does actual intentions to correct. The fact that participants moved only in response to messages about descriptive norms surrounding the behavior adds evidence in support of this argument.

Conclusion

Overall, survey data suggest that the concerns about correction voiced in the interviews we discussed in Chapter 6 are widespread. Many people are worried about correction not being effective or resulting in negative social implications like broken relationships and toxic responses. Several of these beliefs—especially about whether observed correction increases accuracy among the community and perceptions of social norms around correction—meaningfully predict whether people say they will engage in correction themselves. Our experiment confirms exposing people to a single simple message targeting these critical beliefs increased their willingness to say they would correct a specific misinformation post. As such, a campaign to promote these messages about the value of correction represents a viable strategy for increasing the number of willing correctors in the world. If a single message can lead even a few more people to correct, those acts of correction will not only affect the beliefs of their network of observers, but also further heighten the idea that correction is a normal and valuable act, strengthening social norms around correction,[35] and leading to a virtuous circle of correction.

TL; DR

- Concerns about correction—that it won't work, that people won't like it, or that it will damage social relationships—are widely held.
- Showing people that observed correction can increase audience accuracy and that many people like and perform corrections boosts people's willingness to correct.
- Changing people's general willingness to correct is harder than motivating them to correct a specific case of misinformation.

Chapter 8

Constrained Experts

In the previous three chapters, we focused on members of the public as a potential source of correction. These correctors and would-be correctors are particularly important because the scale of misinformation on social media requires lots of corrections, so we need as many people as possible to be able and willing to correct. But members of the public are by no means the only people who can correct. In this chapter, we shift our attention to ask: are other actors in the information ecosystem engaging in public correction?

To answer this question, we spoke with 13 professionals working in communication or outreach offices at 10 health and science organizations and eight fact checkers from eight organizations across four continents about their approach to correction. In addition, we spoke to nine trust and safety professionals from various social media platforms, search engines, and wikis. While we wouldn't expect these platform professionals to be directly correcting in the same way we might imagine fact checkers and health organization professionals, hearing from them helps us to better understand how platform employees are thinking about their role in facilitating correction.

The dedicated health communication and fact-checking professionals, driven by a commitment to the truth, spend their days focused on getting accurate information to the public. You might therefore expect that they would also be directly and publicly correcting misinformation posts on social media frequently. Somewhat to our surprise, we learned that for the most part these experts did not engage in direct public correction. Instead, they are largely *constrained correctors*, who generally believe in the value of correction but are limited by a lack of organizational and financial support, concerns they will face a hostile audience quick to argue back, and uncertainty that corrections work or that they are the best messengers to deliver them (see Figure 8.1). As a result, few of the experts we spoke to were at organizations that encouraged or even (in some cases) permitted them to engage in direct public corrections on social media. Instead,

Observed Correction. Leticia Bode and Emily K. Vraga, Oxford University Press.
© Leticia Bode and Emily K. Vraga (2025). DOI: 10.1093/oso/9780197565896.003.0008

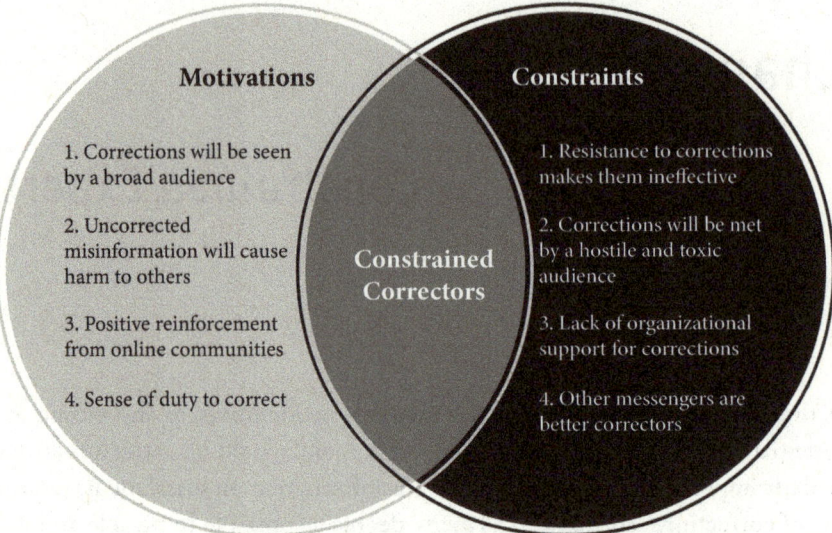

Figure 8.1   Constrained correctors. Credit: Meghan Landsberg, 2024.

organizations largely perceived their core responsibility as creating accessible cu-rated evidence (ACE) that others can use in corrections—something that we'll explore in more detail in the next chapter.

We also identify a subset of professionals and press who *do* engage in systematic correction of social media misinformation. For these experts, their belief that they are helping to reach a broader public with accurate information, the perceived harm of (uncorrected) misinformation, the positive reinforcement that they receive from their audience, and ultimately their feelings of a duty to scientific discourse and an informed society make corrections worthwhile. However, the firsthand experiences described by these individuals also validate many of the concerns of those who are reluctant to correct—the costs incurred in doing so, the hostility of (some) members of the audience, and the inability to eliminate misinformation.

Why These Actors

We chose to talk to professional communicators and fact checkers because we think they're some of the most relevant experts in health and political misinformation. So much of what we experience in the twenty-first century (and for much of recorded history as well) is not firsthand, but is instead mediated through someone else's experience.[1] Most often this mediation occurs through journalism, which remains the main way that most people get information, form opinions, and make sense of the world.[2] This remains true even with the rise of social media.[3] However, expert organizations—health professionals and fact-checking journalists alike—have also prioritized maintaining a social media presence,[4] offering the potential for people to hear directly from them and making it important to consider how they are adjusting their methods (or not) to combat misinformation.

When thinking about efforts to correct misinformation online, three groups are especially important. First, professionals tend to serve as the arbiters of truth, relied upon to define what is accurate versus what is misinformation.[5] Second, within journalism, fact-checking journalists specifically attempt to identify and respond to misinformation.[6] Third, actors at the platforms themselves provide the context in which corrections happen. Obviously, there are other important actors in the ecosystem, who could be engaging in correction as well. But given their importance in the information, misinformation, and correction ecosystem we outlined in Chapter 2, we wanted to hear directly from these individuals to think through whether, when, and how often these experts decide to engage directly with misinformation on social media, and how they think about the affordances of platforms that facilitate or hinder these efforts.

How We Approached This Research

To identify professional communicators willing to talk to us, we leveraged existing relationships we had with health, science, and fact-checking organizations. We also reached out to colleagues and friends to help connect us to people with expertise in this area. After each interview, we asked whether there was someone else we should talk to on the topic and were put in touch with several other experts in that way.

We gave participants the choice of how they would like to be identified, if at all, to allow them greater freedom to speak candidly to us without fear of repercussions to their job or their organization. Although some professionals were comfortable having their identities or organizations named, for consistency we do not identify any individuals by name. Instead, throughout this chapter we'll use a pseudonym to refer to each of these professionals, trust and safety professionals, and members of the press when we quote them. In all cases, these interviews reflect personal experiences and attitudes, and not the official position of any organization. We also don't name any health and science organizations, for the same reason, but they mainly represent US state and federal health and science agencies, as well as three international health organizations (see Table 8.1). We asked professionals about their perceptions of misinformation as part of a broader communication strategy and the organization's social media presence in general, before turning to specific questions about whether and when they (or their organization) directly correct misinformation on social media and how they think about that decision.[7] These

Table 8.1 **Health and Science Professionals We Spoke With**

Pseudonym	Type of Organization
Ana	International health organization
Bill	State health organization
Claudette	National science organization
Danny	National health organization
Elsa	National health organization
Fred	International health organization
Grace	State health organization
Henri	International health organization
Imani	National health organization
Julian	National science organization
Mindy	National health organization
Odette	National health organization
Rose	National science organization

Note: All national and state health organizations were located in the United States; the international organizations represented multiple countries

Table 8.2 **Fact Checkers We Spoke With**

Pseudonym	Organization	Location
Leslie	AfricaCheck	Africa (multiple countries)
Alberto	Boatos	Brazil
Debby	Chequeado	Argentina
Joyce	CheckNews	France
Chris	deCheckers	Belgium
Helene	FactCheck.org	United States
Francine	Lupa	Brazil
Ernesto	Maldita	Spain

interviews took place via Zoom between May and September 2022, each lasting 30–60 minutes.

Fact checkers, on the other hand, were universally comfortable with their organizations being named, so we include this information alongside pseudonyms to give greater context for the information they shared (see Table 8.2).[8] In addition to using our personal networks, we recruited participants for many of our fact-checker interviews at the 2022 Global Fact convening of the International Fact-Checking Network. In our interviews, we asked questions about their relationship with their audience, their social media presence, and how they try to reach the public in different ways.[9] Interviews were conducted primarily over Zoom, with a handful in person and one over email, in June and July 2022, lasting 25–60 minutes.

Table 8.3 **Trust and Safety Professionals We Spoke With**

Pseudonym	Platform Type
Dexter	other
Sebastien	social media
Jerry	search
Pablo	social media
Andrea	social media
Erin	social media
Gabrielle	social media
Karen	social media
Melissa	Wiki

Additionally, we interviewed nine current and (mainly) former employees of social media platforms, search engines, and wikis (see Table 8.3). The platforms themselves along with the names of employees we spoke with are masked to protect their privacy, but they represent many of the major US platforms. We asked a range of questions related to misinformation policy, approaches to dealing with content, and motivations and constraints at the platform(s) they had worked for (for the full interview protocol, please see the online appendix). The interviews were conducted over Zoom in the summer of 2022 and lasted between 17 and 55 minutes.

We'll start by discussing why some of the experts we spoke with did engage in correction, highlighting major themes that came up repeatedly in our interviews. Then we'll discuss the opposite—why so many were reluctant to engage in (direct and public) correction. Throughout this chapter, we'll also hear from platform employees to add context to the decisions made by the public-facing experts.

Why Correct: The Imagined Audience for Correction

Both professional health and science communicators and fact checkers are first and foremost motivated by informing people. Sometimes referred to as a "public service orientation,"[10] this is a key professional norm among journalists and health organizations in general—they see their role as directly improving society, and that underlies the work they do. As a result of this public service orientation, both professional health communicators and fact checkers told us they spend a lot of time thinking about the audience for their work. That is, they think a lot about who sees the information they create and how they are impacted by it. This then shapes how they produce and distribute information. Part of this audience is those they reach directly—for instance, people who subscribe to their content, go to their website, or otherwise seek out the information intentionally.

But from our interviews we learned that a lot of what they think about is the in-direct or secondary audience that social media encourages—those who see their content only when it is shared by others.

COMMUNICATING FOR THE BROADER AUDIENCE

The minority of experts we spoke with who did engage in direct and public cor-rection of misinformation posts on social media were especially likely to mention a broader or secondary audience for their corrections when discussing the value of their work. While these experts remain concerned with the impact of a cor-rection on the person they are directly responding to, more of their attention tends to be focused on other people that may see the interaction. Thus they are intentionally thinking about observed correction, even though they are not us-ing that term. Instead, these online correctors speak about their desire to offer credible information in a conversation "so that more people in that community can see" (Elsa, professional) and to "let the viewer themselves make an informed decision" (Mindy, professional).

But they are also aware that not everyone in the broader audience will be receptive to their corrections. Claudette (professional) spoke to us about the im-portance of focusing on the people you can reach and letting go of the people you can't. As Chris from deCheckers (press) put it, you've

> got those two polarized extremes, [and] the big part in the middle . . . And so the people we target are those people in the middle. And we try to keep that middle as large as possible.

They are right—for all the attention paid to people on the extremes, even on the most contentious issues there are often a lot of people in the middle.[11] And it is this majority in the big middle who are likely most receptive to corrections.[12] This distinction between the louder extremes and the quieter majority was em-phasized by platform employees we spoke with as well. As Pablo (social media) describes it clearly, in the context of politics:

> Most political content is done by people who like fighting. [In] an internal study we found, like the majority of political content is posted by people in the most physical extreme 5% of the two ends. So like the 90% of people who aren't the more extremes, don't by and large post political content, and don't by and large comment on it.

By creating content for this "big middle" (Chris, DeCheckers), "the 90% of people who aren't the more extremes" (Pablo, social media), or the "lurkers" (Julian, professional), experts who engage in public correction are thinking about the kinds of observers who are likely to be most open to corrective information. In doing so, as Elsa (professional) says, they are "trying to provide correct information really to people who are going to be receptive to correct information."

HARM

Like members of the public (Chapter 6), professionals and the press were sensitive to the reality that some of the misinformation proliferating in the world would cause real harm to people. Those who were responding to misinformation publicly saw their corrections as a way they could immediately mitigate those harms. For example, Leslie from AfricaCheck (press) emphasized they prioritized debunks of vaccine misinformation in their WhatsApp voicenotes (delightfully called Whats Crap on WhatsApp), because it was "important for our subscribers to hear" given how harmful vaccine misinformation was perceived to be. Because the press couldn't address all possible misinformation (as we'll hear more about below), they focused their correction efforts on the misinformation they perceived as the most harmful.

Professionals tended to define harm in terms of both the content of the misinformation and its reach, echoing what we heard from platform employees in Chapter 6. For example, Rose (professional) says they "tend to try to weigh in on threads where we see there's already a lot of spread and reach" and that "we just try to tackle the worst ones" when performing direct correction on social media. Danny (professional) explained that his organization largely defines harm in terms of misinformation with "wide reach, high dissemination, and [that] may lead to vaccine refusal and uptake," because vaccine hesitancy represents a clear harm not just to the individual but to society. Mindy (professional) says her organization makes sure to respond, "When there's blatant information that I think we believe can be harmful from a health standpoint." Elsa (professional), whose organization had been responding to misinformation since before COVID-19 emerged, said the pandemic forced them to "focus [their] resources" in responding to misinformation, "trying to identify things that we feel are going to have the biggest burden or damage on those belief systems." Overall, perceptions of misinformation harm proved to be both a motivating force and an orienting mechanism, allowing professionals to prioritize their responses to some misinformation rather than others.[13]

DUTY

Even more so than members of the public, professionals who engaged in public correction often spoke about a feeling of duty. In other words, they expressed a feeling of obligation to correct, and a sense that if experts with the best available information didn't engage in correction, no one would. Again, this is consistent with the professional commitment to public service:[14] both health communicators and fact checkers feel an obligation to improve the information environment, for the good of society. Ana (professional) told us that she felt that sense of duty even though her organization doesn't correct, and that she believed "We absolutely do need to be correcting the records in digital spaces online." Ernesto from Maldita (press) said when he saw a lot of people who were confused or misinformed about a particular topic, that "I have to write something to explain that this is false." Similarly, when asked about the problem of misinformation on social media, Julian (professional) specifically used the word "duty" to describe his impetus to respond because otherwise "misinformation seems like it's more widespread." He makes it clear that he's very much thinking about the community on Facebook when he decides to correct, because:

> It's our mission and our job and the expectation that we will respond to these things. It's part of our brand, it's part of how we're seen, and I can't expect others to push back if I won't push back.

POSITIVE REACTIONS ARE MOTIVATING

Finally, in addition to intrinsic motivations like a duty to inform a broader audience that could be harmed in the absence of a correction, we heard about the motivating role of positive reactions to corrections. Below, we'll talk about the opposite—toxic responses to corrections tend to inhibit willingness to correct. But experts also told us that toxic reactions are coming from a minority of users. Instead, many of those we spoke with had plenty of examples of *positive* interactions after corrections. Chris from deCheckers (press) notes people thanking them for sharing a fact check are quite motivating, and highlights that they get "more positive reactions than negative reactions." Leslie from AfricaCheck (press) concurs, saying that "our loyal subscribers are always sending us really nice feedback" for their work. Julian (professional) also says that he hears from a lot more people who support his corrections, often responding with "hundreds and hundreds of likes and heart emojis." This positive feedback encourages correctors to continue to engage in spite of the many challenges.

Why These Experts Don't Correct Directly and Publicly

Having heard why some experts (and organizations) correct—and other experts think their organization *should* correct even when they don't—we turn our attention to understanding why most organizations don't engage in direct, public correction of misinformation in their professional capacity. Four major reasons emerge (many of which will sound familiar): concerns about the effectiveness of correction, anticipation of a toxic reception to such efforts, the resource constraints that make correction costly, and perceptions of their relative merits as a messenger. Clearly several of these themes overlap with what we heard from the users in Chapter 6, although they are rooted in professional orientations and priorities, rather than interpersonal friction.

PERCEIVED INEFFECTIVENESS OF CORRECTION

Many of the health professionals and fact checkers we spoke with expressed skepticism about whether directly responding to misinformation on social media is effective. Some experts simply were not convinced that people sharing misinformation would be open to correction. For example, Ernesto from Maldita (press) tells us that even if you could find the original sharer of a piece of misinformation, they are likely to be so partisan and convinced of their position that "they're not going to change their way they see things" in response to any debunk on Maldita's part. Similarly, Debby from Chequeado (press) talks about following trending topics on social media to be able to "be part of that conversation and to take more evidence-based conversation there" but that often, trying to step into these so-called debates will "make us lose reputation without necessarily [making] people better informed." Or as Henri (professional) summarized it, people have

> evolutionarily adapted psychological mechanisms that really affect how we process different kinds of information. Based on emotion, based on trust, based on heuristics, based on mental shortcuts, and all this stuff, and it's a fool's errand to correct [misinformation].

But reflecting their broader lens, these experts were often less concerned about their ability to persuade an audience of one (the person sharing misinformation) than about the effects on the larger audience witnessing their interactions. The perception—and often the reality—that attempts at direct correction led to pushback from online communities reinforced concerns about corrections as not just ineffective but problematic, and therefore something to be avoided. Many of the professionals spoke about their concerns that the protracted "back and forth" (Bill, Grace, Mindy) or "duking it out" (Imani) with someone who doesn't accept a correction will "probably spread more misinformation than actually correct the misinformation that's out there" (Imani).[15] In Grace's words:

You end up in this long thread of back and forth, and it just ends up not being fruitful because you know you're not going to be changing the person's mind. And then somebody reading the thread is probably seeing all of these things and . . . it just lends more confusion than clarity, I think. And so, a person's probably left reading that thread going, I don't really know what to do or think right now.

TOXIC REACTIONS

While the previous section focused on the harm that a back-and-forth interaction can cause for the public in terms of their confusion on the topic, this is only one element of the potential backlash that can occur from direct public correction. A second source of reluctance involves the all-too-real fears that corrections would provoke hostile or toxic comments, as well as personal threats or attacks. While this concern echoes what we heard from social media users, it was even more salient for the experts we spoke with, whose social media accounts tend to have many more followers than the average social media user. This means there is both more opportunity for observed correction to occur—but also more risk of toxic blowback.

These concerns about trolling and hostility are realized in the experiences of those individuals and groups who do engage in correction. Each and every one had an example of people reacting to a correction with toxic comments, although it took a variety of forms. For some, it manifested as "nasty comments" (FactCheck.org, Rose, Julian), and hate mail (Chequeado, Lupa, Maldita)—or as Mindy (professional) describes it, "we take a lot of beatings." Julian (professional) highlights the stress of feeling constantly attacked.

> It's very hard to do the comment section. It's hard. It's a mental drain to do it . . . you get shared on, I don't know where, the dark place on the web, and then you get inundated all day, and if I wanted to respond to all the comments, it will take up an entire day. It's only so many times you can be called evil or a Nazi and all these horrible things. It's only so many times you can take of that eventually taking a mental toll on you.

Julian's comments about the mental toll that constant attacks can take were echoed by others as well. Debby at Chequeado (press) described it as "really intense, whether there are violence or trolls or something, it is also difficult in terms of mental health." Her organization even adjusted the workflow of dealing with social media comments in response—whereas they used to have one person who handled all of it, they now rotate through (one person gets each day of the week) to lessen the impact on any given person.[16]

These attacks sometimes get quite personal. Rose (professional) told us about multiple cases where corrections have led to "some threatening type of responses as well," including writing to their bosses to try to get Rose (or others doing correction) fired. While Rose believes her confidence and "thick skin" have protected her, she says this kind of online harassment has caused multiple people to leave their job at her organization.

Research shows that these experiences are not unique, as attacks against journalists and health experts are on the rise,[17] and disproportionately affect women and people of color.[18] These attacks often lead to the same negative emotions described by the participants you just heard from,[19] which the targeted experts are often left to manage on their own with inadequate organizational support.[20] Such experiences can then change how and when these experts engage with controversial topics.[21] For example, research shows that fear of toxic reactions can lead to a tendency to self-censor even in professional arenas, sometimes resulting in a "chilling effect," among both scientists and journalists.[22] That is, fear of being attacked may lead you to not say anything that you think might provoke such an attack.

It's important to note that often these "trolls" do not find journalists, health professionals, or even trust and safety professionals on their own. Coordinated harassment is a documented part of the modern information ecosystem,[23] and often includes hate speech, threats of violence, and sometimes doxing—finding and disseminating personal information about the person online. For instance, Elon Musk's smear of Yoel Roth, the former head of trust and safety at Twitter, directed attacks by online mobs, which eventually forced Roth to move in order to escape the resulting offline harassment.[24] In addition to longtime attacks from the political right on the press in general[25]—recall Donald Trump repeatedly calling them the "lying media"[26]— conservative pundits also regularly attack individual journalists or prominent scientists by name, steering online and offline harassment their way.[27] Another example of this features the journalist Taylor Lorenz, who was repeatedly attacked by celebrity pundit Tucker Carlson. Carlson's attacks, which Lorenz later described as "an attempt to mobilize an army of followers to memorize my name and instigate harassment," led to hate speech and harassment online.[28]

But while toxic comments are a very real fear, many of the experts we spoke with believe this toxicity comes from a small, vocal minority. As Julian put it, "the folks who cause a lot of the issues, it's not like there's a lot of them." Rather, a few bad actors are posting a lot, and Julian has even learned to recognize several of these troll accounts ("there are the characters who I know") and their characteristics ("But I can normally tell who are going to be the problems, oftentimes because they post so many times. If they post on multiple threads at once,

I know they're going to be a problem"). This is consistent with research showing that quite a small minority of superusers on social media is often responsible for much of the violent or hateful rhetoric[29]—and those users tend to be the same users that share misinformation.[30]

Attempts to engage with these trolls were largely seen ineffective. As Fred (professional) put it, "to convince a troll, it's a waste of time," while Chris from deCheckers (press) described it as "maybe even throwing more oil on the fire." Because of this, these experts often tried to distinguish between the people who were likely posting in good faith and willing to be corrected (i.e., spreading *mis*information), others spreading false content maliciously or for profit (i.e., spreading *dis*information), and yet others who were just there for the fight (i.e., trolls). Implicit in a willingness to correct is either a belief that most people fall in the first group, or that one can tell the difference between innocent and ill-intentioned sharers of misinformation. As Ernesto from Maldita (press) put it,

> I don't think it's really a good idea to spend time in doing this kind of thing. If there were a way to make a distinction between people . . . sharing, but if you explain, "No, that's false," it's going to change their mind to, "Oh, okay, it's false. Sorry. I apologize for doing that," and the ones who you are going to take your debunk and they're going to say, "Hey, you, Soros is paying you. Go to hell."

Even here, though, Chris from deCheckers (press) emphasized that convincing the troll was not the point. He points out that "the main purpose of doing it" is not to convince the sharer of misinformation, but rather to ensure that people watching can see "another kind of noise in her timeline."

Likewise, experts also described the value in distinguishing between trolling and simple negative sentiments. Bill (professional) said he was unwilling to engage with "somebody coming at us and telling us we're a bunch of corrupt morons," especially when they do so publicly, but their organization is more willing to respond to a direct (private) message, "even if it is fairly hostile" because it is seen as a genuine attempt to seek information from them, leading them to try to "ignor[e] the more salacious or the more attack-oriented part of the message." Imani (professional) also points to public attacks as evidence of trolls trying "to bait you into engaging in the conversation" to increase their visibility and spread their message further. Similarly, Henri (professional) says when people are spreading misinformation on his organization's social media feed, they might be willing to "do some countering of that online in a neutral and nonaggressive way so as to not to stir the pot." But as soon as it descends into "just defamatory or just blatant lies," their organization disengages and instead flags the posts for the social media platform to potentially address.

In this way, concerns about toxicity actually relate back to concerns about effectiveness—toxic comments are generally perceived to be intentionally "stir[ring] the pot," implying that a correction would be ineffective and is therefore just not worth it.

CONSTRAINTS

This idea of whether corrections are "worth it" relates to our third theme: the recognition that engaging in correction is resource intensive, and this burden falls on organizations with insufficient resources. First, as we discussed above, corrections can have a cost in terms of mental health, especially when they carry the risk of toxicity. Second, correction takes time, and *good* corrections take even more time. Time is a scarce resource for all those we spoke with—they are habitually overworked and understaffed—and there is a strong awareness that doing one activity represents an inherent tradeoff in being able to do other activities. Any given behavior like correction is therefore considered not only on its own merits, but also in relation to what *could* be done if the time spent correcting were instead spent doing something else. Everyone is trying to maximize the impact they can make with the resources they have.

Correction is therefore only a small part of a broader communications portfolio at major health organizations, one that can include misinformation mitigation, but also lots of other things, like promoting new reports, disseminating information, and building relationships with the communities they serve.[31] Similarly, fact checkers told us they are increasingly not only spending time on fact checks, but also on preemptive efforts like media literacy trainings, university partnerships, and collaborations meant to expand their reach.

Because they have many activities and few resources, experts recognize that responding to misinformation limits their ability to engage in other, potentially more fruitful avenues of advancing their goals. Henri (professional) notes that monitoring or responding to health misinformation isn't going to be a top priority for his international organization, which instead is "very much first and foremost motivated by the specific need to just save lives." In some cases, this means that rather than correcting misinformation, his health organization accommodated people's misperceptions. As an example, when confronted with misinformation that a thermometer used at a local clinic was spreading COVID-19, Henri told us his organization just used a different kind of thermometer, rather than directly addressing the misinformation.

For both professionals and the press, time is directly tied to monetary resources. Hiring more people, or redirecting efforts of existing staff, to increase the amount of time they could spend on such corrections all require money. Therefore, lack of resources was perhaps the greatest source of reluctance for both groups. Many (CheckNews, deCheckers, FactCheck.org; Fred, Odette, Rose) bemoaned the fact that they just didn't have enough time, money, or staff to effectively combat misinformation on social media. As Joyce from CheckNews (press) put it succinctly, "So we wanted to do everything, answer to everybody, but we understood that we couldn't and we have limited resources." This was echoed by Chris with deCheckers (press): "The basic problem, it's lack of resources. If you have to publish, publish, publish, publish, you're already with your head in the next piece," and Helene from FactCheck.org (press) told us they couldn't do more video corrections because "it's just a lot. That's a lot of time commitment, and we don't have a big enough staff right now to do that."

This general lack of resources is often exacerbated by the small teams tasked with social media communication, or even misinformation specifically. For example, among our health organizations, both Odette and Fred (professional) described their group as "a very small team." Julian (professional), whose science organization engages in the most systematic correction on social media of anyone we spoke with, notes that there are only two people on their team, despite the perception from their Facebook page that "it's a comment farm somewhere of a team of 30 responding to comments, and not two of us doing it all at once." Rose (professional), who works with Julian, laments that the work of correction drains so many of their resources that could be used for other things:

> We don't have any bandwidth. . . . I feel like we're not getting as much out of our social media as we probably could if we had more resources and a bigger staff to help us.

Platform employees also mentioned the constraint of resources. Obviously multibillion-dollar corporations have more money to play with than scrappy journalists or health organizations, and some are actively choosing not to invest resources in the problem. But it's also worth acknowledging just how complicated and resource intensive properly dealing with misinformation can be.

To start, the platform employees described to us how difficult it is to create a coherent policy about information integrity across many disparate teams of people, often working on different products and with different goals. As Sebastien (social media) put it, "It's very, very difficult to . . . get a consensus across policy and product teams." This is further complicated by the global context in which many platforms work, or as Jerry (search) put it, "functionally, it serves the entire world." That means that any given platform policy has to be enforced in myriad languages and cultures, so the context in which content occurs matters a lot. Jerry (search) gave a good example of this issue:

> Off of misinfo, but take harassment policy. Photo of me and you having a drink in Madrid or wherever . . . not harassing to me or you. Same exact photo taken under the same exact willingness to be photographed for someone in a more conservative society where socializing with the opposite gender or having alcohol [is forbidden], then that's harassment. So how do you write a policy, always, that's perfectly applicable?

This global context also makes fighting misinformation more expensive for the platforms. Although Erin (social media) concedes people might be "incredulous at the idea that these companies don't have resources to do this," she goes on to describe some of the costs:

> Every country, you're going to have to train a machine learning algorithm to identify political misinfo in that country's language. You're going to have to have human reviewers that speak that language. You're going to have to have policy experts who are familiar with that country to deal with escalations when the content moderators don't know what to do with a piece of content. And so the idea that you could have this policy functioning in all places at all times is really, really hard to pull off.

And because this is an expensive problem, it sometimes means enforcement of policies is inconsistent. Platforms have to "make a resource tradeoff between continued enforcement in one place at the expense of enforcement in any other place" (Erin, social media). She goes on to describe this inability to apply policy consistently across time and space as "a huge point of failure."

Much like those working at platforms, professionals and fact checkers also pointed to technical barriers that made responding to misinformation (as well as sharing high-quality information) more difficult. Leslie (press) told us someone at her organization (AfricaCheck) had to add each individual user who wanted to receive a weekly voicenote in WhatsApp—over 5,000 individuals—one at a time to a specific phone designed for the purpose. They used 20 different broadcast lists because of the WhatsApp group limitation of 256 people per group,[32] and sent updates in batches of groups, because "if I do more than seven at a time, then it just doesn't send." Joyce from CheckNews (press) also highlighted that they could do more outreach if they had the ability to semiautomate their communication with those seeking information and send links directly when a new article was published.

Finally, for health professionals and platform employees, there is a *structural* layer of constraint beyond the cost of direct correction. The health professionals we interviewed are part of a larger organizational hierarchy that governs how their social media accounts can be used. These professionals often described their organization's structure as "conservative" (by which they mean overly cautious, Mindy, Ana), with a disconnect between the people working on the front lines on social media to correct misinformation and the higher-ups at the organization who set policy. Imani (professional) spoke about a policy of bringing concerning social media content to a broader team for the "proper checks and balances" before deciding whether to respond—and that decision is almost always to *not* directly respond. Danny (professional) describes a multiple-week review period that essentially eliminates the ability to correct, because "social media doesn't work on a month timeframe." Thus, the affordances of social media and best practices for correction that stress a timely response just don't align with the hierarchical decision-making often in place in health organizations, further limiting the potential for correction.

This also means that the health professionals we spoke to—who were largely directly tasked with communication on behalf of their organization—did not always agree with the higher-ups' policy to not correct. For example, Ana (professional) spoke about her admiration for self-organized groups of healthcare workers who were responding to misinformation online, even though her organization was reluctant to do so. Likewise, Danny (professional) shared his frustration that his organization did not engage in correction or other misinformation mitigation strategies in part because "the people clearing stuff, aren't familiar with the science behind it."[33]

These frustrations were echoed by trust and safety teams at platforms, who often felt like they were severely constrained by those higher up at platforms from doing what they thought was most effective for limiting misinformation. These platform employees were deeply committed to the work they were doing: Gabrielle (social media) said she wanted to "protect" or even "save democracy," while Sebastien (social media) said he took the job because he thought he would be "solving the societal problems and the issues that society was facing and not really caring about [the platform's] interests. And I would say most of the employees who work on this space, that's how they're driven."

But these employees did not feel like their company saw their jobs the same way. For some, it was the opposite: employees told us they felt like their trust and safety teams were primarily designed to reduce bad publicity rather than advance solutions, as both Pablo ("I think the main role of integrity was defense against regulators and PR") and Sebastien ("The thing that they care about first and foremost is how much heat are they going to get for the thing versus actually solving the core thing") suggest. Gabrielle (social media) described it, somewhat tragically:

> There is a way in which a lot of these mid-level jobs at a company like [the social media platform she worked for] are bullshit jobs. And our team was not a bullshit team. We were very committed to not doing bullshit things. And it's just extremely hard to try to not be a bullshit team in a bullshit job situation, when what you were assigned was not a real job and you decide to make it a real job. You are in for a world of hurt.

This "world of hurt" also played out when these employees attempted to get buy-in from the platform for misinformation solutions. Most of the platform employees we spoke with told us about times when they identified an effective way to decrease misinformation on the platform. But when they took their ideas through the organization's hierarchy, they were met with resistance, due to a concern that doing so would decrease user engagement, and therefore profit, for the platform. Like so many things, much of it simply comes down to money. As Sebastien (social media) put it clearly:

> So if you're hurting growth metrics even a little bit, compared to the benefits that you're gaining, you're going to have a really tough time launching.

In other words, growing the user base (and the associated profit that growth represents) remains a top priority for their platforms. Other employees described the same driving motivation in different words, saying that "the company wasn't willing to have the bottom line lose" (Gabrielle, social media). Sahar Massachi, cofounder of the Integrity Institute (an association of trust and safety professionals), described this in a recent speech as "sacrific[ing] the safety of our users for short-term business growth." He went on to argue that such a sacrifice is short-sighted, sacrificing not just user safety but also long-term viability of the platforms themselves—because no user really wants a platform experience full of hostility and lies.

OTHERS DO IT BETTER

Partly because of the costs and difficulties of doing correction, many of the health and fact-checking organizations we spoke with thought that *others* were better positioned to deliver corrections. Many communicators—both professionals and the press—were very much aware that trusted messengers are much more effective communicators, better able to inform, persuade, and motivate behaviors among the public.[34] These benefits also extend to corrections, where trust matters even more than expertise in increasing accuracy.[35]

Therefore, experts acknowledged that in some cases, their organization would *not* be the best messenger for the groups they wanted to reach. Ana (professional) recognizes that around the globe, "Not all communities trust . . . a health authority to be communicating to them," and Debby from Chequeado (press)'s acknowledges that "People don't necessarily trust the news . . . they trust . . . peers" (Debby, Chequeado). Therefore, these organizations must and do work with these trusted messengers in order to be effective.

Sometimes, these trusted messengers are other expert voices, who just have a better connection to the community in question. Elsa (professional) talks about working with different health partners to help them perform corrections, depending on who is most likely to have a community's trust: "And so we really are trying to work with our partners in the communities, faith groups, physicians, educators, and arm them with information that they can use because they tend to be trusted in their community." As another example, during the pandemic Factcheck.org partnered with highly trusted local news organizations serving largely black and Hispanic populations to translate and republish their content "to hopefully reach communities of color, with the idea that there was a lot of misinformation specifically being targeted about COVID-19 to communities of color." Similarly, Chequeado described its partnerships with community radio to reach indigenous populations "translating fact checks in the Native languages" as a way to use trusted community allies to spread their messages more effectively. Grace (professional) talks about the need to engage partners to share high-quality information that can stand in contrast to misinformation "floating around" on social media:

> Engaging other partners and other voices in helping to share information, healthcare providers and others, if people are hearing the same message from those different trusted voices, that can help reaffirm that, okay, this is probably the more accurate thing then that other thing I saw floating around from an article on Facebook, or whatever it might be.

Other times, the trusted voices are not experts but members of the community. Fred (professional) talks about his desire to have his organization create a series of debunking videos using a bunch of different "witnesses" that "people perceive belong to [their] communities," because his experience with previous campaigns found that using "community-based influencers" (which he stressed were *not* celebrities) tended to be more successful in changing minds and generating "lift."

Partnering with members of the community has a second benefit: it allows organizations to operate at a larger scale. Media influence research has long understood that information campaigns only need to reach a small group of interested individuals, who then share the information with their broader networks and other members of the public via a two step flow of information.[36] Therefore, professionals and the press want to reach allies—both social media users and other professionals (first step)—who can then pass on their message to others (second step), therefore amplifying the impact of their messages. Ana (professional) said that part of their portfolio is creating content "that can be taken up by others and remixed and taken up and shared by themselves," and Grace (professional) said they wanted to produce the "factual information . . . so that people are getting it from a credible source and can reference back to it and share with others." Similarly, Helene from FactCheck.org (press) said "hopefully they are sharing [the fact checks] in a nice way with somebody who might be receptive to the information," and Joyce from CheckNews (press) reiterated this idea—"we don't ask to share the article. We want people to share it, but we don't say," as did Leslie at AfricaCheck (press)—"we're hoping they'll just pass it on."

These materials also raise the potential for community allies to also perform corrections themselves. Or as Chris from deCheckers (press) put it, "let's make an army" of volunteer correctors. Mindy (professional) says that creating these materials means that "a lot of times, the community themselves, do their own . . . corrections," in an organic fashion with little direction from any organization. Julian (professional) talks about recognizing the "five or six people" who are "in that comments section more than I am, God bless, correcting people and using links." Or as Bill (professional) put it, their job in public health is to "support the voices who are on the side of the facts, who are putting out good, accurate information," so that they can enable other people to support what their health organization is saying or do the corrections themselves.

These allies are sometimes mobilized through an explicit request: Multiple fact checkers specifically ask users to share fact checks with others (Lupa, Cheqeado, Maldita). They think it's important to "ask them to help us shar[e] that content with their own community" (Debby, Cheqeado, press), and "take our debunk to the group where you find this piece of disinformation in the first place" (Ernesto, Maldita, press). Notably, some fact checkers thought that part of these efforts means equipping users to do that work more effectively. As Ernesto (Maldita, press) said, "maybe we have to . . . give some tips of the best way to take our debunks to the groups."

Sometimes this desire to help other people engage in correction even affects *how* they choose to make information available. Francine (press) said that Lupa's audience often reports encountering misinformation while on WhatsApp. As a result, Lupa sent WhatsApp "cards" to its subscribers,[37] specifically to make it as simple as possible to share the information with others within the platform where they encounter it (see Figure 8.2).[38] Fact-checking organizations have also

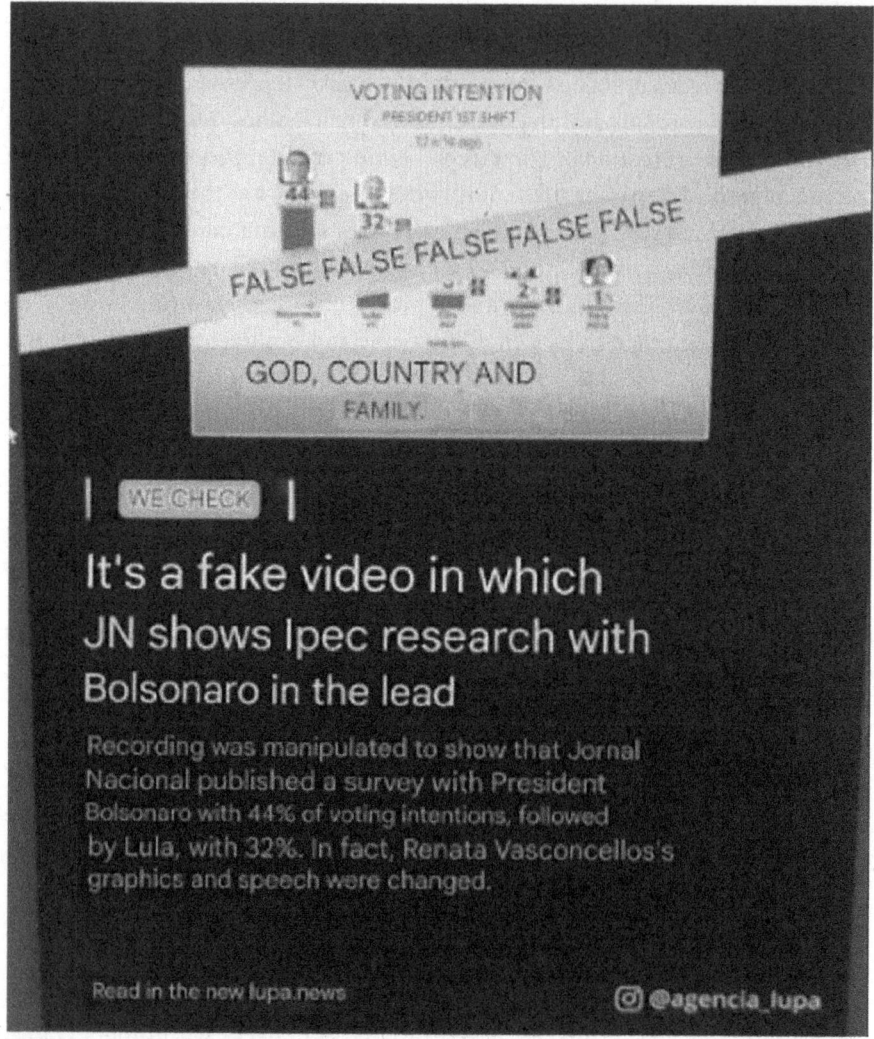

Figure 8.2   Example of Lupa WhatsApp correction card. *Notes:* Given that Lupa works in Brazil, the original WhatsApp card was in Portuguese. We used Google translate to produce the English version shown here. For the full accompanying fact check produced by Lupa, see https://lupa. uol.com.br/jornalismo/2022/08/17/video-jn-ipec-bolsonaro.

examined tools to help them disseminate their materials more effectively, such as relying on a Share the Facts widget designed to make fact checks "easier to find, easier to understand, and easier to share."[39]

In theory, organizations encouraging users to share corrective information should lead to more opportunities for observed correction—professionals and the press are trying to empower people with easily shareable information and urging people to refute misinformation using that information where they see it. Organizations therefore see a core element of their work to be the production of accessible curated evidence (ACE, which we'll discuss in the next chapter), directly supporting users engaging in correction of others. Indeed, in health communication specifically, the WHO has stressed the importance of using a risk communication and community engagement (RCCE) framework to improve response to health threats.[40] This framework argues that proactively communicating accurate information (both what is known and unknown) and actively involving communities as partners are both essential for successful communication.[41] We hear this echoed in the way health communicators talk about their work. Danny (professional) explicitly points to the time and resources dealing with misinformation requires, saying "the juice is better worth the squeeze if you're in a proactive approach instead of a reactive approach with it. Filling those information voids, building resilience to misinformation." Grace (professional) offers a similar comment, suggesting that rather than deal with people one-on-one, she chooses to "kind of take it back, and craft a message, and craft some different materials and push that out through a lot of our different channels . . . having something packaged up that we can make sure is getting out to still a broad audience and the right people." And as we saw above, in doing so they are not only making correction more likely from a range of allies—some of whom may be better messengers given the way they are embedded in communities—but also hopefully creating and reinforcing social norms that correction is something that *ought to* and *can be* done in response to misinformation.

Conclusion

Many of the experts we spoke with said they did not directly and publicly correct misinformation on social media. They expressed concerns about the effectiveness of corrections and whether responding would feed trolls or reinforce the virality of the misinformation on social media. And even those who want to do more lack the resources to support a team to focus on responding to misinformation and must operate within a conservative and controlling hierarchy. Therefore, we think of professionals and the press as *constrained correctors*.

We contrast this with members of the public, who we described as *conflicted correctors* in Chapter 6. The same fundamental conflict—between recognizing the value of correction but also the risks of personally performing it—underpins many experts' perceptions. While they share some of the same sources of reluctance as the users, like fear of toxic reactions and concerns about ineffectiveness, experts are further constrained by a lack of resources and an absence of support from leaders in their organizations. They are also focused on whether direct public correction on social media—done by these individuals or their organizations—is the best way to serve the public and address the problem of misinformation. Most of these experts (or at least their organizations) ultimately decided they could not afford to correct, given the multiple priorities they had and the constraints they were under.

This is also true of platform employees. Despite having more resources, they remain constrained in their ability to adequately address misinformation on their platforms by the difficulties in creating consistent policy and the broader organization goals that prioritize outcomes (especially growth and engagement) other than information integrity.

Instead, most of the professionals and press that we spoke with fulfilled their perceived duty not through directly *correcting* misinformation but through *producing* good quality information for the public. While we think more correction by these individuals and organizations would be valuable to build social norms promoting correction, their focus on information production still has positive downstream effects for observed correction. First, it means the information can be amplified by a variety of trusted messengers who are able to speak more effectively to specific audiences. Second, it enables more people to correct by equipping them with the information needed to do so. There are only so many fact checkers and health organizations in the world. Even if all of them were engaging in direct correction of misinformation in their areas, much misinformation would still go uncorrected. For that reason, it's worth thinking about the content they do produce, how it gets used, and to what effect—which we'll do in the next chapter.

TL; DR

- Few health organizations or fact checkers directly and publicly correct misinformation on social media.
- The press and professionals are constrained correctors, limited by scarce resources, concerns about causing confusion, and toxic harassment that damages mental health.
- Platform employees also feel constrained by the difficulties in addressing misinformation and the corporate priority placed on engagement.
- Organizations that engage in direct correction are motivated by an awareness of the broader audience they can impact, a sense of duty, and support from online allies.

Chapter 9

Accessible Curated Evidence

In the last chapter, we found that the press and professionals are largely constrained correctors, pulled in many directions and sometimes unconvinced of the value of direct public correction. In this chapter, we focus instead on what many of them told us they saw as their primary job: sharing the best available evidence on a topic. We call this content "accessible curated evidence" (ACE), and think of it as the gold standard of what experts should be aiming to produce. We then ask: how is ACE used by the general public and to what effect?

We find that members of the public recognize the importance of ACE for correction. In interviews, they tell us that they rely on ACE to make sense of the information they encounter and to decide what's true. Additionally, members of the public like to use ACE—especially fact checks—when they correct. Finally, an experiment demonstrates that when users include ACE in their corrections, it makes those corrections more effective.

Defining ACE

Before getting into how ACE helps people navigate the information they encounter and facilitates their correction of misinformation, we need to define what we mean by ACE. We'll work through each component of ACE individually, before explaining how combining all three elements creates ACE (Figure 9.1).

First, when we say ACE must contain *evidence*, we don't just mean accurate information (although this is of course necessary). For instance, if someone says that drinking coffee will give you cancer, a correction could simply say "that claim is not true," or "coffee is safe." These are both corrections, in that they are accurate information in direct response to a misinformation claim, but neither offers evidence in support of their (correct) claims. With that said, we take an inclusive

Observed Correction. Leticia Bode and Emily K. Vraga, Oxford University Press.
© Leticia Bode and Emily K. Vraga (2025). DOI: 10.1093/oso/9780197565896.003.0009

Figure 9.1   The components of
ACE. Credit: Meghan Landsberg, 2024.

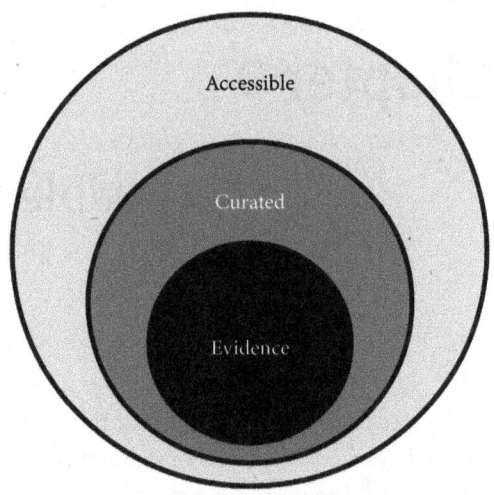

view of evidence, such that it includes personal experiences or narratives, a link
to a primary source (like a scientific article), an explanation of the misleading tactics or goals of someone sharing the misinformation (for example, if the
person claiming coffee causes cancer is selling some kind of cancer-preventing
supplement, or is confusing correlation with causation), or something else that
provides (ideally) concrete and observable data to back up the accurate information. In short, there's a lot of different types of evidence out there that can
be used to support a correction, all of which (i.e., narrative, factual, rhetorical, and source-based) can work to improve accuracy when offered as part of a
correction.[1]

But just because all these are kinds of evidence does not mean all evidence is
equally strong. This leads to the next component of ACE: *curation*. By curated
evidence we mean that someone (probably with expertise or specialized skills)
has identified and brought together the best available knowledge on a topic to
offer a conclusion or recommendation about what the whole body of evidence
says.

A classic example of curation in academic and medical research are meta-
analyses (like the ones we did in Chapters 3 and 4), often considered the gold
standard because they draw conclusions across a body of evidence to illustrate
the state of the field.[2] That is not to say that any individual study isn't valuable *evidence*, but it does not offer the same level of confidence that a meta-analysis does
by virtue of its synthesis across all the relevant studies (evidence) on the topic;
in other words, by *curating* it. So when we think about debunking misinformation claiming coffee will kill you, curated evidence might include a description
of a meta-analysis showing that "light to moderate coffee intake is associated
with a reduced risk of death from all causes".[3] This is very good news for me
(Leticia), as an avid coffee drinker, but I didn't know my daily caffeine fix was

healthy until writing this book (Emily, a tea drinker, is less concerned). This element of curation is important because it does the work of piecing together multiple (sometimes conflicting) pieces of evidence. When there's a new study each week, and this one says coffee is good and that one says it's bad and the next one says it's good again, any given piece of evidence alone can be really confusing and even lead to backlash against health recommendations.[4] The curation involved in ACE is key to helping people make sense of complicated information.

But curated evidence by itself may not be all that useful when it comes to corrections. For example, a nutritionist might share a link to the study we quoted above in response to misinformation on social media. But the study is (likely) complicated and confusing, and most people probably don't have the skillset to understand what a meta-analysis is (or why it's different from a single study), or the specialized statistics associated with it. And almost none of us have time to sit down and make sense of that while we're also dealing with kids and work and feeding the cats and taking out the trash. Plus, the link may well have a paywall (meaning they charge people to access the content) that prevents most people from reading it in the first place.

Which brings us to the final and in some ways most important component of ACE: it is information that has been made intentionally *accessible*. Lots of knowledge that exists in the world is hard to find, access, and understand, like the meta-analysis above. Organizations that produce ACE do so by democratizing information, allowing more people to make use of it—including in corrections. The importance of ACE is that people encounter it and readily comprehend it, even in between all the other stuff that occupies most of their time and attention.

This accessibility can happen in different ways. Sometimes ACE just makes information available that would otherwise be hidden behind paywalls or other access barriers. For instance, if you want to read "Impact of Coffee and Other Selected Factors on General Mortality and Mortality Due to Cardiovascular Disease in Croatia," which is full of useful information about coffee and risk of death,[5] it will cost you $43.95 without an institutional subscription.[6] A summarized version is more accessible simply because it is free.

Sometimes ACE makes things that are super complicated or filled with jargon easier to understand. The meta-analysis showing that coffee drinking reduces risk of death is full of this kind of specialized vocabulary, and most of us just don't know what a "U-shaped dose response relationship," "oxidative DNA damage," and "phenolic acids" are.[7] Academic research sometimes needs specific words to explain things clearly to other academics—but it makes it difficult for most people to make sense of. By simplifying and explaining that language, ACE can make evidence more useful as well as boost its credibility.[8] For instance, rather than talking about oxidative DNA damage, ACE could explain in simple language that cells in an oxygen-rich environment regularly become damaged from exposure to oxygen, which in extreme cases leads to diseases like cancer.[9] The Department of Veterans Affairs calls this principle of communication being "conversational," which they describe as using "everyday human words and plain language whenever possible. We talk like a human, not like Government."[10]

And sometimes ACE takes lots of different sources of credible information and synthesizes their findings into something that's comprehensive. For instance, the graphic in Figure 9.2 summarizes lots of research on coffee consumption and categorizes it into pros and cons of drinking coffee. It cites sources so people can read more, but also effectively synthesizes those sources so people don't have to look them up for themselves. Note that this sounds a lot like curation—and it is! But the act of curating all this evidence for people also makes it more accessible (I don't have to go to each study individually), so long as it's written in a clear, straightforward manner.

Importantly, ACE by itself does not constitute a correction. But ACE can be used effectively and made even more powerful when used strategically as part of a correction, as we'll discuss below. Thus, personal anecdotes, stories, or narratives—which we would call accessible evidence but are not *curated*, may be especially powerful when paired with curated evidence. Combining both (in the context of vaccine misinformation, for instance) has been shown to be more effective than either strategy alone.[11] Telling someone your 100-year-old

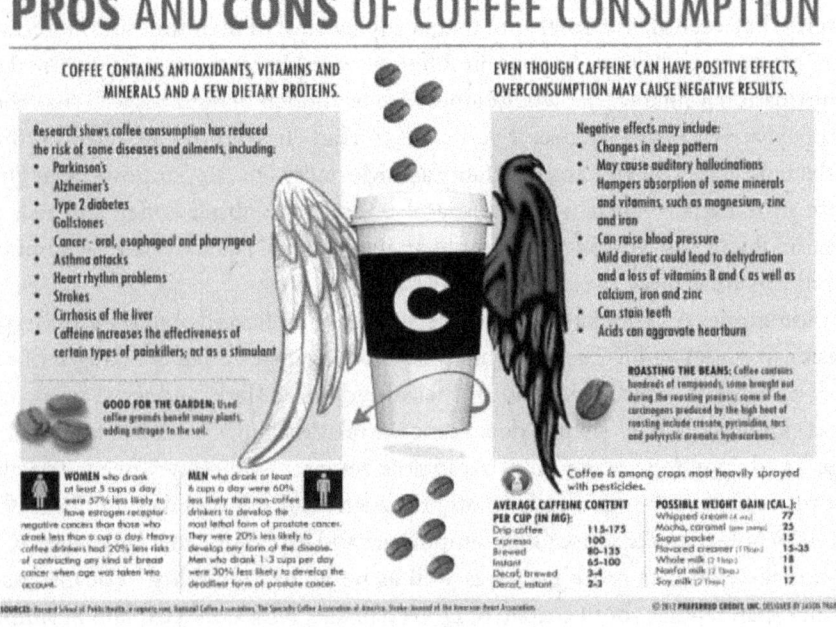

Figure 9.2 An example of ACE. Credit: Jason Tham.

grandmother drinks coffee every day might be convincing accessible evidence, but should be even more credible if paired with curated evidence about the science on the matter, explaining that this is true for a lot of people's grandmothers. And personal narratives may have other benefits as well, like fostering respect for opposing views as well as encouraging more accurate beliefs.[12]

Fact Checkers and Health Communicators Think of Themselves as ACE Creators

Now that we've established what ACE is, let's think about where it comes from. ACE can come from lots of different places; technically anyone can create ACE. But creating high-quality ACE is difficult: it requires knowing what the best evidence is and being able to put it together in simple terms. Many well-intentioned purveyors of information just don't have those skillsets. As we heard in the last chapter, fact-checking journalists and public health communicators see creating high-quality content as the most important part of their jobs. We therefore return to these conversations within the specific context of ACE.

For all the experts we spoke with, relying on the best available *evidence* is at the heart of their mission. Among health professionals, Ana describes her team as "very evidence and science-based," Bill says "it's very much a part of the culture of our department to be an evidence-based organization," and Danny's organization puts "disseminating factual information" front and center in their core goals. This is also true of fact checkers. As Helene from Factcheck.org (press) put it, "we're thinking about what's the best evidence that we have to show." This sentiment was echoed by Debby from Chequeado (press): "We think that we should have a really evidence-based and data-driven article." Finally, some platforms—especially those that generally focus on information rather than entertainment, like search engines (as opposed to social media platforms)—also described surfacing accurate information (and not misinformation) as "foundational" to what they do (Jerry, search). Clearly, all the potential suppliers of ACE recognize that what they create (or promote) must be based in evidence.

Second, *curation* is baked into the process at journalistic and expert organizations. Indeed, curation is inherent in the very definition of journalism, which focuses on finding and presenting the best evidence about a topic from a wide variety of sources.[13] This was reflected in our interviews with the fact checkers, who emphasized their role in bringing expert knowledge to their audience, or as Ernesto from Maldita (press) said: "Tak[ing] the knowledge of these experts [they specifically named top scientists, experts, doctors] to the people" because "it's kind of difficult for [the experts] to get to the public" without relying on journalists. One way Maldita does this is by utilizing their database of vetted experts (which they call "superpoderes," or "superpowers" in English) on a wide range of topics to help them fact check claims. Fact checkers recognize that expert knowledge is often inaccessible to the public, and they help bridge that gap by making it easier to understand—essentially combining curation of experts with accessibility.

Many professionals (Bill, Danny, Grace, Henri, Imani) similarly told us that they would share public questions, concerns, and potential misinformation with experts in the field to be able to identify "what do the subject matter experts in their very educated perspective, what do they deem to be a credible reliable point of fact" (Bill, professional). When Henri's (professional) team identifies potentially problematic content, they rely on "a desk of medical profiles, maybe an epidemiologist, comms people with technical support from headquarters offices to brainstorm what's the best way of addressing this given all the information we have." As Bill summarizes, "Generally speaking, we're not producing original content. We are synthesizing content from a lot of different sources."

But both fact checkers and public health communicators are focused on creating curated evidence not just for it to exist in the world, but also with an eye toward making information they think will be useful and easy to understand (*accessible*). For fact checkers, this is especially salient. There is a fundamental understanding among the fact-checking community that evidence on its own is not enough—it needs to be evidence that can get through to a busy and distracted audience. As Debby at Chequeado (press) put it, "our principles are always: be as simple as possible, as short as possible, and . . . you don't need to be boring, to be good." Accessibility is at the heart of fact checkers' mission; they are keenly aware that if they provide evidence that is too complicated, they will lose the attention of their readers. As Ernesto from Maldita (press) said:

> Our audience is probably people who's been working eight, nine hours this day, and they arrive home and they want to read something. If we are too complex, if we use very high-level language, we're losing them. We have to be simple, direct, and . . . to use expression and words that everybody can understand.

Health organizations had similar things to say about the accessibility of the information they produce and disseminate. Ana (professional) emphasized that "how we publish information is as important as correcting false information," further elaborating that health organizations need to be "making sure that the health information is effectively available to the people." Imani (professional) echoes this point, talking about working with experts when responding to public questions or concerns, making sure that they are "actually meeting the needs and answer[ing] the question that's being posed" in an approachable way—in other words, making their corrections usable or accessible for the audience.

Importantly, the creation of ACE combats misinformation even if it is never used in a direct correction. For instance, using ACE to reiterate the scientific consensus that vaccines are safe, rather than debunking the specific vaccine misinformation that vaccines cause autism, can reduce belief in the link between vaccines and autism.[14] By bypassing misinformation related to genetically modified foods through sharing accurate information, rather than correcting the misinformation directly, belief in misinformation was also reduced.[15] As these examples highlight, ACE can work to make people more accurate, even if it doesn't meet our narrow definition of "correction" on social media.

Platforms Promote ACE

Much like the professionals and press, who were more comfortable creating ACE than correcting publicly, platforms, too, described their investment in ACE. Platforms have long been criticized for lacking strong policies toward the promotion of reliable (or evidence-based) information.[16] When they do promote high-quality information it is often concentrated within just a handful of health-related issues—generally those where there has been substantial public or regulatory pressure.

A few examples of platforms elevating ACE include Facebook connecting people to official sources for vaccine misinformation,[17] Pinterest directing searches for "vaccine" content to information from public health organizations,[18] and Instagram offering expert resources for help when users search for eating disorder content.[19] Research suggests that these changes lead to higher quality information on the platforms,[20] though critics argue platforms need to be doing more on this front.[21]

The COVID-19 pandemic supercharged the promotion of ACE on platforms. As Jerry (search) put it when talking about search engine changes made during the COVID-19 pandemic "the amount of prime real estate, we have handed over to the CDC, local health authorities, for COVID, it's unprecedented." In fact, all of the major public social media platforms—including Facebook, Instagram, YouTube, and Twitter—engaged in health promotion activities surrounding COVID-19, including increasing the visibility of authoritative content, providing advertising credits to public health partners, and compiling credible information that was easily accessible to users.[22]

This approach of explicitly linking ACE to contentious content has been applied in other limited contexts, including the 2020 US Census, the 2020 US presidential election, and health and scientific issues where expert consensus is extremely high, most notably climate change and vaccination. For example,

Twitter posted ACE to the top of people's feeds before the 2020 US presidential election, providing them with facts about mail-in voting that were designed to inoculate people against misinformation on the topic (see Figure 9.3). [23] TikTok pursued a similar strategy around the 2024 European Union elections, setting up election centers in the app to connect people with reliable information. [24]

The people we spoke to at platforms described this as a broader content strategy. Erin (social media) talked about the policy at her platform of linking posts on contentious topics—she mentions elections, COVID, and vaccinations as examples—"append[ing] every piece of content with a redirect to a reputable source of information." Similarly, Jerry (search) describes this idea of linking contentious or possibly misleading content with high-quality information: "Folks use [search engines] to fact check stuff and so it seems natural to ... have the counterspeech attached to the speech, to have them travel together more easily." Andrea (social media) described the goal of these strategies simply: "We're not just removing it, we're trying to inform people too." And research broadly suggests this kind of contextualization of misinformation can work; indeed, our inspiration for studying observed correction was spurred by our idea that if related stories appearing after misinformation in the Facebook feed offered corrective information, they could reduce misperceptions—something that we and others found to be effective. [25]

Promoting ACE is worthwhile in lots of ways, but this approach also benefits the social media platforms. By attaching ACE to entire categories of content, platforms don't have to wade into the messy area of deciding what's true—something platform employees told us they *really* don't want to do. Erin (social media) explicitly linked her platform's policy of appending "reputable

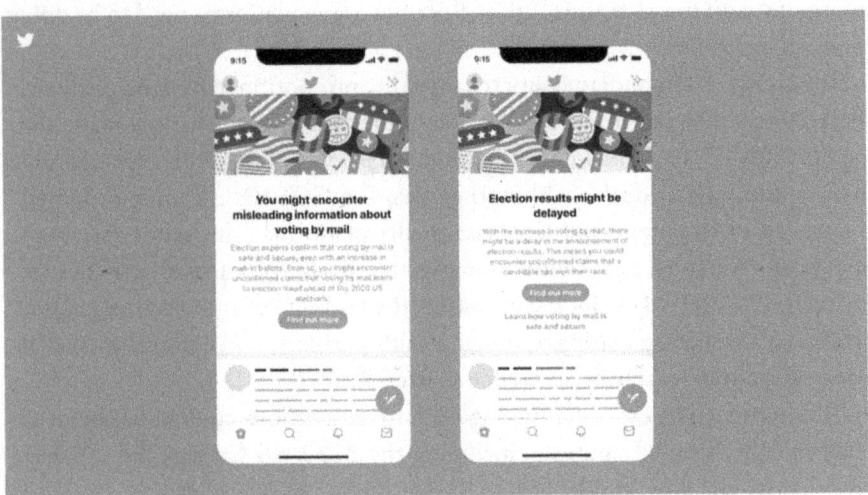

Figure 9.3   ACE about voting by mail on Twitter.

information" to the fact that "they [the platforms] didn't want to have to deal with . . . these determinations at scale," something scholars have argued would be functionally impossible even if attempted.[26] She went on to describe this as "reticence of not wanting to be in the business of calling things misinformation," and later said bluntly: "Do we really want private corporations doing this?" As Pablo (social media) described in detail, this is a question of power as much as one of policy, and employees at the platform he worked for were

> very uneasy with the idea of a centralized power control. Having too much control of what is said and what isn't said. Because even if they believe that they themselves would use it wisely, once powers exist, who knows who's going to use them in the future? And there's a lot of like unease. Even though we knew there's lots of bad stuff floating in the system, about if [the platform] legitimizes having this current lever, governments and other creepy people are going to want to control that lever. We don't necessarily know how much the leaders of [the platform] themselves can be trusted to use that lever ethically. Are we setting up a North Korea-like situation where we just control truth and control elections?

Jerry (search) also highlights the need for distance between the platforms and truth determinations because "the more it becomes the political battleground, which it has, then you go from Texas to Britain where you see things saying, 'Don't touch misinformation whatsoever, or you're going to get sued.'" Therefore, promoting ACE becomes a way for platforms to avoid the decision of what is misinformation, helping them stay out of politics, out of the courtroom, and generally out of trouble. This reasoning may apply to YouTube's decision in 2023 to abandon a prior policy of removing misinformation related to the 2020 presidential election from the platform, and instead focus on showing people looking for election information so-called authoritative sources.[27]

But while promoting ACE from expert organizations can offer platforms some cover in deciding what is or is not misinformation, it is not without its own risks. Platforms recognized this as well, describing the importance but at times impossibility of selecting sources to surface that are respected by diverse audiences—as Pablo (social media) put it, the choice of sources "gets very icky fast because who decides what stuff is reliable?" Jerry (search) said the platform he worked for wanted to rely on sources that have EAT: "expertise, authoritativeness, and trustworthiness." But EAT is not enough—Sebastien (social media) emphasized that any sources they relied on needed to be "very robust sources that are nonpartisan . . . noncontroversial sources that are pretty reliable." Given the politicization of many issues in recent decades (or as Pablo (social media) says more colorfully, "everything gets swallowed in some political dumpster fire"), this task has become increasingly difficult over time. As Erin (social media) puts it, "they tried to engage in this counterspeech from nonpartisan elites, and then, through time, that elite becomes considered to be partisan, so then it doesn't work anymore." While this question of partisanship may feel especially salient in the hyperpolarized two-party system of the US, it is in fact exacerbated in many places around the world, where government data may be corrupt, unreliable, or generally not trustworthy.[28]

Basically, platforms are generally wary of doing too much and have concluded that doing less is more defensible than doing something that turns out to make things worse. ACE—while certainly a useful counter to misinformation—also allows them to avoid difficult choices, by outsourcing the decisions of what is true and what is credible to other organizations.

ACE for the People

So far, we've heard from health professionals, fact checkers (the press), and platforms that they prefer ACE to correction because it better aligns with their core mission, values, or priorities. They also told us (in Chapter 8) that they think other people may be more effective correctors. ACE should theoretically make these corrections by others easier to perform.

Turning our attention now to the *public*, we find that ACE plays three main roles in the (mis)information landscape: first, in assisting people in deciding whether something is misinformation; second, in helping them feel more confident in correcting misinformation, and third, in making those corrections more effective.

ACE as a Truth Determinant

First, people often told us they were quite skeptical of the information they saw on their social media feeds. And this is true not just of the folks we talked to, but of people around the world. A Pew study from 2022 found that only 33% of US adults said they had some or a lot of trust in the information they get from social media.[29] Or as Tobias (user) told us of his experience, "It's all misinformation. Especially on social media. Dear God, I mean, everything there is . . . It's just not true."

As a result, many of the social media users we talked to spoke about "doing research" (Walter and Julia, both users) when they saw red flags in online content. This process is alternately referred to as corroboration, verification, or authentication of information on social media in the academic literature.[30] It's worth acknowledging that verification is by no means a panacea; sometimes people are verifying information or relying on fact checks not for accuracy motivations but instead to reinforce their existing beliefs—what some call "affirming fact checkers."[31] But verification processes at least introduce opportunities for new information to enter one's thought process.

Different people had different versions of their own verification processes, but ACE was often mentioned, either directly or indirectly. This is especially true of fact checks, which were frequently mentioned as a specific source people rely on to help them make sense of what is true or not (Colin, Martin, Shary, Franklin, all users). As Martin (user) put it, once something is verified "from the fact-checking organizations, then I can feel confident that it's like, okay, this is actually a true situation." Likewise, Bret (user) says, "I've seen these fact checks everywhere, and I love to read them because they give you a better perspective." Others mentioned the press more broadly (rather than fact checkers specifically) as being a way of deciding what's true (Walter, Martin, Shary, Nigel, all users). As Nigel (user) described this process, "I will double check the social media post against other sources, maybe like news sources." Generally, research supports the value of verification through fact-checker ratings (like the *Washington Post*'s Pinocchio scores,[32] or Politifact's "Truth-o-meter" featuring the famous "Pants on Fire" rating[33]), which also help people decide what's true[34] and lead them to share misinformation less often.[35]

But this reliance on fact checkers is not universal, and others raised concerns about the validity of fact checks. For example, Don (user) said that he "[doesn't] trust fact checkers, to be honest with you because I feel like they're also leading people to one way or the other" and Owen (user) expressed his feelings that fact checks are "often just another source of potential misinformation." The fact that some participants relied on fact checks while others were skeptical aligns with public opinion research showing that only about half the American public believes fact-checking organizations deal fairly with all sides. In the US, this belief is quite polarized: 69% of Democrats believe this but only 28% of Republicans do.[36] This is not necessarily true around the world though; one study of fact checking in the United Kingdom during COVID-19 found broad support for *more* fact checking from journalists.[37] This highlights the difficulties in finding agreed-upon authoritative sources of information, and just how much those trusted sources depend upon context.

Users were less likely to bring up professionals, like public health organizations or government sources, as sources they might rely on to verify information. Only one person (Julia, user) spoke of specifically looking for content from professionals when trying to decide if something is true or false in a public health context, saying that "some of the sources I might trust could be my own doctor or websites of public health organizations or professionals." This represents a missed opportunity: all of the public health and science organizations thought that providing this credible information is a critical part of their job (Bill, professional, says "I feel like a big part of our job is to be the source of record, to be the reference point that others can use"), yet those kinds of sources were not top-of-mind for the social media users we spoke with. Health organizations might therefore consider how they can do even more to publish information that is easy to find, use, and share (i.e., the accessible part of ACE).

The Dominant Role of Search in Looking for ACE

Overwhelmingly, though, rather than go directly to ACE suppliers (fact checkers and health organizations), the users we spoke with described an even more mediated way of deciding what's true. You've probably found yourself there—someone makes a claim that doesn't sound quite right to you in conversation, and you have to figure out where to start to try to figure out whether they're right. I (Leticia) was recently told by my mom that you don't need to (and therefore shouldn't, because yikes) bring a snake that has bitten you when you go to the emergency room for treatment (my parents and I have some interesting conversations).[38] This surprised me because I thought anti-venom (used to treat venomous snake bites) was specific to the snake that bit you, so assumed doctors would need to know what the snake was (maybe just take a picture rather than bringing the whole snake with you, but the point remains). When I wanted to find out how anti-venom worked, I went straight to Google, and within 10 minutes had a layperson's understanding of the topic (and my mom was right! Anti-venom in the US—but not everywhere[39]—is "polyvalent," which means it works against all the venomous snakes you would find in the country. So leave your snakes at home, guys).

Like me, many of the social media users we talked to discussed going to Google as a key part of their information verification strategy (Richard, Nicole, Danielle, Karl, Owen, Walter, Lisa, Shary, Tobias, Alberto, and Don—interestingly the only person who also said he used Bing, all users). There are obviously lots of search engines, but almost all the people we spoke with about this mentioned Google by name, reflecting its dominance in the field—Google has 93% of the global search engine market.[40] That search process would then refer them to other sources, but Google was very often the first stop in their truth-seeking journey. Karl (user) describes this well:

> So if I saw like a meme on Instagram that had some sort of content that I kind of thought was inaccurate, I will literally go to Google and just type what it says . . . And I'm pretty much guaranteed to get something back.

The experiences described by the participants we spoke with are consistent with other data showing that most people go to Google to find reliable information (65% of Americans say they get news from Google or other search engines).[41]

One benefit of Google our participants described is the feeling that they could verify the information using lots of different sources. For example, Shary (user) said that for her, "most important is to Google and see how many different news sources, legitimate news sources like BBC and Politico and a lot of those kind of mainstream news sources" all have the same story. Similarly, Karl (user) says the "good thing" about a search engine is that "I'm going to have access to a lot of different perspectives," while Owen (user) describes "open[ing] several tabs on the results that seem to be the most relevant and credible" before deciding whether information is true or not. In other words, people sometimes like doing their own curation of information sources, and search engines help them do that efficiently.

Fact checkers were very much aware of this audience reliance on Google and were vocal about making sure their content would show up there. An important way they make sure the people who need to see a fact check are being exposed to it is by engaging in Search Engine Optimization (SEO) to make sure their content shows up in relevant Google searches. As Joyce (press) from Check-News put it, they prioritize "SEO and how people are searching on Google and to have the right keywords . . . [to] make your article appear" to the people who are searching for related information. This is a way to expand their audience, Debby from Chequeado (press) describes: their organization has to be "easy to find on Google" because the people searching on Google are not searching for a specific organization or even necessarily for a fact check—they are just looking for reliable information. By doing so they are reaching an audience beyond those that subscribe to their content or visit their website.

Problems with Search

In general, turning to search engines to find ACE may be an effective strategy, but there are several clear downsides of this approach. First, search engines are not immune to misinformation themselves. For example, Google has been criticized for their search results linking to misinformation both about the Zika virus[42] and COVID-19,[43] as well as broader concerns about search turning up racist and sexist content and images.[44] An audit of conspiracy theory content on Google, Bing, DuckDuckGo, Yahoo, and Yandex revealed that most search engines often return "conspiracy-promoting results" in their top results.[45] Given how rarely people scroll past the top few results on Google,[46] what they see at the top of the feed matters. As Debby from Chequeado (press) succinctly puts it: "We know that if they Google it and don't find a good credible or evidence-based info, they're going to believe what they find."

The risks of search contributing to misinformation may be even more stark when thinking about the current shift from traditional search to using other technological tools like smart speakers (Amazon's Alexa, Google's Assistant, Apple's Siri, etc), as well as tools like ChatGPT and other AI summaries that rely on large language models to parse text into answers to queries. Early research on smart speakers suggests that the information they provide is often misleading—39% of queries posed to smart speakers related to the HPV vaccine, for instance, returned inaccurate information.[47] Additionally, a majority of their answers do not contain the source of the data on which they rely,[48] making assessment of their credibility even more difficult (as compared to traditional search engines, for instance, where the source is more obvious). Similarly, early research on the accuracy of large language models like ChatGPT is mixed. For example, when asked to evaluate 12,784 fact-checked claims, ChatGPT only correctly identified the claims as true or false in 72% of cases.[49] Various large language models were only intermittently accurate when asked a series of questions about the 2024 European elections.[50] Other studies have shown higher accuracy on specific topics like common cancer myths,[51] and accuracy seems to be improving as large language models develop.[52] But ChatGPT can also generate misinformation by "hallucinating" or making up nonexistent but seemingly expert references,[53] further bolstering the credibility of low quality information. Given this, providers of information need to adjust their tactics as technologies change what kinds of information are surfaced and how users interact with them. No matter what the technology, an overreliance on search will likely sometimes expose people to misinformation despite their best intentions.

Second, for some issues, turning to Google may produce very little information at all—making it more likely to become a target of opportunity for those pushing misinformation. This problem of a lack of (easily found) reliable information is sometimes called a "data void"[54] and research has found that when people use search engines to evaluate the veracity of misinformation claims and the search engines return low-quality information, it can actually increase belief in misinformation.[55] Google previously responded to this issue by including "data void warnings" on fast-changing issues where quality information does not yet exist.[56] Search engines we spoke with also hoped these types of warnings could help fact checkers and other content producers be aware of the need for information by "potentially giv[ing] the heads up to producers of news of quality content, that, 'Hey, in this space looks like it would be beneficial if we . . . write about this stuff. Filling those voids'" (Jerry, search). However, recent research suggests Google is no longer providing data void warnings.[57]

Third, relying on search engines to get content to the people who need it can be gamed by other interested actors, motivated by money or their own issue agendas. So-called keyword squatting means that sometimes related content that shows up in a Google search is swamped (and therefore effectively hidden) by bad actors pushing an agenda, such as the Internet Research Agency—a purveyor of propaganda backed by the Russian state—creating content related to Black Lives Matter.[58]

All the actors we talked to were aware of and often pursuing different means of mitigating these downsides of relying on search. First, social media users did not blindly trust the information they found on Google. Much like their skepticism of social media platforms, people acknowledged the limitations of Google. They described its known biases: "I'm always cautious of the Google searches as well because I know a lot of times they're not very accurate or they can be providing links that are manipulative" (Lee, user), and were quick to acknowledge that it doesn't replace expertise. Tobias (user) says the fact that Google can provide quick answers as both the "best" and "worst" thing, because "nevermind the fact that you have a medical degree, I just Googled it." Or as Nicole (user) puts it simply: "I usually go online. That's crazy. Go online to find out whether some other online information is accurate."

From the platform side, search engines described a focus on promoting or elevating high-quality content, to avoid people being exposed to misinformation via their platforms. Search engines are incentivized to ensure that they are returning high-quality, accessible content, because few people are likely to continue using a search engine that consistently fails to meet their needs, and accuracy remains a fundamental goal for information search.[59] Along those lines, Google has worked with fact checkers to make their content more visible in search results. Jigsaw, part of Google, partnered with the Duke Reporters Lab to develop the Share The Facts widget, which allows fact checkers to standardize their content and surface it to Google. That way, when relevant fact checks are available for a search, they get pushed to the top of search results and labeled as a fact check.[60] For instance, if you Google why Obama's Hawaii house was spared by the tragic 2023 wildfires, a fact check indicating that his house is on a different island than where the fires burned is labeled as such (see Figure 9.4). Notably, though, the label is small and gray—and we know from Chapter 4 that makes it less visible, less memorable, and therefore less likely to effectively change beliefs.

ACE Empowers Correctors

So people rely on ACE to know what's true, and count on search engines to help them find it. But beyond using ACE to determine whether something is true or false, ACE can also be used to make correction itself easier. Among social media

Figure 9.4 Labeled fact checks in Google search results.

users, there was broad consensus that a good correction requires evidence, something ACE should allow them to provide more easily. The users we spoke with varied in what they deemed a credible source, although they tended to parallel the sources they turned to for information verification in the first place. Most commonly, they spoke about turning to the press: a "fact checker" (Earl) or a "trusted, verified news source" (Bonnie). A few users also mentioned original scientific evidence, or as Alex (user) said:

> Ideally, I would like to get a link from maybe some journal or some website that does scientific article . . . [or] I try to find a news site that posted an article that references, like I mentioned, research or some sort of statements from medical experts or scientists.

Providing a source was seen as offering several advantages. First, providing a source allows the person being corrected the opportunity to seek more (accurate) information for themselves, or as Richard (user) says he likes to share a link so that "they can themselves go and see that whatever they posted was false." Likewise, Hermine (user) says she also includes links when she's correcting so "they can become more educated," even while expressing skepticism that people actually want to learn more (as she puts it, "they just want to post what they want to post"). By making those sources readily available, they are enabling people to (theoretically) verify the information for themselves.

Offering a source as part of the correction can also be a way to signal respect for the person sharing misinformation. Bonnie (user) says that providing a source allows her to correct without "trying to show them I'm not like, I'm right, you're wrong, but more like, 'Here's some additional information that shows that this thing you shared is misinformation.'" Sharing a credible source was also seen as a way to find common ground with those they were correcting.[61] Sean (user) says it's important that the "proof" he provides to support his correction is from "a source that both of us can trust," and Lisa says she will "go out of my way to find something that supports what I'm saying by sources that they believe." Importantly, these efforts to find common ground and to engage in civic cross-cutting conversations in the context of politics may have other downstream benefits, as both have been shown to decrease misperceptions about social divides as well as reduce animosity between the parties.[62] However, one user (Gaston) disagreed, worrying that offering a source made a correction less conversational and more confrontational, saying you can't just "go to someone with an article," as it instantly makes them defensive.

But perhaps most importantly, most people we spoke with believed that including a source makes their corrections more effective. Or as Colin (user) puts it, when he responded to misinformation on social media, he "just hit him back with this is I respect your attitude, but these are the numbers. These are the facts." As such, most of the discussion of correction centered around finding and providing a source that offers *facts* and *expertise*. Expertise matters—and when experts engage in correction, they increase accuracy.[63] But given that most of us are not experts, we rely on the expertise of others to be persuasive.[64] This may serve as a signal that we know what we are talking about and may also give additional information people can rely on to learn more.[65]

But trust matters even more than expertise for successful correction.[66] Trust in a social media correction can come from different places. The person performing a correction may or may not be trusted, and corrections from those with whom one has a close relationship (people you trust) work better than those from unknown others.[67] Trust can also come via the source you share in a correction. When drawing upon ACE to bolster the *expertise* side of the credibility equation, thinking about the most appropriate *trusted* sources for your audience remains critical. For these reasons, we need a lot of different organizations producing ACE, allowing those engaging in correction to find not just an expert, but a trusted expert to share with the audience they are trying to reach.

ACE Makes Observed Correction More Effective

People clearly believe in the value of incorporating trustworthy information into corrections, especially to make corrections more effective. But does the evidence bear this out? To answer this question, we'll consider one of the experiments that we showed you in Chapter 3. We'll compare conditions that either include or do not include links to credible information from the press and prominent health organizations. This will help us see whether including ACE makes correction more effective.

Our data collection in the spring of 2016 showed participants an ordinary user sharing a story with a headline claiming that the Zika outbreak was "caused by the release of genetically modified mosquitoes in Brazil." We then had two unknown users (i.e., members of the public) correcting the misinformation, but in one case, those users simply said the information was "false" and "discredited" while in the second, they supported these claims with links to Snopes (a fact checker) and to the CDC (see Figure 9.5, which shows the Facebook version of the experiment that included links; there was also a Twitter version).

The results suggest that providing a link was critical for observed correction to increase accuracy about the (false) claim that GM mosquitoes caused Zika (see Figure 9.6). On both (simulated) Facebook and Twitter, accuracy improved somewhat when the users did not offer a link to support their claims that the news story was false; the increase in accuracy was noticeably larger (and statistically significant as compared to the control) when the user corrections included links to reputable sources.[68]

Notably, this study offers only the bare minimum to count as ACE. As you can see in Figure 9.5, the ACE condition only shows headlines and links to seemingly expert sources, which were not clickable for participants. The only information making a difference is therefore a brief description available in the link preview (e.g., "Despite articles suggesting otherwise, there is no proof that GM mosquitoes have helped the spread of Zika"). Given that very few people actually click on links on social media,[69] this likely imitates a typical experience for

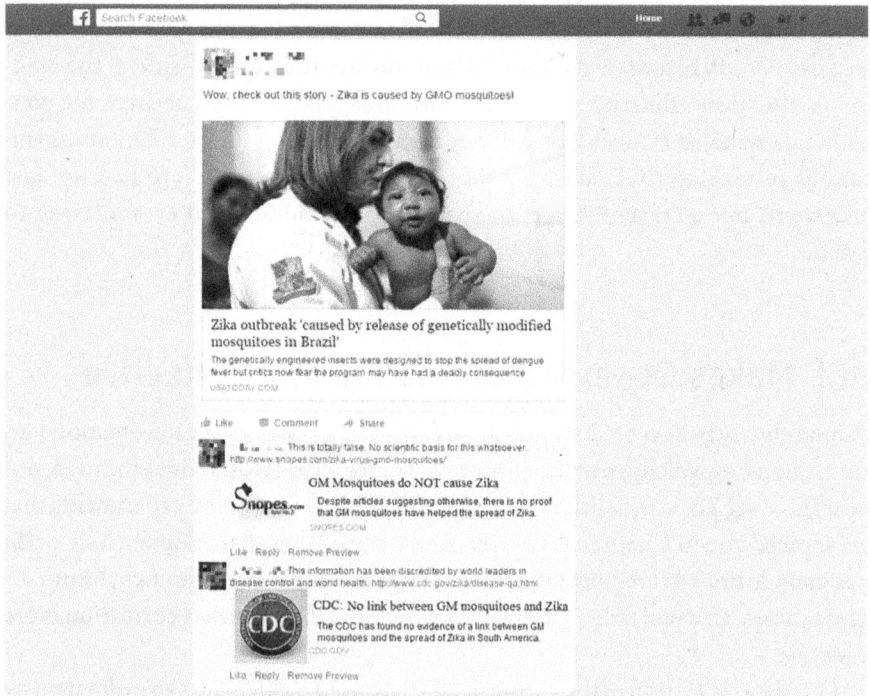

Figure 9.5 Example of user corrections with sources.

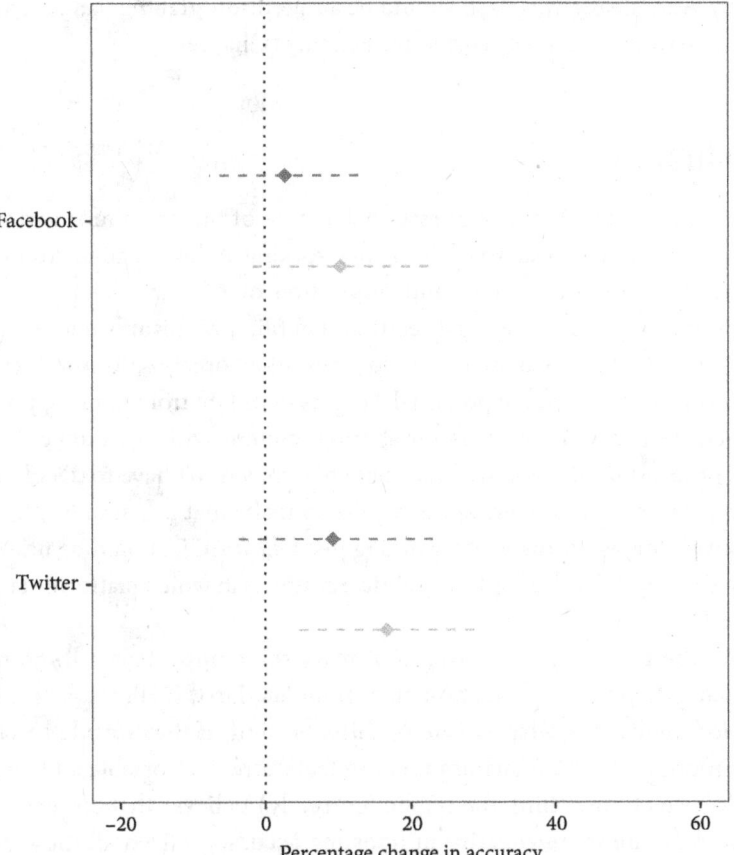

Figure 9.6   Effects of including ACE with corrections on accuracy in the US. *Notes:* The y-axis represents the simulated social media platform people were randomly assigned to see in this single experimental study. The x-axis represents the percentage change in accuracy comparing the experimental condition to the control group. We use different color diamonds to represent whether the correction did or did not include a link to an expert source. The x-axis represents the percentage change in accuracy between the correction and control condition, where results to the right of the vertical dotted line represent increased accuracy and those to the left represent decreased accuracy. The diamonds represent the averaged percentage change, and the horizontal dashed line represents the 95% confidence interval for this difference. Values further from the dotted line indicate stronger effects. When the confidence interval crosses the vertical dotted line, the relationship is not statistically significant.

those navigating social media. That is, most people on social media will rely only on the information available to them with zero effort.

It's critical, then, that creators of ACE consider how to best optimize their content for social media to make it truly *accessible*, without requiring that users leave the platform they're using. We expect that the effects of including ACE will be even stronger when it fully leverages each of these components, making corrective material with curated evidence presented in a format that is easily accessible to many. And ideally, this ACE should be as attention-grabbing and memorable as possible to strengthen its corrective benefits (Chapter 4).

Conclusion

ACE is an often overlooked but essential feature of the (mis)information landscape, and one that appeals to all the actors working in these spaces. Professionals and the press see the creation and promotion of ACE as their primary role, much more so than responding directly and publicly to misinformation. The advantages of this approach are multifold: they allow organizations to focus their limited resources, avoid the potential dangers of online trolls, and support allies who may be better messengers for sharing content with the public. For platforms, promoting ACE has different benefits: they don't have to decide what is true or false and can rely on someone else to make that decision for them. The biggest risk for platforms is determining just *which* ACE should be utilized—a risk that is shaped by the multiple political contexts in which platforms engage in this work.

From the public's perspective, ACE plays three important roles in helping them navigate online information environments. First, it allows people to discover for themselves what is true or false. Second, if they decide to respond to misinformation, ACE enables them to feel more comfortable and confident in their corrections. Third, the public (correctly) believes that corrections that include ACE are more effective in boosting accuracy. Given all these positive potential and actual uses of ACE, more organizations should invest in creating accessible curated evidence for the public.

TL; DR

- Professionals and the press see the creation of ACE as their primary job.
- Platforms prefer promoting ACE to correcting misinformation to sidestep the job of deciding what is true and false.
- The public primarily relies on search engines to find ACE.
- The public uses ACE to determine what is true or false, to increase their confidence in correcting, and to bolster the credibility of their corrections.
- Corrections that incorporate ACE boost accuracy more than those that do not.

Chapter 10

Conclusions

We started this book by acknowledging that misinformation has been around as long as people have communicated with each other. With that said, many people point to social media as a culprit in making misinformation a more pernicious problem for society.[1] This book doesn't say they are wrong, but flips this script on its head to ask: How can the affordances of social media be leveraged to also offer an (incomplete) solution to the misinformation that rapidly spreads online? To answer that question, we describe *observed correction*, which happens when people witness someone else being corrected after sharing misinformation. This is something that can (and does) happen in a lot of spaces, but the affordances of social media—especially in terms of the persistence and visibility of interactions and the association of diverse groups through social networks—make online observed correction especially powerful in reaching a lot of people with accurate information.

We've shown that observed correction consistently improves people's accuracy (Chapter 3), and these effects are even stronger when people can recall what the correction said (Chapter 4). Therefore, an important path forward is thinking about how we can make public corrections more visible, salient, and memorable. We need to up our game—those spreading disinformation are making their content as engaging and evocative as possible,[2] and corrections need to be equally engaging on the side of truth.

Saying that observed correction can improve accuracy doesn't matter unless people are willing to correct. We know that people perceive correction to be happening on social media (Chapter 5) and computational studies have charted public social media corrections of controversial topics like COVID-19 vaccinations and politics.[3] But when we spoke with social media users about their perceptions and experiences, we learned they are conflicted correctors (Chapter 6). On the one hand, they tell us they think correction is valuable and can tell us about times they might correct or have corrected someone else on

Observed Correction. Leticia Bode and Emily K. Vraga, Oxford University Press. © Leticia Bode and Emily K. Vraga (2025). DOI: 10.1093/oso/9780197565896.003.0010

social media. On the other hand, they expressed concerns, often based on lived experiences, that correction won't work, that it will harm their social relationships, that it will cause them to the be the target of a hateful mob, or that it is just too hard. Some of these concerns can be mitigated—telling people about the effectiveness of and public approval for social media corrections led people to say they would be more willing to correct specific cases of misinformation (Chapter 7). Other concerns, however, aren't as easily addressed and will require larger changes to the built environment, not just on social media but in society more broadly.

The Limitations of Observed Correction

We've just spent an entire book convincing you of the benefits of observed correction. Obviously, we're also convinced, but we want to be clear about the ways in which observed correction is limited.

First, the book focuses on the ability of observed correction to increase people's accuracy, but accurate knowledge about a topic does not automatically translate to behaviors. For example, previous research has found that showing people that a politician lied about a fact may lead people to be more accurate about that fact, but largely doesn't change their perception of the politician or their willingness to vote for them.[4] And this is to be expected. People's evaluations of an individual or a topic—let alone the actions they take in response to those evaluations—are a complicated constellation of a lot of different beliefs, so even if one is shown to be false, others may remain true, or at least still feel true to them. We think that people are less likely to change their broader attitudes or behaviors in response to correction when they are thinking about an issue on which they have strong opinions, when their identity is tied to the issue, or when the issue relates to key values they hold.[5] In those cases, the impact of observed correction on behaviors or evaluations beyond accuracy about a specific component of the issue is probably quite limited. For this reason, correction efforts might be most effectively directed toward issues that do not have those characteristics—so-called everyday misinformation.[6] But narrowing the focus of correction efforts still leaves a lot of misinformation that can be corrected relatively easily. In general, most of the misinformation people encounter online is not about hot button topics but instead about crime, medical mistakes, or false deaths.[7]

Along those same lines, observed correction is almost certainly more difficult in hyper-polarized environments. When people strongly disagree with each other, that disagreement can foster intensely negative feelings against those with whom we disagree (sometimes called affective polarization).[8] If we perceive the other side as evil, we're motivated to do whatever we can to prevent them from gaining power—including accepting, embracing, and endorsing misinformation. In those circumstances, it becomes more difficult to accept any correction that goes against our preferred group. That is, if I'm a Democrat and I see misinformation that favors Democrats, it will be harder for me to accept a correction that shows the misinformation is inaccurate because I care so much about Democrats succeeding. As more issues become politicized, especially in the context of health,[9] polarization will make corrections for those topics harder as well. But hard does not mean impossible. Despite affective polarization, there remains a lot more common ground than people realize, and stressing our common identities can supersede partisanship.[10] Even for political topics—which are more explicitly tied to the strong mega-identity of party affiliation[11]—corrections have been shown to change attitudes about current policies,[12] the degree of affective polarization that divides people,[13] and lots of other issues too.[14] In other words, there are still many opportunities to make people more accurate.

Another limitation revolves around the fact that people can't engage in effective correction without having access to reliable information. If you don't know what's true, it's impossible to identify misinformation, let alone correct it (Chapter 9). This makes some topics more difficult to correct. For example, when we started writing this book at the beginning of the COVID-19 pandemic, we were dealing with a *novel* coronavirus, so definitive information was hard to come by. Even the experts didn't know how it spread (remember when people were washing their groceries?), who was most likely to get infected, or who was most likely to die from the virus. Emerging events will always be rife with misinformation[15] and knowing what is true is especially hard in these contexts. But this is also a space where sharing the best information that we have is particularly important, while remaining transparent about what we do and don't know. We've been talking about correction in response to clearly false information, but it is also likely valuable in responding to information that is simply misleading or incomplete.

Many of the strengths of observed correction, including its scalability and adaptability, are contingent on its reliance on people. People are great! We love people! But they are also relatively slow, compared to other ways of generating information content. This means that misinformation shared on social media can reach many people before someone is able to effectively respond. And this speed differential may only be growing, given new concerns about the ability of bad actors to generate lots of disinformation content using large language models like ChatGPT.[16] With the significant development of artificial intelligence in the past couple of years, disinformation can be generated much faster, and possibly even more effectively. But there is a hopeful side to this as well, and we see a lot of potential from developments in artificial intelligence. People are already employing AI-generated corrections from models that are trained to optimize on accuracy and politeness,[17] and conversations with AI-generated bots arguing against conspiracy theories have shown to be effective in early trials.[18] Artificial intelligence might also accelerate the ability to create more effective ACE without specialized skills. While correction is adaptable to this new environment, it will need to compete with the speed and effectiveness of (often very motivated) disinformation spreaders,[19] but also not sacrifice both careful scrutiny for accuracy and thoughtful balancing of ethical imperatives.

It's also worth keeping in mind that the fight against misinformation is like an arms race. Any advantage those fighting against misinformation gain will be thwarted in some way by the purveyors of disinformation. For instance, several platform employees told us about just how good disinformation actors are at adapting to new policies the platforms develop, tailoring their content to avoid them. Dexter (other) said one of the most frustrating parts of his job is "how aggressively and quickly all of the purveyors of misinformation have adapted their techniques to the rules of each individual platform" and that sometimes it only takes weeks before someone sharing misinformation can "perfectly evade" any new policies developed. Likewise, Sebastien (social media) marveled at how "the adversarial actors in this space have gotten very, very good at toeing the line on it." All of this means that, as Jerry (search) puts it, "every policy is a tombstone." Platforms create a policy against a new form of misinformation, and the motivated sharers of disinformation figure out a way around it.

So, once they realize the effectiveness of the correction format, disinformation campaigns will likely weaponize it to further spread misinformation, rather than truth. Indeed, when we ran an experiment in which someone shared truth and was "corrected" with misinformation posing as a fact check, the participants in the experiment were convinced by the fake correction.[20] There may be no escape from this arms race, but critically assessing the ways in which corrections can be improved, to limit misunderstandings as well as misrepresentations, will help us to keep up.

An Updated Understanding of Swiss Cheese

In addition to those specific limitations, we want to be absolutely clear that observed correction is not an end-all be-all solution to the problem of misinformation. It helps. But even in the best-case scenario—when people are paying enough attention to remember what it says, on an issue they don't know much about and are willing to update their beliefs on—it still only improves accuracy about 40%. Even if everything goes right, that is not enough to fully address people's inaccurate beliefs about the world.

But we still think observed correction is an important part of a concerted approach to misinformation mitigation. First and foremost, correction will always be necessary because there is no perfect solution to misinformation. Observed correction offers the ability to increase the public's accuracy across a wide range of spaces and issues. While there's more all of us can do to make observed correction even more valuable (as we discuss below), we also know that observed correction can work no matter how the social media environment changes. So long as there are people willing to correct and others to witness such corrections, observed correction can happen. The fact that so many people say they value correction even while they talk about the risks and constraints of doing so personally, suggests it is something that has buy-in from a lot of different actors in society.

However, the process of writing this book has convinced us that the approach we described as a Swiss cheese model in Chapter 1,[21] where multiple layers of protection reduce the overall level of misinformation in a system, is oversimplified. Misinformation mitigation is not just a linear process through which a bit of misinformation is filtered out of the information ecosystem at each stage. In contrast, all the different layers of Swiss cheese interact with each other in complicated ways (Figure 10.1). Those interactions sometimes make one layer stronger than it would be on its own, but sometimes may have the opposite effect. To better understand this, we'll unpack a few examples of how different layers of the model interact symbiotically with observed correction: the importance of quality information, rebuilding trust, and developing strong social norms around the value of truth.

Because corrections are more effective when they contain evidence, observed correction works best in contexts in which there is an abundance of high-quality information in the world that all members of society can readily access and understand (ACE, Chapter 9). But corrections also require trust to increase accuracy.[22] For ACE to be an effective part of corrections, we have to all agree on which sources of information are trustworthy and which are not. Misinformation is made worse when it's hard to know what information to trust. If all information is suspect, you might choose to either believe nothing you see (including misinformation) or everything you see—and both of these responses are problematic.[23] For that reason, rebuilding trust in institutions that produce and disseminate high-quality information, including governments, health organizations, and journalism, is a critical aspect of making ACE an effective source of evidence, thereby increasing the value of observed correction. Likewise, increasing trust in one another will make observed correction more effective, because users are the primary vehicle by which public corrections happen.[24] There is a lot of room for improvement in trust of government (only 16% of the US public said they trust the federal government to do the right thing at least most of the time[25]), journalism (only 32% of Americans reported they trust the mass media at least a fair amount[26]), health organizations (only 26%

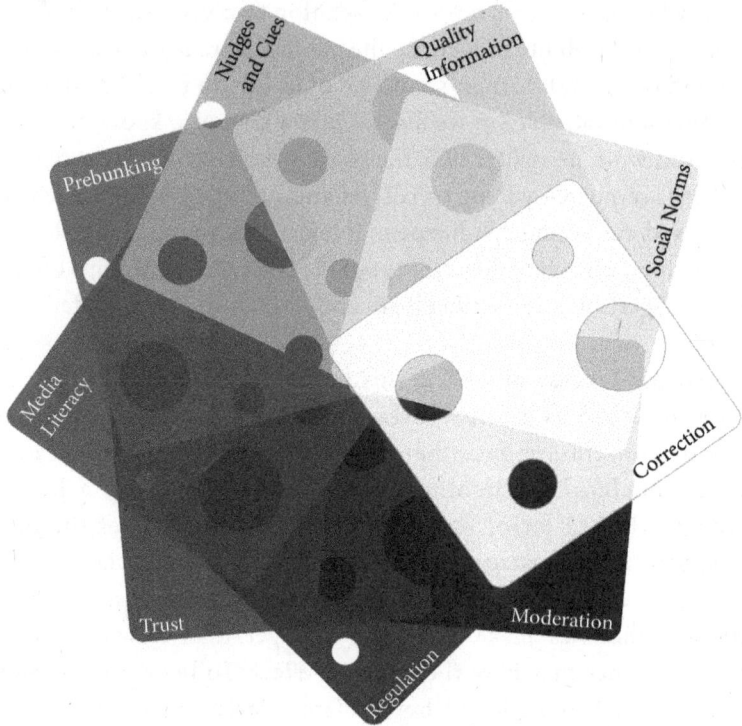

Figure 10.1   Updated Swiss cheese model Credit: Meghan Landsberg, 2024.

of Americans trust their local public health departments a great deal and 37% trust the CDC[27]), and our fellow citizens (only 37% of the US public said most people can be trusted[28])—both in the United States and globally. Of course, rebuilding trust does not come easily, nor should it be granted unreservedly, so organizations and institutions need to consistently behave in ways that deserve trust.

Along the same lines, stronger norms around the value of truth would also strengthen the power of observed correction. Obviously people say that they (and often do in fact) value truth,[29] but commitment to truth is often sacrificed to other priorities like winning elections or validating a strongly held identity when deciding what to believe and how to behave.[30] Stronger societal norms of how much truth matters—not just in the abstract, but relative to other considerations—could make observed correction more effective by increasing the weight people give to it.

Greater commitment to truth could also result in positive downstream effects: passing policies that fund organizations that prioritize truth (and therefore create more ACE), electoral repercussions for those who act dishonestly (thus increasing trust in government), and a general willingness to accept corrections when they occur. When people are committed to verifiable information, and acceptance of corrections in the face of evidence, we see amazing things take place. Consider Wikipedia. As a Wikimedia spokesperson[31] told us in an interview,

> People just want to, they just believe in the project.... We have this goal of creating free knowledge for all, and have this goal that everybody will be able to join us in this goal. And people do. They want to share knowledge.

Within that community, verified information is the driving goal, and people act accordingly. And Wikipedia has been stunningly successful in creating a space where accurate information thrives—while it isn't perfect, its errors are usually of omission rather than inaccuracy.[32] For correction to be most effective, we would have to see a concurrent shift in norms along those lines, such that individuals, groups, and societies value truth over other motivations like winning, feeling smart, earning money, or gaining political power.

Just as observed correction can be strengthened by rebuilding trust or recommitting to truth, observed correction can also strengthen other layers of misinformation mitigation. When users, experts, and platforms engage in correction, that may in turn increase the value we collectively ascribe to truth and to corrections—that is, social norms. These social norms matter, because they can create virtuous cycles encouraging more correction—knowing people like and perform correction makes me more willing to do it (Chapter 7), which then makes other people realize that people like it, and so on.[33] When corrections take place in such a way that they go against one's natural incentives—like when I correct someone in a way that is detrimental to my preferred political party, or my favorite sports team—that not only makes the correction more effective,[34] but likely also increases both social norms around truth *and* trust in the corrector, yet another layer of the model.

Finally, it's also worth noting that various platforms have been excising one slice of the Swiss cheese from this model by moving away from content moderation approaches. Both Twitter and Meta have pulled away from previous efforts to reduce misinformation exposure, which had involved making content deemed to be misinformation less visible (or sometimes removing it entirely). For years, Meta worked directly with many of the fact checkers we spoke to for this book, in order to critically ascertain untrue content and label it accordingly. Recently they have announced a move away from this partnership, and will instead be relying on the Meta community itself to weigh in on what is true or not true.[35] This choice intersects with another layer of the model, though, in that Meta has said it will not change course in its European markets, where it must abide by the Digital Services Act (i.e., policymakers).[36] At the same time, a new wave of social media platforms, like Mastodon and Bluesky, have emerged that are federated – that is, with less centralized power and control than the traditional platforms.[37] Content moderation on those platforms is generally given over to users to control, deciding for themselves what types of content they want to see, with what kinds of curation and filters. The changing nature of content moderation fundamentally interacts with other layers of the model, impacting how people get information, how they think about trust, and what opportunities they have to correct.

Collaboration Among the 5 Ps

Beyond the synergy between layers of the Swiss cheese model, a second important synergy is among the different actors who are involved in the (mis)information landscape, who we introduced as the 5 Ps—platforms, professionals, press, public, and policymakers—way back in Chapter 2. Although we've often talked about these actors separately throughout the book, it has actually been quite difficult to do so, because observed correction relies upon—and is greatly enhanced through—the combined efforts of all these actors.

We've probably spent more time in this book talking about users—the public in our 5 Ps—compared to any other actor. That's no accident, since we think that users have a crucial role to play in making observed correction work. But this emphasis on users should not be interpreted as an intention to impose the full burden of combatting misinformation on members of the public. That's not reasonable nor is it what we expect the public to do in other areas of society. Think about food safety. We expect people to be generally aware of and comply with the best practices that health organizations put forward based on research: they should wash their vegetables and cook their meat to the right internal temperature to reduce their risks of food-borne illnesses.[38] But we don't expect them to go to the farm where their food was grown to see if they have safe irrigation techniques, to test the chickens for salmonella, or to visit factories to see if their food may have been produced near an allergen. Instead, we rely on an integrated system of protection. The government is responsible for passing and enforcing food safety legislation. When there is a foodborne outbreak, we expect government health organizations to monitor the situation and issue food recalls when appropriate. The press is tasked with sharing this needed information with the public, who then must comply with any updated guidelines, like throwing out possibly contaminated foods.

Likewise, we shouldn't expect people to be fully responsible for determining the health and safety of the information they consume. Instead, we think all the various actors in society can contribute to the solution. Members of the public offer a scalable way for correction to happen, but their work is made much easier when it is supported by the other 4 Ps.

ACE is perhaps the best example of this sort of collaborative effort. The press and professionals already prioritize creating ACE and see its benefits as not only maximizing scarce resources but broadening who they can reach by equipping the right messengers (which often are *not* the expert organizations directly) with the right message (Chapter 8). Platforms seem more willing to promote ACE for at least some topics and would rather do so than decide for themselves what counts as misinformation. And members of the public rely on ACE to determine what's true, while also recognizing the utility of including it in their corrections (Chapter 9).

While ACE represents a kind of ideal type of collaborative efforts among the 5 Ps, there is more to be done. First, we can broaden the playing field in terms of who is creating ACE. While we've focused largely on controversial health topics where there is a lot of known misinformation, any organization committed to producing evidence-based content should be considering how those materials could be leveraged in cases where misinformation might emerge. Having ACE ready to be deployed on a variety of key topics will help prevent people from believing misinformation in the first place and enable allies to offer corrections quickly and effectively if and when misinformation begins to spread on that topic.[39] This should also serve as a call to experts in all fields to invest in making information more accessible. This means information can't be behind a paywall, it should show up when I look for it with a search engine, and it must be easy to understand. If it doesn't meet those requirements, it's unlikely to be found or absorbed by people looking for information about an unverified claim, and that means they can't use it to correct others. Finally, organizations should also be thinking specifically about the affordances of social media in creating that content. Creating visible and appealing graphics that communicate the necessary accurate information without requiring users to click through to another website[40] should boost their corrective potential.

We use the word invest deliberately—creating ACE takes resources. It is not easy to do, and it is often undersupported, in terms of time, skills, and money. For instance, both fact checkers ("Young people are on TikTok and Reels," Debby, Chequeado) and platforms ("Our younger users are going to always go click the video because they just prefer consuming content that way," Jerry, search) highlighted that younger users have a strong preference for video content. Creating videos—especially good videos—is more time consuming and requires different skills than creating text, but also will broaden the reach and impact of ACE for new segments of the population. As a society, we should be spending more resources on making sure knowledge is findable and found by those who are looking for it and putting it into the types of formats that are most useful to the people who need it. This is a space where policymakers can create needed structural changes. More funding for organizations involved in creating ACE—journalists, fact checkers, health organizations, and others— is essential. For years, we've seen declines in funding for public health[41] and journalism;[42] to successfully combat misinformation we must reverse those trends.

A second place where we need more coordination among the 5 Ps is addressing the bad actors who often deter correction. Everyone doing the work of correction—whether members of the public, the press, or the professionals— spoke about their very real fears of a toxic mob that was going to attack them for daring to share accurate information they didn't want to hear. Research has found that such attacks, especially for journalists and public health officials, have increased in recent years, and infrastructure to support those under attack is sorely lacking.[43] These attacks have real chilling effects on whether people are willing to correct misinformation (as we heard in Chapters 6 and 8), what they say publicly more generally, and even whether they stay in the profession at all.[44] Platforms need to enforce their terms of service more consistently to reduce hateful, toxic, or dangerous speech,[45] especially from repeated offenders. Of course, that will not solve the problem of misinformation—people can still politely respond to corrections with misinformation—but if people know they can engage in corrections without risking their mental or physical safety, we're going to get a lot more people willing to do it.

To ensure this happens, we can enact regulations that require social media companies to crack down on bad actors spewing hate or encouraging violence, and otherwise improve the pro-social design of their products,[46] even if it harms engagement. We can look to other countries for models. Regulations like the Digital Services Act in the European Union require "countering and quickly reacting" to various harmful content, including hate speech and harassment,[47] while Australia requires that platforms take down abusive posts, including those related to bullying and harassment.[48] In the US, policymakers have been reticent to act similarly.[49] But they could leverage their power to create incentives (platforms) or financial support (press, professionals) to enable the production and dissemination of accessible curated evidence, and its safe and effective use in online environments, ultimately contributing to a more informed society.

3 Vs to Make Correction More Impactful

In thinking about ways to increase the impact of observed correction, we'll organize our recommendations into three categories. Observed correction is a better (partial) solution when we increase the volume, visibility, and value of corrections.

INCREASING THE VOLUME OF CORRECTIONS

As we heard from both users (Chapter 6) and experts (Chapter 8), there are many personal and professional reasons to avoid correcting others publicly on social media. Most of these reasons deal with the costs of doing so—sometimes financial but more often in terms of time and effort, damage to personal friendships, threats of toxicity and harassment, and fears of it being ineffective. Despite these concerns, rather than rejecting corrections entirely, people remain either conflicted (public) or constrained (press, professionals) correctors. Therefore, there are a lot of people who could be motivated to correct—increasing the *volume* of corrections—under the right set of circumstances.

Our book showcases two approaches that seem particularly important to increasing correction volume. First, we must boost the efficacy of people who might correct. Making ACE more widely available should boost internal efficacy (am I able to correct?), reduce the work (and thus costs) of doing correction well, and give people the confidence needed to offer an accurate correction. We can also boost external (will people listen to my correction?) and response (if they listen, will they change their minds?) efficacy by making sure that people know that observed correction does in fact make people more accurate (one of the main arguments of this book). Given the vast literature showing that feeling efficacious tends to produce behaviors,[50] we should be focusing on how to encourage *correction efficacy* to motivate corrections.

Second, we must nurture social norms that support correction. People tend to say they *personally* like corrections (Chapter 5) more than they believe *others* like corrections (Chapter 7). We must close this perceptual gap between individual and perceived social injunctive norms. Motivating more people to correct more often doesn't just directly increase the volume of corrections in the moment, but also communicates the descriptive norms that further encourage future correctors. In Chapter 7, we demonstrated that even short messages about the effects of correction and social norms around correction encouraged people to say they would correct misinformation. This sets the stage for a more sustained strategic communication campaign to embolden correctors among the public, when it feels safe and comfortable to do so.

INCREASING THE VISIBILITY OF CORRECTIONS

Second, corrections are most impactful when they are *visible* (Chapter 4). There are lots of ways to make corrections more visible, and different actors have different roles to play in making corrections show up.

The people doing the corrections—whether they're members of the public, the press, professionals, or others—can make choices that make those corrections more visible. A first step to increasing visibility is providing a link or some kind of visual information. In some of our previous research, when we showed people a feed with 120 posts on different topics and with different features, posts that included links or pictures tended to receive more attention than text-only posts,[51] in part because they just take up more space on the screen. More importantly, when we asked people to tell us in an open-ended question which posts they paid most attention to, the top three posts mentioned all contained links to news stories.[52] Additionally, including a link in a correction can itself boost its effectiveness (Chapter 9), although we think the best ACE will go beyond just a link.

Platforms can also work to make corrections more visible. They can give more real estate to information that is corrective or potentially corrective, through highlighting ACE or making comments that are likely to contain corrections more prominent, bolder, or more vivid. They can also choose to prioritize or amplify accurate or verified information, therefore making it more visible to users. This logic underpins three common strategies that many social media platforms have pursued in addressing misinformation: the three D's of downranking (making low quality content less visible),[53] deplatforming (removing repeated or egregious offenders of content rules),[54] and demonetizing (eliminating the ability to make money off certain types of content).[55] We see these processes as the inverse of our argument about the importance of making corrections visible—by making the misinformation less visible, especially as compared to accurate information, it should improve the information environment. But platforms can do more to explicitly prioritize corrective information.

We want to take a moment to highlight the special role that search engines play in this process. We learned in Chapter 9 that many people start with search engines when trying to figure out whether something is true or false, so it is especially important that search engines make sure the most visible content is accurate. Yet research suggests that is not always the case; especially in situations where misinformation is new or quickly evolving, trying to search for evidence online can actually make people more susceptible to misinformation.[56] As we finish this book, major search engines like Google are also starting to increasingly rely on AI to generate a summary of search results. While often their AI curates a lot of information in an effective way, the slipups in the technology are (sometimes hilariously) apparent. For instance, when asked how many presidents have graduated from the University of Wisconsin (our joint alma mater), the Google search summary (see Figure 10.2) pulled information from a light-hearted article describing graduates of Wisconsin with presidential *names*,[57] and therefore returned the answer that 13 US presidents have graduated from UW. But in reality, the answer is none.[58] While many of these examples are funny errors, others could prove dangerous, like the suggestion that glue should be added

△ AI Overview   Learn more ⋮

Thirteen US presidents have attended the
University of Wisconsin-Madison and
earned 59 degrees in total:

- Andrew Jackson: Graduated in 2005
- William Harrison: Graduated in 1953 and
  1974
- John Tyler: Graduated in 1958 and 1969
- Andrew Johnson: Earned 14 degrees,
  including classes of 1947, 1965, 1985, 1996,
  1998, 2000, 2006, 2007, 2010, 2011, and
  2012
- James Buchanan: Graduated in 1943,
  2004, and 2013
- Harry Truman: Graduated in 1933
- John Kennedy: Graduated in 1930, 1948,
  1962, 1971, 1992, and 1993
- Gerald Ford: Graduated in 1975 ⌃

Ⓦ Wisconsin Alumni Association ⋮
Presidential Badgers |
Wisconsin Alumni...

Figure 10.2   An example of inaccurate AI-enabled search engine results.

to pizza.[59] As the nature of search evolves, it's important to continue to think
about the ethical questions involved and the possible downstream impacts. Ensuring that search results contain clear and accurate information will make it both
more likely people are accurate in their knowledge about controversial topics and
make it easier for them to use such evidence in their corrections.

INCREASING THE VALUE OF CORRECTIONS

Beyond increasing the volume (both the number of correctors and the number of
corrections) and visibility of corrections (with the goal of increasing recall), we
also need to make each correction more *valuable*, by which we mean more effective in increasing accuracy. There are many steps that people can take to improve
the likelihood their corrections will work. First and most importantly, people
should be thinking about the ways in which they can correct others that are right
for the situation. Observed correction can work in many different ways—it can
be someone simply addressing the factual inaccuracies and saying what we know

to be true,[60] it can focus on the misleading tactics used in the misinformation and explain why they are leading to false conclusions,[61] it can undermine the credibility of the misinformation creator, especially when confronting disinformation being spread for political or financial gain,[62] or it can offer a personal narrative that directly rebuts the misinformation being spread.[63] This versatility means that each person can decide the best way to address misinformation as they see it, depending on what they know, what they find, the experiences they have, what they think their intended audience will be most receptive to, and what is comfortable for them.

But in general, offering some kind of evidence or explanation for what is true (what misinformation researchers call an "alternative explanation") makes corrections more effective.[64] This is yet another opportunity for ACE creators. To make ACE more potentially corrective—as well as more valuable in and of itself—in addition to simply clearly describing existing evidence, they should also precisely explain *how* or *why* this evidence leads to a particular conclusion. From our food safety example above, it should be more effective to not just tell people that they should wash their vegetables, but *why* exactly washing vegetables reduces the risk of getting sick, and *how* to go about washing your vegetables to minimize that risk.[65]

It's also important to consider the kinds of sources the intended audience for a correction is likely to believe. We all turn to and trust different sources of information when we're trying to figure out what's true and false (Chapter 9). Therefore, correctors need to think about who will be a credible source for their audience.[66] This is also a space where multiple corrections help. Not only does repetition itself make corrections more effective,[67] if different correctors are using different approaches or relying on different sources to support their corrections, those corrections can reach more diverse audiences.

We also want to stress the importance of corrections that are civil and empathetic. Even if being uncivil doesn't necessarily make the correction itself less effective in increasing belief accuracy,[68] it can have negative downstream consequences like harming the credibility of the person offering the correction[69] and fomenting anger.[70] It's never going to hurt to be humble, empathetic, and kind. Despite studying misinformation now for nearly a decade, we're quite positive that we both have unintentionally shared misinformation, because all that means is that we were wrong or unaware of new evidence on a topic. If we've all done it, we need to be more understanding when it happens to others.

And, much as we described above with the layers of Swiss cheese and the 5 Ps, these different Vs will interact with each other. Efforts to increase the *visibility* of corrections are likely to encourage perceptions of social norms (other people are doing it) that will lead to a greater *volume* of corrections, as well as making each individual correction more *valuable* by boosting recall. You can sum up best practices for effective correction with the acronym, REACT:[71] repeated, empathetic corrections that offer alternative explanations (or evidence) using credible sources offered in a timely way. Ultimately, as this acronym suggests, and as the book itself has argued, people should react, responding when they see misinformation in the way that feels right and safe to them.

Conclusion

People often point out that misinformation is more of a symptom than a cause of a problem with our information environment.[72] We don't disagree with this idea.

But just because misinformation is the symptom rather than the cause of the problem doesn't mean we should ignore the symptom. You still take Tylenol when you have a headache, even if the headache is caused by something else like dehydration, stress, or drinking too much alcohol. My (Leticia) kids' pediatrician, Dr. Baldwin, calls this "supportive care." In the moment, we sometimes need to focus on alleviating our symptoms to remain functional.

But that shouldn't take away from solving the underlying problem. People should demand that our leaders behave in ways that earn trust. Health organizations should own up to the mistakes made over the years that undermined trust in them. The press should strive to communicate what leaders do that is trustworthy, genuine, and useful to society in a way that competes with other information in the crowded information space (and fights against the negativity bias of media) and includes all corners of society in their coverage. Policymakers should hold each other accountable, even when it hurts their own goals. And there should be electoral consequences when leaders behave in a way that is misleading, corrupt, hurtful, or otherwise counter to the greater good. To extend the metaphor too far, we should hydrate, meditate, and drink less, even while we use supportive care to alleviate our current misinformation headache.

Notes

Chapter 1

1. Forestal (2021).
2. Glassman and Kuznetcova (2022); Waltenberger, Höferlin, and Froehlich (2023).
3. Bob Woodward (@realBobWoodward), reddit, https://www.reddit.com/r/PoliticalHumor/comments/13giqj4/worst_smell_ever/.
4. Elon Musk rebranded Twitter as X in July of 2023. We'll continue to refer to it as Twitter throughout the book to signal that we are referencing the platform that existed at time of all of our data collections and the majority of our writing, with the affordances implied.
5. Chou, Gaysynsky, and Cappella (2020); Kuklinski et al. (2000); Southwell et al. (2022); Swire-Thompson and Lazer (2020); Vosoughi, Roy, and Aral (2018).
6. Budak et al. (2024); Guess, Nagler, and Tucker (2019).
7. For this definition we draw from our previous work, Vraga and Bode (2020b), and Southwell et al. (2022). Other scholars have offered other definitions of misinformation; if you are interested in this you could refer to the works of Nielsen and Graves (2017); Southwell et al. (2022); Tandoc, Lim, and Ling (2018); and Wardle (2017), to name a few.
8. Jack (2017); Swire-Thompson and Lazer (2020).
9. Canadian Centre for Cyber Security (2022); Cybersecurity and Infrastructure Security Agency (n.d.).
10. Berinsky (2023); Eismann (2021); Rath et al. (2018); Kuklinski et al. (2000); Thorson and Abdelaaty (2023).
11. Kuklinski, Quirk, Jerit, Schwieder, & Rich (2000); Thorson & Abdelaaty (2023).
12. Butler, Koopman, and Zimbardo (1995); Jolley and Douglas (2014).
13. Reedy, Wells, and Gastil (2014).
14. Einstein and Glick (2013); Karpf (2019, December 10); Kim and Cao (2016).
15. Directorate-General for Communications Networks (2018); Ekström, Lewis, and West-lund (2020).
16. Barlow et al. (2012); Swami (2012).
17. Jolley et al. (2019).
18. McDonnell and Sanchez (2021); Uscinski and Parent (2014).
19. Mozur (2018, October 15); Reeves (2017).
20. Wright et al. (2021).
21. Barua et al. (2020).
22. Thorburn and Bogart (2005).
23. Benedetti et al. (2023); Peterson, Swire-Thompson, and Johnson (2020).
24. Craciun and Baban (2012); Kata (2010); Ognyanova et al. (2021).
25. Serrano (2022, September 22).
26. Beaujon (2020, December 4).
27. FDA (2024).

28. Langer et al. (2012).
29. FDA (2024).
30. Branswell (2024, April 29).
31. Southwell et al. (2019).
32. Vraga and Bode (2017), 624. We make two adjustments to our previous definition of what we used to call *observational correction* in this book. First, we now refer to it as *observed correction* to emphasize the behavioral piece of witnessing the correction. Second, our previous definition argued observed correction "occurs when social media users update their own attitudes after witnessing another user being corrected" (Vraga & Bode, 2017, p. 623). We have decided to focus specifically on *witnessing* a correction, which is separate from whether or not it effectively reduces misperceptions. In other words, when someone sees a public direct correction on social media, it is observed correction whether or not they adjust their attitudes on the topic. Though as we'll see in Chapter 3, they often do.
33. This raises an interesting conceptual distinction between debunking (or what we call correction throughout this book) which includes direct responses to specific pieces of misinformation and prebunking, which is meant to inoculate people against misinformation they haven't yet seen. That is, correction comes after exposure to misinformation, whereas prebunking comes before it. But as others have already pointed out (Van der Linden, 2023), in many cases this distinction is theoretical. While a direct correction to misinformation is inherently debunking in that it helps people adopt more accurate beliefs in the face of misinformation, it may also have inoculative benefits so that if I see that misinformation again later, I will know it is false.
34. Naylor (2017, November 29).
35. Bode and Vraga (2015); Bode and Vraga (2018); Vraga and Bode (2017); Vraga and Bode (2018).
36. Garvey (2022, November 17).
37. Cleveland Clinic (2022, December 20).
38. In fact, Minneapolis airport only got about 13 inches of snow (Winter Storm [2023, February 24]), reinforcing that what is misinformation (or not) is very much dependent on the best information available at the time, and can change as new information becomes available Vraga and Bode (2020b).
39. Mutz (2006); Mutz (2008); Schudson (1997); Wells et al. (2017).
40. Lewandowsky et al. (2022).
41. Compton (2020); Lewandowsky and van der Linden (2021); Roozenbeek, Linden, and Nygren (2020).
42. Chan (2024); Guess et al. (2020); Tully, Vraga, and Bode (2020); Vraga et al (2021).
43. Funk et al. (2019, August 2); Jaiswal, LoSchiavo, and Perlman (2020); May (2020).
44. Golebiewski and Boyd (2019).
45. Pennycook et al. (2020); Pennycook et al. (2021).
46. NewsGuard Ratings (2022).
47. Courchesne, Ilhardt, and Shapiro (2021); Maruf (2022, February 26).
48. Brown and Peters (2018); Helberger (2020); Marsden, Meyer, and Brown (2020); Yang, Broniatowski, and Reiss (2019).
49. Bode and Vraga (2021a).
50. Mackay (2020, December 26); Reason et al. (1990).
51. Bode and Vraga (2021a).
52. Bode and Vraga (2015); Vraga and Bode (2017); Vraga and Bode (2020a).
53. Janmohamed et al. (2021); Porter, Velez, and Wood (2023); Porter and Wood (2019); Walter et al. (2020); Walter et al. (2021); Walter and Murphy (2018).
54. Bode (2019); Stout (2019, July 8).
55. Mercier (2016).
56. Gravelle et al. (2022); Leiserowitz et al. (2022, January 12).
57. Berinsky (2023); CCDH (2021).

58. Varshney (2020).
59. Lukoff et al. (2021). User autonomy is often prioritized from an academic perspective, but rarely a major concern when it comes to social media design. See Lorenz-Spreen et al. (2020). Critics suggest that respect for human autonomy needs to be articulated as a key ethical consideration in any artificial intelligence approaches to content, including recommendation algorithms. See Milano, Taddeo, and Floridi (2020); Varshney (2020).
60. Bode and Vraga (2021c).
61. Bode and Vraga (2015).
62. McCorvey (2023, February 10).
63. X Transparency Center (2022, July 28); Associated Press (2022, November 29).
64. Roth (2023, June 2).
65. McMahon, et al. (2025).
66. Marks (2022, February 21).

Chapter 2

1. Fisher (2022); Kaplan and Haenlein (2010); Ronzhyn, Cardenal, and Batlle Rubio (2022).
2. Bode and Vraga (2015); Smith (2017).
3. Smalley (2022).
4. Morrison (2023); Wheeler (2023).
5. Besley and Dudo (2022).
6. Of course, there is a lot of debate over what scholars mean by "the press," "journalism," or "publishers." Carlson (2016); Nielsen & Gantner (2022); Schudson (2003); Shapiro (2014); Zelizer (2005). We are using a simple and inclusive definition, but acknowledge that the boundaries around who counts as a member of the press can be blurry.
7. Shearer (2021, January 12).
8. Saks and Tyson (2022).
9. Croteau and Hoynes (2006).
10. Agarwal and Barthel (2015); Hallin and Mancini (2004).
11. Conrad (1999); Merkley (2020).
12. Amazeen (2020b); Graves (2016).
13. Beagan et al. (2022); Brann and Himes (2010); Jamieson (1995); Thomas-Hunt and Phillips (2004).
14. Kirzinger et al. (2023, March 7).
15. Funk et al. (2019, August 2); Gadarian, Goodman, and Pepinsky (2022); Nadeem (2022, February 9); Pollard and Davis (2022).
16. Amazeen (2020a); Humprecht (2020); Stencel, Ryan, and Luther (2022, June 17).
17. Norris (2022).
18. Evans et al. (2017); Ronzhyn, Cardenal, and Batlle Rubio (2022); Treem and Leonardi (2013).
19. Forestal (2021).
20. Ellison and Vitak (2015); Evans et al. (2017); Gibson (1977); Pearce and Malhotra (2022); Treem and Leonardi (2013). This is not an exhaustive list of all affordances, and there can be disagreement among scholars in where affordances operate and how to define them. We are focusing on those most relevant to our argument and where there is general agreement. We are also not the first to connect affordances of social media to misinformation and correction—see Apuke and Omar (2021); Pearce and Malhotra (2022).
21. Of course, these platform choices can change at any time, so these examples may be specific to when this book was written. Many platforms, like reddit, allow both users and moderators of subreddits (or other communities) to decide how to sort comments, including best, old, top, Q&A, controversial, and new comments. Platforms may also make it easier or harder to change this sorting.

22. Note that platforms often refer to these sets of rules as "policies" and therefore think of themselves as policymakers—but we are using the more generic "rules" to distinguish them from policies put in place by governments. For that reason, we do not include those that create platform policies in our policymakers category of actors.
23. Thorson and Wells (2016).
24. Broussard (2018). While some of these decisions—about who to follow, what groups to join, or what content to like—are within an individual's control, many of the choices platforms make are essentially unknown to users, happening only behind the scenes and often invisible and untraceable.
25. Snapchat (2023).
26. Bakshy, Messing, and Adamic (2015); Marwick and boyd (2011).
27. Vaidhyanathan (2022).
28. Indeed, there is an entire section on *The Onion*'s Wikipedia page dedicated to prominent cases where people accidentally took something from the satirical publication seriously.
29. Darlenski and Tsankov (2020).
30. Davis and Jurgenson (2014); Marwick and boyd (2011).
31. Kaplan and Haenlein (2010).
32. Vaidhyanathan (2022).
33. Emigh (2021); Nielsen and Ganter (2022).
34. Freelon, McIlwain, and Clark (2016); Mundt, Ross, and Burnett (2018); Shahin, Nakahara, and Sánchez (2021).
35. Quan-Haase et al. (2021).
36. Earl et al. (2010); Harlow et al. (2020).
37. González-Bailón et al. (2024); Singh et al. (2020); Vosoughi, Roy, and Aral (2018).
38. Ajzen (2011); Aral (2020); Chung and Kim (2021); Cialdini, Kallgren, and Reno (1991).
39. Gimpel et al. (2021); Koo et al. (2021).
40. Janmohamed et al. (2021); Walter et al. (2021).
41. Porter, Velez, and Wood (2023); Walter et al. (2021); Walter and Murphy (2018).
42. Berinsky (2023); Nyhan et al. (2020); Swire-Thompson et al. (2020); Thorson (2024).
43. Thorson and Abdelaaty (2023).
44. Brashier and Marsh (2020); Ecker et al. (2022); Young (2023).
45. Flynn, Nyhan, and Reifler (2017); Kunda (1990).
46. Blumgart (2022, June 30); Descant (2023, January 8).
47. Festinger (1957); Kahan (2015); Taber and Lodge (2006).
48. Fiske and Taylor (1991).
49. Cacioppo and Petty (1979); Chaiken (1980).
50. Camaj (2019); Redlawsk (2006); Schaffner and Roche (2017).
51. Pennycook and Rand (2019).
52. Bartels (1996); Kuklinski et al. (2000); Li and Wagner (2020).
53. Bardon (2020); Pyszczynski and Greenberg (1987).
54. Redlawsk, Civettini, and Emmerson (2010).
55. Bago, Rand, and Pennycook (2020); Brashier and Marsh (2020); Ecker et al. (2022); Pennycook et al. (2020); Fazio (2020).
56. Lyons et al. (2020).
57. Boulianne et al. (2021).
58. Shin and Thorson (2017).
59. Ellison, Steinfield, and Lampe (2007); Vraga, Bode, and Troller-Renfree (2016).
60. Bode (2016a); Fletcher and Nielsen (2018); Tewksbury, Weaver, and Maddex (2001).
61. Brashier and Marsh (2020); Ecker et al. (2011); Ecker et al. (2022); Thorson (2016).
62. Ecker et al. (2011); Kendeou et al. (2019); Kendeou and O'Brien (2014).
63. Altay and Mercier (2020).
64. Altay, Hacquin, and Mercier (2022).
65. Bode and Vraga (2015); Vraga, Bode, and Tully (2022b); Vraga and Bode (2017).
66. Schmid and Betsch (2019); Van der Linden (2023); Vraga et al. (2020).

67. Ecker, Butler, and Hamby (2020); Krishna and Amazeen (2022).
68. Lewandowsky et al. (2012).
69. Ecker and Antonio (2021); Guillory and Geraci (2013).
70. Margolin, Hannak, and Weber (2018).
71. Bode, Vraga, and Tully (2020); Vlasceanu and Coman (2022).
72. Robinson (2023).
73. Shabayek, Vincent, and Théro (2022).
74. Sobieraj (2020).
75. Suler (2004); Udris (2014).
76. Yuan (2018, August 6).
77. Note it didn't actually ban TikTok outright, but passed legislation designed to force its parent company, ByteDance, to sell TikTok or face a ban. AP News (2024, April 24). And the question of the TikTok ban is still in flux as of this writing.
78. Jones and Kaminski (2020); Lomas (2021, April 29).
79. European Commission (2024b); European Commission (2024a).
80. Humprecht, Esser, and Van Aelst (2020).
81. Goh et al. (2017); Song et al. (2021).
82. Duke Reporters' Lab (2022, November).
83. Norris (2022).
84. Sørensen et al. (2015).
85. Gallup (2018).
86. Norris (2022).
87. Sears and Valentino (1997).
88. WHO (2024b).
89. Bond (2020, October 30); Stabile et al. (2019); Thakur and Hankerson Madrigal (2022); Timberg and Stanley-Becker (2020, August 26).
90. Birhane (2019, July 18); Noble (2018); Turner Lee (2018).
91. Bailey et al. (2017); Feagin and Bennefield (2014); Gravlee (2020).
92. Bigman et al. (2019); Coles and Lane (2023); Freelon, Pruden, and Malmer (2023); Kuo and Marwick (2021).
93. Stromback et al. (2022).

Chapter 3

1. Note that we focus on misinformation topics so that we can be more confident that something is true or false. We rely on expert consensus on the topics we use to establish what is true. See Vraga and Bode (2020b). However, we would expect observed correction to work similarly with different categories of false or misleading information, like malinformation.

2. In those four experiments, we incorporated a second factor that manipulated whether people also saw a news literacy message (of different type and format) as part of the experiment. In this book, we're focused on the effects of observed correction so we do not use any of the conditions that included a news literacy message—but we have a lot of published work with Melissa Tully that you can refer to if you want to read more about news literacy and how it does (and mostly does not) intersect with misinformation and correction efforts. See Tully, Vraga, and Bode (2020); Vraga, Bode, and Tully (2020b); Vraga, Tully, and Bode (2022).

3. We required participants to spend a minimum amount of time (typically 10 seconds) on the simulated feed to ensure they saw our manipulations.

4. We have some evidence that these debriefings are working as intended to increase accurate beliefs. In our COVID-19 study, as part of the debriefing all participants were told the scientific consensus that taking a hot bath cannot prevent COVID. In our follow-up survey one week later, all participants—including those in the control and misinformation conditions—had more accurate beliefs, suggesting the debriefing itself served its purpose as a correction. For more details see Vraga and Bode (2021).

5. You might notice there are some differences between our simulated Twitter feed and how Twitter/X looks today. The appearance and affordances of social media platforms change over time, so this simulated feed resembles how Twitter looked in 2017, when we performed this study.

6. We generally try to use gender-neutral names and profile pictures, to prevent the perceived gender of either the misinformation poster or the corrector from playing a role in the experiment.

7. Rainie and Funk (2015, January 29).

8. In different experiments, we asked participants to rate their agreement on five- or seven-point scales or asked them about the veracity of the information (from definitely false to definitely true) on five-point scales. Our online appendix has more information about each of the design choices for these studies (please see https://bode.vraga.org/).

9. When using percentage change in accuracy, we are reporting descriptive statistics rather than empirical tests of significance. To ensure these results are not due to chance, we also report on the results of a mini-meta analysis, which allows us to statistically test the effects of observed correction across our studies. We include the confidence interval for these differences in all figures, so people can see for themselves which results are or are not significant.

10. Walter et al. (2021); Wang et al. (2019).

11. Fombonne et al. (2020); Gravelle et al. (2022).

12. An alternative would be to ask people their attitudes on a topic both before and after seeing correction. We do this in several experiments (see Bode and Vraga (2015); Vraga, Bode, and Tully (2022a); Vraga and Bode (2017), but this runs the risk of sensitizing people to what we're interested in. In other words, if I ask your beliefs on a topic (even among other topics), then show you content on that topic, you may be inclined to pay more attention than you otherwise would, altering your responses to the misinformation and its correction. In some cases, where the topic of misinformation is well-known and the attitude questions are hidden by other questions, this concern may be less pertinent. But where the misinformation is relatively new or novel, asking people in advance about their beliefs may be especially likely to skew our results. Because we only ask about pre-test beliefs in a subset of the experiments that we include in this book, we rely on the comparison between the control and correction conditions as described when comparing across studies. We use the pre versus post-test measures of accuracy in two studies (GMO foods and flu vaccine) for specific analyses in Chapter 4.

13. We chose to use the median, which looks at the middle number in a series to gauge average size, rather than the mathematical mean, to account for the outlier of raw milk, which had a much larger increase in accuracy than most other studies. The mean increase in accuracy is 7.3%.

14. It's also worth noting that in the post-replication crisis era we've learned that effect sizes are often smaller than we were traditionally led to believe (Schäfer & Schwarz, 2019).

15. Grewal, Puccinelli, and Monroe (2018); Haidich (2010); Walter et al. (2021).

16. Goh, Hall, and Rosenthal (2016).

17. More information on the meta-analysis is also available in our online appendix (see https://bode.vraga.org/).

18. Which we define as anything above a "neutral" or "mixed" response in terms of the veracity of true information (or the falsity of inaccurate information).

19. Bode and Vraga (2015); Lyons et al. (2023).

20. Gorman and Gorman (2017); Vraga et al. (2023).

21. As political elites talk more about the issue of raw milk, there's an increased risk it becomes politicized and associated with partisan identities (Armour, 2025).

22. Freelon et al. (2022); Suarez-Lledo and Alvarez-Galvez (2021); Walter et al. (2021); Wang et al. (2019).

23. Silverman et al. (2017).

24. Vraga et al. (2020).

25. Vraga, Bode, and Tully (2022b).

26. Kligler-Vilenchik (2022); Kuru et al. (2022); Rossini et al. (2021); Vijaykumar et al. (2021).
27. Heiss et al. (2024).
28. Bode, Vraga, and Tang (2024).
29. Micallef et al. (2020).
30. An observant reader may notice that this number is higher than the median effect for observed correction overall. We did not systematically vary user versus expert correction sources across studies, so other elements of studies, especially the topic, may contribute to differences between correction sources. Because our studies are not generally designed to test this difference, we do not read too much into these numbers. We have tested this comparison directly in two studies: in one we found that the expert corrector was more effective than a user corrector; see Vraga and Bode (2017). In the other, we found no differences between an expert and a user corrector; see Vraga and Bode (2021).
31. Cook (2020).
32. Wittenberg et al. (2021).
33. Benway (1998).
34. Vraga et al. (2022a).
35. CDC (2022, December 19); Schmid et al. (2017).
36. Bode and Vraga, (2015); Larson (2020); Nyhan and Reifler (2015).
37. Vraga, Bode, and Tully (2022a).
38. Dixon, Lerner, and Bashian (2024); Feldman et al. (2014).
39. Berinsky (2023); Sui and Zhang (2021).
40. Funk et al. (2019, August 2); Gauchat (2012); Hamilton (2015).
41. Gauchat (2011); Hamilton (2015); Hamilton and Safford (2021); Kennedy, Tyson, and Funk (2022, February 15); Krause et al. (2019).
42. Gottfried and Liedke (2021, August 30).
43. DeVerna et al. (2022); Jennings and Stroud (2021).
44. Age has been shown to matter for a number of social media experiences, including misinformation. Digital divides between younger and older people persist in terms of who can access the internet and what they do there. See Chinn and Fairlie (2007); Dijk (2020); Hargittai (2021); Prieger (2003); van Deursen and van Dijk (2019); Yu et al. (2016). Older adults are more likely to see and share misinformation on social media. See Chadwick and Vaccari (2019) and Guess, Nagler, and Tucker (2019). However, this can be differentially impacted by such exposure. See Ahmed, Madrid-Morales, and Tully (2022); Nan, Wang, and Thier (2022). This makes it important to see whether corrections have stronger or weaker effects depending on age.
45. A second characteristic we consider is level of education, which is often associated with greater trust in science and scientists, as well as more trust in the news media. See Gauchat (2011) and Gottfried et al. (2019). This might make educated groups more receptive to correction. Alternatively, education can reinforce motivated reasoning (the accuracy motivation we described in Chapter 2), as people not only have the *motivation* but the *skills* to appropriately reinterpret media messages to match their predispositions. See Taber and Lodge (2006). Therefore, it is an open question as to whether observed correction works differently among those with higher versus lower education.
46. In online spaces, women experience more social media conflict and harassment than men. See Sobieraj (2020). They may also be targeted with disinformation campaigns; see Banet-Weiser (2021); Di Meco and Wilfore (2021, March 8); Nan, Wang, and Thier (2022); Stabile et al. (2019). This may translate into a different experience with observed correction.
47. Racial and ethnic minorities are frequently targets of disinformation campaigns. See Bond (2020, October 30); Freelon and Lokot (2020); Kuo and Marwick (2021); Timberg and Stanley-Becker (2020, August 26). They are also targets of online misrepresentation; see Noble (2018). Moreover, both historical and ongoing systematic racism could make minorities in the US less receptive to correction as well, given the expert sources provided for

such corrections. See Feagin and Bennefield (2014); Gravlee (2020); Jaiswal, LoSchiavo, and Perlman (2020).

48. Although we are studying health topics where partisan identity may seem less relevant, that is not to say it is absent altogether. Political polarization (especially in two-party systems like the US), clear elite partisan cues, and heavy media coverage all make partisan identity more salient. See Flynn, Nyhan, and Reifler (2017).

49. An additional possible moderator is pre-existing beliefs on the topic. There is substantial disagreement about whether a correction works less well when it runs counter to people's pre-existing beliefs. See Chan and Albarracín (2023); Nyhan and Reifler (2010); Taber and Lodge (2006). This may be due to motivated reasoning; see Flynn, Nyhan, and Reifler (2017); Kahan (2015); Kunda (1990); Taber and Lodge (2006). There is also disagreement as to whether corrections increase accuracy even among those with misperceptions. See Porter and Wood (2019); Porter and Wood (2021); Walter et al. (2021); Walter and Murphy (2018). In our own work, we have consistently found that observed correction effects are actually *stronger* among those who start out with less accurate beliefs on the topic. See Bode and Vraga (2015); Vraga, Bode, and Tully (2022a); Vraga and Bode (2017). This may reflect differences between observed correction and other types of correction, but clearly is a place where more research is needed.

50. Coppock, Hill, and Vavreck (2020).

51. To get into the weeds, for each selected individual characteristic, we fit a linear regression model using PROCESS, model 1 (version 3.3), estimating an interaction between exposure to a correction (as compared to the control condition) and the individual characteristic in predicting misperceptions on that topic. Using PROCESS allows us to examine the full range of the individual characteristic as a continuous variable (i.e., considering specific age rather than grouping it into categories).

52. We only examine education and age for adult samples, as student samples are inherently limited to largely young, educated adults. Analyses for these two variables are therefore limited to 10 of the 24 possible comparisons. All other variables were measured in all 24 comparisons.

53. This average effect could be obscuring real differences in response to correction if those effects are not consistent. For example, women might have been more receptive to correction on some topics (such as misinformation about Zika, which given its effects on pregnancies was likely of greater concern for people who might become pregnant) than others (such as misinformation about COVID-19, to which men proved more vulnerable). See Bwire (2020). When we consider each case separately, however, only very rarely do we find significant effects, and these differences are not directionally consistent (see our online appendix, https://bode.vraga.org/).

54. Margolin, Hannak, and Weber (2018).

Chapter 4

1. When replicating the analyses in chapter 3 (among all participants) for only the 10 conditions for which we have recall data in chapter 4, we come up with the same increase in accuracy: 4.1%.

2. The 95% confidence interval ranges from .34 to .52.

3. Field (2018, p. 88).

4. Fazio, Hong, and Pillai (2023); Swire-Thompson et al. (2023).

5. Schulz et al. (2010); Tripepi et al. (2020). Limiting analyses to people who pass a so-called manipulation check is also common in communication and psychology, especially when studying memory. See, for example, Jones, Crozier, and Strange (2018); Rich and Zaragoza (2016); Uner and Roediger (2018); Vraga, Bode, and Tully (2022b); Amazeen and Krishna (2022).

6. Acharya, Blackwell, and Sen (2016); Montgomery, Nyhan, and Torres (2018).

7. Montgomery, Nyhan, and Torres (2018).

8. Smith, Coffman, and Hudgens (2021).
9. Thorson and Wells (2016).
10. King et al. (2019).
11. Buschman and Miller (2007); Lang (2000); Vraga et al. (2019).
12. Bode, Vraga, and Troller-Renfree (2017); Garrett (2009); Knobloch-Westerwick (2014); Sears and Freedman (1967).
13. Fazekas (2023); Wichmann, Sharpe, and Gegenfurtner (2002).
14. Lang (2000).
15. Frost (2000); Lang (2006).
16. Many models of memory incorporate an additional step between encoding and retrieval—that of information storage in long-term memory. But because our recall measures occur so quickly after the encoding process, directly after people see the simulated social media feed, storage is less important to the process so we do not elaborate on it here. For those interested in studying how memories of correction endure or decay over time, this element may be more important. See, e.g., Kemp et al. (2022); Rich & Zaragoza (2016); Swire-Thompson et al. (2023).
17. Schwarz and Oyserman (2001).
18. Bullock et al. (2015); Prior, Sood, and Khanna (2015); Schaffner and Luks (2018); Yair and Huber (2020).
19. Berinsky (2018); Graham and Yair (2024). And at least some misrepresentations in surveys are just trolling—unrelated to other characteristics like partisan identity. See Lopez and Hillygus (2018).
20. Guess (2015); Vraga, Bode, and Troller-Renfree (2016).
21. Bradburn, Rips, and Shevell (1987); Prior (2009a).
22. This difficulty is amplified the longer the time period—there is no way I can accurately report how often I made chicken in the last month, for instance.
23. Junco (2013).
24. We test this using logistic regression predicting correction recall separately for each of our five datasets only among the correction conditions. In each analysis, we control for the correction condition (when there are multiple) but do not report those in the table. We include a figure and the full results of this regression analysis in our supplemental appendix (https://bode.vraga.org/).
25. Bode, Vraga, and Troller-Renfree (2017); Garrett (2009); Knobloch-Westerwick (2014).
26. Edwards and Smith (1996); Taber and Lodge (2006).
27. Bullock et al. (2015); Prior, Sood, and Khanna (2015).
28. For the GMO study, pre-test GMO belief accuracy was positively associated with correction recall (B=.23, SE=.11, p=.04, Exp(B)=1.25). For the flu study, pre-test flu belief accuracy was positively associated with correction recall (B=.28, SE=.11, p=.01, Exp(B)=1.32).
29. King et al. (2019).
30. N=61. There were two types of corrections, one humorous and one not. For these analyses, we do not consider the differences in the types of correction given the small sample size, but you can learn more about this research. See Kim, Vraga, and Cook (2021).
31. In this case, participants were only given two options for correction recall: that the reply tweet about HPV vaccination either said the HPV vaccine does (incorrect) or does not (correct) cause autoimmune disorders.
32. A logistic regression predicting recall suggests that the relationship between time spent looking at the correction and accurate recall is marginally significant when controlling both for initial HPV accuracy and correction message type (humorous and not-humorous); B=.14, S.E.=.09, p=.10, Exp(B)=1.15.
33. Feng et al. (2015); Fisher (2022); Stroud (2017).
34. Bode, Vraga, and Troller-Renfree (2017).
35. Specifically, a logistic regression predicting correction recall showed that both time spent on the correction (b=.14, S.E.=.09, p<.10) and pre-existing beliefs (b=.67, S.E.=.40, p<.10) are separately associated with higher correction recall. These results are both marginally significant given the small sample size, so we must be cautious in their interpretation.

36. My (Emily) earlier published work with Sojung and John suggests that this process is instead mediated: that more attention specifically to the correction images tended to reduce perceptions of the credibility of misinformation itself, and it is those credibility perceptions that affected belief accuracy. For more details, see Kim, Vraga, and Cook (2021). This is also the same dataset we used in the analyses earlier in this chapter.

37. We formally test this with a regression model predicting change in HPV belief accuracy (higher numbers reflect more belief accuracy after exposure to the correction than entering the experiment). We find that recall relates to change in belief accuracy, $B=.23$, $p=.07$, whereas time spent on the correction does not, $B=.09$, $p=.48$, controlling for pre-existing HPV beliefs and correction condition.

38. Vraga, Bode, and Troller-Renfree (2016).

39. Borkin et al. (2013); Fazekas (2023); Wichmann, Sharpe, and Gegenfurtner (2002).

40. Forestal (2021).

41. Vaidhyanathan (2022).

42. McPhedran et al. (2023); Sharevski et al. (2022).

43. Garcia-Pueyo et al. (2022).

44. Martel and Rand (2023, p. 2).

45. Vaidhyanathan (2022).

46. Neyman (2017).

47. Bhargava (2023).

48. Baughan et al. (2022).

49. Borkin et al. (2016).

50. Bylinskii et al. (2015); Isola et al. (2014).

51. Wichmann, Sharpe, and Gegenfurtner (2002).

52. Isola et al. (2014).

53. Bateman et al. (2010); Borgo et al. (2012).

54. Borkin et al. (2013).

55. Fazekas (2023).

56. Borkin et al. (2016); Thomas (2020).

57. Kim, Vraga, and Cook (2021). This is also the same dataset we used in the analyses earlier in this chapter.

58. Klein et al. (2020); Vraga, Bode, and Troller-Renfree (2016).

59. Amazeen et al. (2018).

60. Bachmann and Valenzuela (2023); Porter, Velez, and Wood (2022).

61. Carnahan and Garrett (2019).

62. Swire-Thompson et al. (2023); Fazio et al. (2023).

Chapter 5

1. Krumpal (2013); Larson (2019); Nederhof (1985); Schwarz and Oyserman (2001).

2. We limit our analysis to those who passed an attention check, and weight the data based on gender, race, age, education, party, and political ideology to adjust for biases in online data collection.

3. Buchanan et al. (2022); Edgerly et al. (2020); Tandoc, Lim, and Ling (2020); Walter, Edgerly, and Saucier (2021); Xiao (2022).

4. In different datasets, we've asked people about their experiences with misinformation and correction differently. To enhance comparability between these data sources, we performed an experiment in April of 2022 with 733 participants from Amazon's Mechanical Turk, testing the effects of differences in response options (yes/no versus how often). The results point to two conclusions. First, the number of response options offered produces a substantive and significant effect. When offered a frequency scale, only 18—32% of people say they "never" performed correction on their social media in the past week; when offered it as a binary yes/no choice, between 45—58% said they had not performed correction. Logistic regression, controlling for the question wording manipulation, confirms these effects are significant: the four-point and five-point response options produce

significantly (p<.001) higher estimates of observed correction than the binary scale when never is compared the other frequency options. However, subsequent analyses demonstrate that combining the "rarely" response with the "never" response for our frequency measures substantially reduced—but importantly did not eliminate—differences between the frequency and binary response options. While we cannot speak to which measurement strategy produces more accurate responses, only that a frequency measure produces higher self-reported exposure to correction, we used a more conservative approach to interpreting what it means to be a corrector in these datasets to account for these differences. For more information on this experiment, please see our online appendix.

5. For example, early studies found very few people corrected misinformation; 12% of Singapore social media users in 2016 left a comment when reading misinformation. See Tandoc, Lim, and Ling (2020). Chadwick and Vaccari (2019) found that 21% of UK social media users did so in 2018. More recent work suggests the numbers may be higher: one cross-national study from 2019 found that over 60% of WhatsApp users in Singapore, Turkey, and the US had performed correction; see Kuru et al. (2022). Another study in 2021 found about a quarter of social media users in France, the UK, Canada, and the US had corrected misinformation in the past month. See Tang et al. (2024). Because of differences in samples, question wording, and context, these various estimates are difficult to directly compare. But the disparate responses further support our argument that self-reported measures of correction are likely to be imprecise, reflecting estimates and norms more than actual behavior.

6. He, Ahamad, and Kumar (2023); Ma et al. (2023).

7. Larson (2019); Nederhof (1985).

8. Burden (2000).

9. Tourangeau and Yan (2007).

10. Bond and Garrett (2023); He, Ahamad, and Kumar (2023); Ma et al. (2023).

11. Ajzen (2011); Borsari and Carey (2003); Chung and Kim (2021); Cialdini, Kallgren, and Reno (1991).

12. Norman, Conner, and Bell (1999).

13. Bhochhibhoya and Branscum (2018).

14. Ajzen (1991); Ajzen (2011); Ajzen (2020).

15. Besley and Dudo (2022).

16. Bautista, Zhang, and Gwizdka (2021); Chen and Fu (2022); Pundir, Devi, and Nath (2021).

17. Additionally, the same experiment described in note 4 from this chapter suggested that using the term "correction" rather than "telling someone they are wrong" produces substantially higher estimates of performed correction (42% said they "told" someone else they were wrong, whereas 55% said they had "corrected" someone), which we suspect speaks to the social norms around correction.

18. Bode and Vraga (2021d).

19. When Pew asked Americans who they thought had the most responsibility to reduce the amount of made-up news and information in 2019, the public was deemed the second most responsible, after the news media. See Mitchell et al. (2019, June 5).

20. Amazeen, Vargo, and Hopp (2019); Chadwick and Vaccari (2019); Huber, Borah, and Gil de Zúñiga (2022); Kuru et al. (2022); Tandoc, Lim, and Ling (2020); Vijaykumar et al. (2021).

21. Brashier and Schacter (2020); Grinberg et al. (2019); Guess, Nagler, and Tucker (2019).

22. Kuru et al. (2022); Tang et al. (2024).

23. Bode (2017); Van Duyn, Peacock, and Stroud (2021).

24. Berinsky (2023); Ecker and Antonio (2021).

25. Tang et al. (2024).

26. Edelmann (2013); Nonnecke and Preece (2000); Sun, Rau, and Ma (2014); Zhu and Dawson (2023).

27. Antelmi, Malandrino, and Scarano (2019); Nielsen (2006, October 8); Priedhorsky et al. (2007).

28. These numbers are not quite comparable with our own US-based surveys, as the cross-country surveys ask about seeing correction in the past *month* (rather than the past week) and most importantly are limited to people who said they saw misinformation at least rarely. Additionally, these surveys did not specify the topic of misinformation as did ours. But the major takeaway is that observed correction is something people say they see on social media across countries. France appears to be somewhat of an outlier, with fewer people saying they have witnessed someone else being corrected on social media in the recent past. Interestingly, the experience of observed correction appears to have declined, particularly in the US and the UK, from 2019 to 2021.
29. Prior (2009b).
30. Bradburn, Rips, and Shevell (1987); Vraga et al. (2019).
31. Thorson (2020); Thorson and Wells (2016).
32. Amazeen, Vargo, and Hopp (2019); Shin and Thorson (2017).
33. Bapaye and Bapaye, (2021); Guess, Nagler, and Tucker (2019); Seo et al. (2021).
34. Bode and Vraga (2021a); Chadwick and Vaccari (2019); Tandoc, Lim, and Ling (2020).
35. Bode and Vraga (2021a); Kuru et al. (2022).
36. Bode and Vraga (2021a).
37. Brashier and Schacter (2020); Grinberg et al. (2019); Guess, Nagler, and Tucker (2019).
38. Garrett and Bond (2021); Guess, Nagler, and Tucker (2019); Lawson and Kakkar (2022).
39. Koliska and Bode (2023); Samples (2019).
40. Thorson (2020); Thorson et al. (2021).

Chapter 6

1. We use the definition of reluctance from Bussink-Voorend et al., 2022, but research on the idea of reluctance is diverse, including everything from serving as a caregiver (Burridge, Winch, and Clavarino, 2007) to getting vaccinated (Bussink-Voorend et al., 2022) to engaging in international "provision of order" (Destradi, 2017) or becoming a whistleblower (Hollings, 2013), to name a few.
2. Goffman (1959); Leary and Kowalski (1990); Hayes et al. (2005); Walther (1996); Leary and Kowalski (1990); Rosenberg & Egbert (2011).
3. Bartsch and Subrahmanyam (2015); Harris and Bardey (2019); Rousseau (2021).
4. Social problems like FOMO (fear of missing out) and low self-esteem can result from these tendencies. See Wright, White, and Obst (2018); Powers et al. (2019); Thorson (2014); Vraga et al. (2015); Wu (2021).
5. Tandoc, Lim, and Ling (2020); Davison (1983); Gunther (1995); Perloff (1999); Rojas (2010).
6. Chen and Fu (2022); Geesaman and Crissman (2023); Koo et al. (2021).
7. See Table 8.3 for more information about these interviews with platform employees.
8. Lasorsa (1991); Matthes, Rios Morrison, and Schemer (2010); Matthes, Knoll, and von Sikorski (2018); Neuwirth, Frederick, and Mayo (2007).
9. Chaudhry and Gruzd (2020); McKeever and McKeever (2019, September 13); Mustafaraj et al. (2011); Tully, Bode, and Vraga (2020).
10. Huang and Wang (2022); Krishna and Amazeen (2022); Lazić and Žeželj (2021).
11. Kubin et al. (2021); Levendusky (2023).
12. Riker and Ordeshook (1968).
13. Hines, Hungerford, and Tomera (1987).
14. Lehmann et al. (2014); Mo, Wong, and Lam (2019).
15. Porter and Wood (2019); Swire-Thompson et al. (2022); Walter et al. (2021).
16. Hart and Feldman (2014); Hart and Feldman (2016).
17. Hayes, Glynn, and Shanahan (2005); Neuwirth, Frederick, and Mayo (2007).
18. Condon and Holleque (2013).
19. Hart and Feldman (2016); Kenski and Stroud (2006); Verba, Schlozman, and Brady (1995).
20. Festinger, Riecken, and Schachter (1956).

21. Cutrona and Troutman (1986); Schaefer, Coyne, and Lazarus (1981).
22. Zhou and Gao (2008).
23. Vaidhyanathan (2022).
24. Baines, Ittefaq, and Abwao (2021); Schmidt et al. (2018); Williams et al. (2015).
25. Arguedas et al. (2022); Barbera et al. (2015); Dubois and Blank (2018); Fletcher et al. (2021).
26. Bakshy, Messing, and Adamic (2015); Barberá et al. (2015); Dubois and Blank (2018); Fletcher, Robertson, and Nielsen (2021).
27. Lang and Pearson-Merkowitz (2015).
28. Sunstein (2018).
29. Bucher (2018).
30. Desai et al. (2022); Fisher (2022); Jiang and Wilson (2018); Zollo et al. (2017).
31. Wagner (2023).
32. Wells et al. (2017).
33. Anderson and Jiang (2018).
34. Bode (2016b); Goyanes, Borah, and Gil de Zúñiga (2021); Kim, Jones-Jang, and Kenski (2022).
35. Matthes, Knoll, and von Sikorski (2018); Neuwirth, Frederick, and Mayo (2007); Noelle-Neumann (1974).
36. Van Duyn (2021).
37. Gearhart and Zhang (2015); Gearhart and Zhang (2018).
38. Pearce and Malhotra (2022).
39. Malhotra (2023).
40. Verba, Schlozman, and Brady (1995).
41. Toff and Nielsen (2018), 637.

Chapter 7

1. We weighted this survey data (much like we did for the surveys we described in Chapter 5) so that the sample approximates the US population in terms of age, education, race, and party affiliation.
2. We used seven-point scales to measure responses for each of these statements. To simplify data display, here we combine people who said they strongly disagree, disagree, or somewhat disagree into "disagree," combine those who said somewhat agree, agree, or strongly agree into "agree," and label the people who said "neither disagree or agree" as the neutral category.
3. Margolin, Hannak, and Weber (2018).
4. Nyhan (2021); Wood and Porter (2019).
5. Bode and Vraga (2021d).
6. Miller (2023); Mutz (1998).
7. Perloff (1999); Sun, Pan, and Shen (2008).
8. Bicchieri et al. (2014).
9. Geesaman and Crissman (2023); Koo et al. (2021).
10. Dixon et al. (2020); Dixon, Lerner, and Bashian (2024).
11. Koo et al. (2021); Sun et al. (2022); Tandoc, Lim, and Ling (2020).
12. The specific wording of questions varies—for instance, sometimes they give people several different options of how they would respond to misinformation, including correction, but also reporting the misinformation or ignoring it. See Koo et al. (2021); Tandoc, Lim, and Ling (2020). Other questions ask about responding to specific people sharing misinformation, like friends, family, strangers (Sun et al., 2022).
13. CDC (2023a).
14. Tully, Bode, and Vraga (2020).
15. CDC (2023b); Sander et al. (2020).

16. In 2023 Democrat Alexandria Ocasio Cortez and Republican Mike Lee were reportedly working together on bipartisan legislation to loosen regulations on American sunscreen. Eilperin (2014, November 18); Larsen (2023, August 19).

17. Vraga, Bode, and Tully (2022b).

18. He et al. (2023).

19. We use a series of linear regression models to test the relationships between each concern and (1) specific and (2) general willingness to correct misinformation. These models control for the same demographic variables tested in Chapter 5 but are not displayed in the figure for parsimony. Please see our supplemental appendix for more information.

20. Ajzen (1991); Bautista, Zhang, and Gwizdka (2021); Chen and Fu (2022).

21. Böhm and Betsch (2022); Nielsen, Tyran, and Wengström (2014).

22. Margolin, Hannak, and Weber (2018).

23. Kim, Vraga, and Cook (2021); Sülflow, Schäfer, and Winter (2019).

24. Vraga and Bode (2020a); Walter et al. (2021).

25. Ajzen (1991); Chen and Tang (2023); Hart and Feldman (2016).

26. Bode and Vraga (2021d).

27. Bode and Vraga (2021a); Chadwick and Vaccari (2019).

28. Ajzen (1999); Besley and Dudo (2022); Koo et al. (2021).

29. Cheng, Danescu-Niculescu-Mizil, and Leskovec (2015); Fisher (2022).

30. Meta (2023a); Twitter (2023, April); YouTube (2023a).

31. Matias, Simko, and Reddan (2020, June 25).

32. While the claims are supported by theory and existing evidence, the actual size of the results represented in these graphs are not perfectly accurate. We prioritized making sure that the messages themselves—not the size of the effects—were what drove our results, so we consistently showed a 25% difference between the two bars.

33. These analyses use a series of T-tests to compare each experimental condition to the control condition separately. We describe these results in detail in our appendix (https://bode.vraga.org/).

34. T-tests confirm that only the perform corrections condition produced significantly higher willingness to correct than the control condition.

35. Tapp et al. (2016).

Chapter 8

1. Lippmann (1922).

2. Anwar et al. (2020); Heikkilä and Ahva (2015).

3. Nielsen and Ganter (2022).

4. Agarwal and Barthel (2015); Harris, Mueller, and Snider (2013); Jha, Lin, and Savoia (2016); Nelson (2023).

5. Vraga and Bode (2020b).

6. Amazeen (2020a); Graves (2016).

7. For the full interview protocol, please see the online appendix (https://bode.vraga.org/).

8. When we reference multiple fact checkers who are telling us something similar, we will use the organizational name rather than an individual's pseudonym to provide this contextual information. For any direct quotes or stories, we will provide both the pseudonym and organization.

9. For the full interview protocol, please see the online appendix. https://bode.vraga.org/.

10. Agarwal and Barthel (2015); Hallin and Mancini (2004).

11. Fiorina (2010); Gravelle et al. (2022); Leiserowitz et al. (2022, January 12).

12. Fisher (2022); Gorman and Gorman (2017).

13. This emphasis on harm also echoes what many in the scholarly community have been urging: that we need to focus on identifying and correcting misinformation that is most likely to be consequential in changing behaviors. See Southwell et al. (2019); Thorson (2014); although as we point out in Chapter 1, it can be hard to determine just what misinformation is or will be harmful.

14. Agarwal and Barthel (2015); Hallin and Mancini (2004).
15. Emerging research gives a mixed picture about the effects of these kinds of back-and-forth exchanges. One study found that a rebuttal to a correction message mitigated its beneficial impact on belief accuracy, even when that rebuttal was subsequently also corrected. See Mourali and Drake (2022). Another found that highly interactive posts—where the original poster and the corrector go back and forth several times regarding the misinformation—were *more* effective in reducing misperceptions than a single correction. See Borah et al. (n.d). To respond to experts' concerns about public corrections, more research is needed to understand how different kinds of responses to correction influence the effectiveness of correction, and best practices for expert voices to respond in turn.
16. Nölleke et al. (2023).
17. CDC (2016, January 1); Larkin (2021); Lewis, Zamith, and Coddington (2020); Waisbord (2020); Ward et al. (2022).
18. Carlson and Witt (2020); Waisbord (2022).
19. Kim and Shin (2022).
20. Belair-Gagnon et al. (2024); Burke et al. (2023); Holton et al. (2023); Nelson (2023).
21. Carlson and Witt (2020); Nölleke, Leonhardt, and Hanusch (2008).
22. Kempner (2008); Nölleke, Leonhardt, and Hanusch (2023); Posetti et al. (2022); Väliverronen and Saikkonen (2021).
23. International Press Institute (2021, January 29); Jaźwińska (2024); Posetti et al. (2022); Westcott (2019, September 4).
24. Danner (2022, December 12).
25. Kurtzleben (2022, August 7).
26. Talbot (2016, September 28).
27. Carlson, Robinson, and Lewis (2021); Hotez (2023); Oreskes and Conway (2019).
28. Armus (2021, March 11).
29. Fisher (2022).
30. Bellutta, Uyheng, and Carley (2022); Mosleh, Cole, and Rand (2024).
31. Guidry et al. (2017); WHO (2020).
32. This has limit was raised to 1,024 in October of 2022, but was 256 at the time of the interview.
33. These disagreements also persist among the correctors themselves: Julian and Rose (professionals) were from the same organization but had quite different orientations toward their efforts, with Rose expressing more skepticism about the value of corrections.
34. Besley and Dudo (2022); Maibach, Frumkin, and Ahdoot (2021); Pornpitakpan (2004).
35. Ecker and Antonio (2021); Guillory and Geraci (2013).
36. Katz (1957); Nisbet and Kotcher (2009).
37. Since the time of our interview, Lupa is no longer relying on these cards, telling us via email that they were too resource intensive to create, which meant that they couldn't disseminate them fast enough to be effective—another way that constraints and resources play a role.
38. We largely did not see this same level of tailoring of messages by platforms among health organizations, who were generally constrained in terms of both resources as well as government rules about which platforms they can use. For pretty much every health organization, it's "Primarily, it's Facebook and Twitter for us, for our audiences" (Mindy), with many others talking about their Instagram (Rose, Grace, Fred, Imani, Henri) or YouTube (Danny, Grace, Julian) accounts. Government health organizations are also limited by what platforms they are even allowed to be on; for example, government prohibitions against Tiktok in the US Merchant (2022, December 20); The White House (2023, February 27).
39. Graves and Anderson (2020), p. 349.
40. WHO (2020).
41. Gonah (2020); Tambo et al. (2021); WHO (2024a).

Chapter 9

1. Krishna and Amazeen (2022); Lazić and Žeželj (2021); Schmid and Betsch (2019); Vraga et al. (2020); Walter et al. (2021).
2. Gøtzsche (2000); Grewal, Puccinelli, and Monroe (2018); Haidich (2010).
3. Zhao et al. (2015, p. 1282).
4. Nagler (2014); Nagler et al. (2022).
5. Jazbec et al. (2003).
6. And a subscription is not a panacea—it can still be a pain to try to figure out how to actually read something to which you theoretically have access.
7. Zhao et al. (2015).
8. Besley and Dudo (2022).
9. Cadet and Davies (2017).
10. Department of Veterans Affairs (2023, April 18).
11. Lazić and Žeželj (2021).
12. (Amazeen & Krishna, 2022; Kubin et al., 2021).
13. Guerrini (2013); Howarth (2015).
14. Van der Linden (2023).
15. Calabrese and Albarracín (2023).
16. Altay et al. (2023); Ceylan, Anderson, and Wood (2023).
17. Combatting Vaccine Misinformation (2019, March 7).
18. Ozoma (2019, August 28).
19. Meta (2024, January 9).
20. Gu et al. (2022); Guidry et al. (2020).
21. Allen (2024, February 13); Conger, Browning, and Woo (2021, October 22).
22. Krishnan et al. (2021).
23. Van der Linden (2023).
24. Kroet (2024, February 14).
25. Bode and Vraga (2015); Bode and Vraga (2018); Smith and Seitz (2019).
26. Vaidhyanathan (2022).
27. YouTube (2023b, June).
28. Norris (2022).
29. Liedke and Gottfried (2022, October 27).
30. Aoun Barakat, Dabbous, and Tarhini (2021); Aruguete et al. (2023); Chan (2024); Majerczak and Strzelecki (2022); Müller and Schulz (2019); Torres, Gerhart, and Negahban (2018).
31. Edgerly et al. (2020); Shin and Thorson (2017); Walter et al. (2020).
32. Kessler (2024, February 22).
33. Holan (2024, January 12).
34. Porter and Wood (2019); Walter et al. (2020).
35. Celadin et al. (2023).
36. Walker and Gottfried (2019, June 27).
37. Cushion et al. (2022).
38. I didn't remember this, but my mom says the conversation started from this *Texas Monthly* article she read, Solomon (2022, November 21).
39. If you're wondering, Wikipedia has a helpful table of whether antivenom in your area is likely to be monovalent or polyvalent; see https://en.wikipedia.org/wiki/Snake_antivenom#Types. Also, this may sound funny, but 100,000 people die from snake bites every year, and another 400,000 have permanent injuries. See Médecins Sans Frontières (2015, September 4).
40. StatCounter (2023).
41. Shearer (2021).
42. Venkatraman et al. (2016).
43. Cuan-Baltazar et al. (2020).
44. Baker and Potts (2013); Noble (2018).
45. Urman et al. (2022).
46. Kammerer and Gerjets (2012); Lewandowski and Kammerer (2021).

47. Ferrand et al. (2020).
48. Dambanemuya and Diakopoulos (2020).
49. Hoes, Altay, and Bermeo (2023).
50. Simon et al. (2024, June 6).
51. Johnson et al. (2023).
52. Haze et al. (2023); Wang et al. (2023).
53. Athaluri et al. (2023); Bhattacharyya et al. (2023); Metz (2023, November 6).
54. Golebiewski and Boyd (2019).
55. Aslett et al. (2024).
56. Hern (2021, June 25).
57. Robertson et al. (2025).
58. Acker and Donovan (2019).
59. Kunda (1990).
60. Google News Initiative (2017, July 6).
61. Levendusky (2023).
62. Druckman et al. (2022); Levendusky (2023).
63. Vraga, Bode, and Tully (2022a); Vraga and Bode (2017); Walter et al. (2021).
64. Young (2023).
65. Vraga and Bode (2018).
66. Ecker and Antonio (2021), 631; Guillory and Geraci (2013).
67. Margolin, Hannak, and Weber (2018).
68. Vraga & Bode (2018).
69. Gabielkov et al. (2016).

Chapter 10

1. Allen (2022, November 3); Aral (2020); Ceylan, Anderson, and Wood (2023); Fisher (2022).
2. Silva et al. (2023); Vosoughi, Roy, and Aral (2018); Zimdars and Mcleod (2017, February 16).
3. Bond and Garrett (2023); He, Ahamad, and Kumar (2023); Ma et al. (2023); Margolin, Hannak, and Weber (2018).
4. Swire-Thompson et al. (2020). It's worth noting that while this was true in the US, people did update their opinions about the politician when the same experiment was implemented in Australia; Aird et al. (2018). This highlights the importance of context (see Chapter 2), and norms and expectations around truth (which we'll talk more about later in this chapter).
5. Jennings and Stroud (2021).
6. Chadwick, Vaccari, and Hall (2022).
7. Silverman, Lytvynenko, and Pham (2017, December 28).
8. Iyengar et al. (2019).
9. Fowler and Gollust (2015); Gadarian, Goodman, and Pepinsky (2022); Gollust, Lantz, and Ubel (2009); Gostin (2018).
10. Levendusky (2023).
11. Mason (2018).
12. Thorson (2024).
13. Ahler and Sood (2018); Druckman et al. (2023).
14. Porter and Wood (2019).
15. Calleja et al. (2021); Monahan and Ettinger (2018); Shu et al. (2017).
16. De Angelis et al. (2023); Hacker, Engel, and Mauer (2023).
17. He, Ahamad, and Kumar (2023).
18. Costello, Pennycook, and Rand (2024).
19. DeVerna et al. (2023, August 21).
20. Vraga and Bode (2022). The format of those "corrections" made such a misleading application possible. In our example, the "correcting" users shared fact checks that had

question-based headlines ("Can the bite of a reverse zombie tick make you allergic to red meat?"), rather than ones that state the definitive truth ("Zombie tick bites can make you allergic to red meat"). Because we know that many people will never read past a headline or click through to the actual story (Gabielkov et al., 2016; Liu et al., 2019; Rosenstiel et al., 2015; Sepúlveda-Torres et al., 2021), these headlines may be the only content they see. Headline writers can ensure that their headlines are not misused in this way by delivering the key accurate information in the headline itself. And this is something that fact checkers have recognized and largely addressed—indeed, best practices now suggest that fact-check headlines should include the answer and not the question; AFP (2022, November 16).

21. Bode and Vraga (2021c); Krause et al. (2020).
22. Ecker and Antonio (2021); Guillory and Geraci (2013).
23. Karpf (2019, December 10); Norris (2022).
24. Micallef et al. (2020).
25. Bell (2023, September 19).
26. Brenan (2023, October 19).
27. SteelFisher et al. (2023).
28. Ortiz-Ospina, Roser, and Arriagada (2024).
29. Kunda (1990); Pennycook et al. (2021).
30. Berinsky (2018); Schaffner and Luks (2018); Young (2023); Walker and Gottfried (2019, June 27).
31. The Wikimedia employee explicitly told us that we could use their platform affiliation (but not their name) in this book. We do so in this case because Wikipedia is such a unique platform.
32. Brown (2011); London et al. (2019).
33. Belle and Cantarelli (2021); Nyborg et al. (2016); van Nunspeet and Ellemers (2023).
34. Berinsky (2023).
35. Silverman (2025).
36. McMahon (2025).
37. Masnick (2019).
38. FDA (2023, November 6); USDA (2023, December 6).
39. Jones et al. (2022).
40. Gabielkov et al. (2016); Rosenstiel et al. (2015).
41. Gadarian, Goodman, and Pepinsky (2022); Goodman and McPhillips (2023, July 14); Komamura (2023); Weber et al. (2020, July 1); World Bank (2023, June 8).
42. Haji (2020, December 7); UNESCO (2022); Walker (2021, July 13).
43. Belair-Gagnon et al. (2024); Burke et al. (2023); Holton et al. (2023); Van Noorden (2022); Waisbord (2020); Ward et al. (2022).
44. Dye et al. (2020); Miller (2023); Ward et al. (2022).
45. DeCook et al. (2022); Meta (2023a); Meta (2023b; Twitter (2023, April); YouTube (2023a).
46. Prosocial Design Network (2021).
47. European Commission (2024b).
48. eSafetyCommissioner (2021).
49. Scharf (2024, January 11).
50. Eden (1993); Hart and Feldman (2016); Song et al. (2023).
51. Vraga, Bode, and Troller-Renfree (2016).
52. Vraga et al. (2019).
53. This may happen for individual pieces of content likely to contain misinformation (for example, linking to content that has been debunked by fact checkers), or may happen over time for repeat offenders by reducing the reach of people or pages who share misinformation repeatedly (e.g., Meta, 2024 March), although these platform policies are always subject to change.

54. Perhaps the most famous example of deplatforming was when Twitter and other platforms permanently banned the account of US president Donald Trump (though the official reason given was related to inciting violence, rather than misinformation; Twitter, 2021, and his account has since been reinstated).

55. For instance, following the Russian invasion of Ukraine, both Meta and YouTube demonetized Russian state-sponsored media as a means of reducing the misinformation and propaganda being spread by those sources (Maruf, 2022; Courchesne, Ilhardt, and Shapiro, 2021).

56. Aslett et al. (2024).

57. Rademacher (2016, November 9).

58. Novach and Ropek (2024, May 28).

59. Kelly (2024, May 31).

60. Swire-Thompson et al. (2021); van der Meer and Jin (2020); Vraga, Bode, and Tully (2022a).

61. Schmid and Betsch (2019); Vraga, Kim, and Cook (2019).

62. Campos-Castillo and Shuster (2021); Guess et al. (2020).

63. Ecker, Butler, and Hamby (2020); Huang and Wang (2022); Ophir et al. (2020).

64. Lewandowsky et al. (2012); Lewandowsky, Cook, and Lombardi (2020).

65. USDA (2024); Weinardy (2019, January 15).

66. Ecker and Antonio (2021); Guillory and Geraci (2013).

67. Sanderson et al. (2022); Swire-Thompson et al. (2023).

68. Bode et al. (2020).

69. Kim and Masullo (2021); Masullo and Kim (2021).

70. Lee and Seo (2023).

71. Vraga et al. (2023).

72. Altay (2022); Hornsey and Fielding (2020); Moore (2017); Pavliuc et al. (2023).

Bibliography

Acharya, A., Blackwell, M., & Sen, M. (2016). Explaining causal findings without bias: Detecting and assessing direct effects. *American Political Science Review, 110*(3), 512–529. https://doi.org/10.1017/S0003055416000216

Acker, A., & Donovan, J. (2019). Data craft: A theory/methods package for critical internet studies. *Information, Communication & Society, 22*(11), 1590–1609. https://doi.org/10.1080/1369118X.2019.1645194

AFP. (2022, November 16). AFP fact-checking stylebook. Fact Check. https://factcheck.afp.com/afp-fact-checking-stylebook

Agarwal, S. D., & Barthel, M. L. (2015). The friendly barbarians: Professional norms and work routines of online journalists in the United States. *Journalism, 16*(3), 376–391. https://doi.org/10.1177/1464884913511565

Ahler, D. J., & Sood, G. (2018). The parties in our heads: Misperceptions about party composition and their consequences. *Journal of Politics, 80*(3), 964–981. https://doi.org/10.1086/697253

Ahmed, S., Madrid-Morales, D., & Tully, M. (2022). Social media, misinformation, and age inequality in online political engagement. *Journal of Information Technology & Politics, 1–17.* https://doi.org/10.1080/19331681.2022.2096743

Aird, M. J., Ecker, U. K. H., Swire, B., Berinsky, A. J., & Lewandowsky, S. (2018). Does truth matter to voters? The effects of correcting political misinformation in an Australian sample. *Royal Society Open Science, 5*(12), 180593. https://doi.org/10.1098/rsos.180593

Ajzen, I. (1991). The theory of planned behavior. *Organizational Behavior and Human Decision Processes, 50*(2), 179–211. https://doi.org/10.1016/0749-5978(91)90020-T

Ajzen, I. (2011). The theory of planned behaviour: Reactions and reflections. *Psychology & Health, 26*(9), 1113–1127. https://doi.org/10.1080/08870446.2011.613995

Ajzen, I. (2020). The theory of planned behavior: Frequently asked questions. *Human Behavior and Emerging Technologies, 2*(4), 314–324. https://doi.org/10.1002/hbe2.195

Allen, J. (2022, November 3). Misinformation amplification analysis in the US midterm elections. Integrity Institute. https://integrityinstitute.org/blog/election-misinformation-amplification

Allen, J. (2024, February 13). Why is Instagram search more harmful than Google search? Integrity Institute. https://integrityinstitute.org/blog/why-is-instagram-search-more-harmful-than-google-search

Altay, S. (2022). How effective are interventions against misinformation? Department of Political Science, University of Zurich. https://doi.org/10.31234/osf.io/sm3vk

Altay, S., Berriche, M., Heuer, H., Farkas, J., & Rathje, S. (2023). A survey of expert views on misinformation: Definitions, determinants, solutions, and future of the field. *Harvard Kennedy School Misinformation Review.* https://doi.org/10.37016/mr-2020-119

Altay, S., Hacquin, A.-S., & Mercier, H. (2022). Why do so few people share fake news? It hurts their reputation. *New Media & Society, 24*(6), 1303–1324. https://doi.org/10.1177/1461444820969893

Altay, S., & Mercier, H. (2020). Relevance is socially rewarded, but not at the price of accuracy. *Evolutionary Psychology, 18*(1), 1474704920912640. https://doi.org/10.1177/1474704920912640

Amazeen, M. A. (2020a). Journalistic interventions: The structural factors affecting the global emergence of fact-checking. *Journalism, 21*(1), 95–111. https://doi.org/10/gf8pn8

Amazeen, M. A. (2020b). Resisting covert persuasion in digital news: Comparing inoculation and reactance in the processing of native advertising disclosures and in article engagement intentions. *Journalism & Mass Communication Quarterly.* https://doi.org/10/hdct

Amazeen, M. A., & Krishna, A. (2022). Processing vaccine misinformation: Recall and effects of source type on claim accuracy via perceived motivations and credibility. *International Journal of Communication, 17,* 560–582.

Amazeen, M. A., Thorson, E., Muddiman, A., & Graves, L. (2018). Correcting political and consumer misperceptions: The effectiveness and effects of rating scale versus contextual correction formats. *Journalism & Mass Communication Quarterly, 95*(1), 28–48. https://doi.org/10.1177/1077699016678186

Amazeen, M. A., Vargo, C. J., & Hopp, T. (2019). Reinforcing attitudes in a gatewatching news era: Individual-level antecedents to sharing fact-checks on social media. *Communication Monographs, 86*(1), 112–132. https://doi.org/10/ggjk25

Anderson, M., & Jiang, J. (2018). Teens' social media habits and experiences. Pew Research Center. https://www.pewresearch.org/internet/2018/11/28/teens-social-media-habits-and-experiences/

Antelmi, A., Malandrino, D., & Scarano, V. (2019). Characterizing the behavioral evolution of Twitter users and the truth behind the 90-9-1 rule. *Companion Proceedings of the 2019 World Wide Web Conference,* 1035–1038. https://doi.org/10.1145/3308560.3316705

Anwar, A., Malik, M., Raees, V., & Anwar, A. (2020). Role of mass media and public health communications in the COVID-19 pandemic. *Cureus.* https://doi.org/10.7759/cureus.10453

Aoun Barakat, K., Dabbous, A., & Tarhini, A. (2021). An empirical approach to understanding users' fake news identification on social media. *Online Information Review, 45*(6), 1080–1096. https://doi.org/10.1108/OIR-08-2020-0333

AP News. (2024, April 24). What a TikTok ban in the US could mean for you. AP News. https://apnews.com/article/tiktok-divestment-ban-what-you-need-to-know-5e1ff786e89da10a1b799241ae025406

Apuke, O. D., & Omar, B. (2021). Social media affordances and information abundance: Enabling fake news sharing during the COVID-19 health crisis. *Health Informatics Journal, 27*(3), 146045822110214. https://doi.org/10.1177/14604582211021470

Aral, S. (2020). *The hype machine: How social media disrupts our elections, our economy, and our health—And how we must adapt.* Penguin Random House.

Arguedas, Robertson, C. T., Fletcher, R., & Nielsen, R. K. (2022). Echo chambers, filter bubbles, and polarisation: A literature review. In *Reuters Institute for the Study of Journalism.* https://reutersinstitute.politics.ox.ac.uk/echo-chambers-filter-bubbles-and-polarisation-literature-review

Armour, S. (2025, January 29). Led by RFK Jr., Conservatives Embrace Raw Milk. Regulators Say It's Dangerous. KFF Health News. https://kffhealthnews.org/news/article/raw-milk-rfk-conservatives-regulators-mark-mcafee/

Armus, T. (2021, March 11). Tucker Carlson keeps attacking a New York Times reporter after the paper calls his tactics "calculated and cruel." *Washington Post.* https://www.washingtonpost.com/nation/2021/03/11/tucker-carlson-taylor-lorenz-fox/

Aruguete, N., Bachmann, I., Calvo, E., Valenzuela, S., & Ventura, T. (2023). Truth be told: How "true" and "false" labels influence user engagement with fact-checks. *New Media & Society*, 14614448231193709. https://doi.org/10.1177/14614448231193709

Aslett, K., Guess, A. M., Bonneau, R., Nagler, J., & Tucker, J. A. (2022). News credibility labels have limited average effects on news diet quality and fail to reduce misperceptions. *Science Advances*, 8(18), eabl3844. https://doi.org/10/grjtd5

Aslett, K., Sanderson, Z., Godel, W., Persily, N., Nagler, J., & Tucker, J. A. (2024). Online searches to evaluate misinformation can increase its perceived veracity. *Nature*, 625(7995), 548–556. https://doi.org/10.1038/s41586-023-06883-y

Associated Press. (2022, November 29). Twitter will no longer enforce its COVID misinformation policy. NPR. https://www.npr.org/2022/11/29/1139822833/twitter-covid-misinformation-policy-not-enforced

Athaluri, S. A., Manthena, S. V., Kesapragada, V. S. R. K. M., Yarlagadda, V., Dave, T., & Duddumpudi, R. T. S. (2023). Exploring the boundaries of reality: Investigating the phenomenon of artificial intelligence hallucination in scientific writing through ChatGPT references. *Cureus*. https://doi.org/10.7759/cureus.37432

Bachmann, I., & Valenzuela, S. (2023). Studying the downstream effects of fact-checking on social media: Experiments on correction formats, belief accuracy, and media trust. *Social Media + Society*, 9(2), 20563051231179694. https://doi.org/10.1177/20563051231179694

Bago, B., Rand, D. G., & Pennycook, G. (2020). Fake news, fast and slow: Deliberation reduces belief in false (but not true) news headlines. *Journal of Experimental Psychology: General*, 149, 1608–1613. https://doi.org/10/ggjw97

Bailey, Z. D., Krieger, N., Agénor, M., Graves, J., Linos, N., & Bassett, M. T. (2017). Structural racism and health inequities in the USA: Evidence and interventions. *The Lancet*, 389(10077), 1453–1463. https://doi.org/10/b5cw

Baines, A., Ittefaq, M., & Abwao, M. (2021). #Scamdemic, #Plandemic, or #Scaredemic: What Parler social media platform tells us about COVID-19 vaccine. *Vaccines*, 9(5), 421. https://doi.org/10.3390/vaccines9050421

Baker, P., & Potts, A. (2013). "Why do white people have thin lips?" Google and the perpetuation of stereotypes via auto-complete search forms. *Critical Discourse Studies*, 10(2), 187–204. https://doi.org/10.1080/17405904.2012.744320

Bakshy, E., Messing, S., & Adamic, L. A. (2015). Exposure to ideologically diverse news and opinion on Facebook. *Science*, 348(6239), 1130–1132. https://doi.org/10.1126/science.aaa1160

Banet-Weiser, S. (2021). Misogyny and the politics of misinformation. In H. Tumber, & S. Waisbord (Eds.), *The Routledge Companion to Media Disinformation and Populism* (pp. 211–220). Routledge.

Bapaye, J. A., & Bapaye, H. A. (2021). Demographic factors influencing the impact of coronavirus-related misinformation on WhatsApp: Cross-sectional questionnaire study. *JMIR Public Health and Surveillance*, 7(1), e19858. https://doi.org/10/gpxbx4

Barberá, P., Jost, J. T., Nagler, J., Tucker, J. A., & Bonneau, R. (2015). Tweeting from left to right: Is online political communication more than an echo chamber? *Psychological Science*, 26(10), 1531–1542. https://doi.org/10.1177/0956797615594620

Bardon, A. (2020). *The truth about denial: Bias and self-deception in science, politics, and religion*. Oxford University Press.

Barlow, F. K., Paolini, S., Pedersen, A., Hornsey, M. J., Radke, H. R. M., Harwood, J., Rubin, M., & Sibley, C. G. (2012). The contact caveat: Negative contact predicts increased prejudice more than positive contact predicts reduced prejudice. *Personality and Social Psychology Bulletin*, 38(12), 1629–1643. https://doi.org/10.1177/0146167212457953

Bartels, L. M. (1996). Uninformed votes: Information effects in presidential elections. *American Journal of Political Science*, 40(1), 194. https://doi.org/10.2307/2111700

Bartsch, M., & Subrahmanyam, K. (2015). Technology and self-presentation: Impression management online. In L. D. Rosen, N. A. Cheever, & L. M. Carrier (Eds.), *The Wiley handbook of psychology, technology, and society* (pp. 339–357). John Wiley & Sons.

Barua, Z., Barua, S., Aktar, S., Kabir, N., & Li, M. (2020). Effects of misinformation on COVID-19 individual responses and recommendations for resilience of disastrous consequences of misinformation. *Progress in Disaster Science, 8*, 100119. https://doi.org/10.1016/j.pdisas.2020.100119

Bateman, S., Mandryk, R. L., Gutwin, C., Genest, A., McDine, D., & Brooks, C. (2010). Useful junk? The effects of visual embellishment on comprehension and memorability of charts. *Proceedings of the 28th International Conference on Human Factors in Computing Systems—CHI '10*, 2573. https://doi.org/10.1145/1753326.1753716

Baughan, A., Zhang, M. R., Rao, R., Lukoff, K., Schaadhardt, A., Butler, L. D., & Hiniker, A. (2022). "I don't even remember what I read": How design influences dissociation on social media. *Proceedings of the 2022 CHI Conference on Human Factors in Computing Systems*, 1–13. https://doi.org/10.1145/3491102.3501899

Bautista, J. R., Zhang, Y., & Gwizdka, J. (2021). Healthcare professionals' acts of correcting health misinformation on social media. *International Journal of Medical Informatics, 148*, 104375. https://doi.org/10/gjpr2x

Beagan, B. L., Bizzeth, S. R., Sibbald, K. R., & Etowa, J. B. (2022). Epistemic racism in the health professions: A qualitative study with Black women in Canada. *Health*, 13634593221141605. https://doi.org/10.1177/13634593221141605

Beaujon, A. (2020, December 4). The comet ping pong shooting was four years ago today. We had no clue what was about to happen. https://www.washingtonian.com/2020/12/04/the-comet-ping-pong-shooting-was-four-years-ago-today-we-had-no-clue-what-was-about-to-happen/

Bélair-Gagnon, V., Searles, K., Vraga, E., Holton, A. E., & Edson C. Tandoc, J. (2024). Attacks on journalism as an occupational hazard. *International Journal of Communication, 18*, 4603–4622.

Bell, P. (2023, September 19). Public trust in government: 1958–2023. Pew Research Center. https://www.pewresearch.org/politics/2023/09/19/public-trust-in-government-1958-2023/

Belle, N., & Cantarelli, P. (2021). Nudging public employees through descriptive social norms in healthcare organizations. *Public Administration Review, 81*(4), 589–598. https://doi.org/10.1111/puar.13353

Bellutta, D., Uyheng, J., & Carley, K. M. (2022). The missing link between user engagement and misinformation's impact on online behavior. In R. Thomson, C. Dancy, & A. Pyke (Eds.), *Social, Cultural, and Behavioral Modeling* (pp. 79–89). Springer International Publishing.

Benedetti, D. J., Hammack-Aviran, C. M., Diehl, C., & Beskow, L. M. (2023). Landscape of pediatric cancer treatment refusal and abandonment in the US: A qualitative study. *Frontiers in Pediatrics, 10*. https://doi.org/10.3389/fped.2022.1049661

Benway, J. P. (1998). Banner blindness: The irony of attention grabbing on the world wide web. *Proceedings of the Human Factors and Ergonomics Society Annual Meeting, 42*(5), 463–467. https://doi.org/10/fzpjfs

Berinsky, A. J. (2018). Telling the truth about believing the lies? Evidence for the limited prevalence of expressive survey responding. *Journal of Politics, 80*(1), 211–224. https://doi.org/10/gcvbzr

Berinsky, A. J. (2023). *Political rumors: Why we accept misinformation and how to fight it.* Princeton University Press.

Besley, J. C., & Dudo, A. (2022). *Strategic science communication: A guide to setting the right objectives for more effective public engagement.* Johns Hopkins University Press.

Bhargava, H. (2023). Infinite scroll: Addiction by design in information platforms. https:// questromworld.bu.edu/platformstrategy/wp-content/uploads/sites/49/2023/06/PlatStr at2023_paper_48.pdf

Bhattacharyya, M., Miller, V. M., Bhattacharyya, D., & Miller, L. E. (2023). High rates of fabricated and inaccurate references in ChatGPT-generated medical content. *Cureus*. https://doi.org/ 10.7759/cureus.39238

Bhochhibhoya, A., & Branscum, P. (2018). The application of the theory of planned behavior and the integrative behavioral model towards predicting and understanding alcohol-related behaviors: A systematic review. *Journal of Alcohol & Drug Education, 62*(2), 39–63.

Bicchieri, C., Muldoon, R., & Sontuoso, A. (2014). Social norms. *The Stanford Encyclopedia of Philosophy*. Retrieved from https://plato.stanford.edu/archives/win2018/entries/social-norms

Bigman, C. A., Smith, M. A., Williamson, L. D., Planey, A. M., & Smith, S. M. (2019). Selective sharing on social media: Examining the effects of disparate racial impact frames on intentions to retransmit news stories among US college students. *New Media & Society, 21*(11–12), 2691–2709. https://doi.org/10.1177/1461444819856574

Birhane, A. (2019, July 18). The algorithmic colonization of Africa. *Real Life*. https://reallifemag. com/the-algorithmic-colonization-of-africa/

Blumgart, J. (2022, June 30). Washington Metro is a transit system in deep trouble. Governing. https://www.governing.com/now/washington-metro-is-a-transit-system-in-deep-trouble

Bode, L. (2016a). Political news in the news feed: Learning politics from social media. *Mass Communication and Society, 19*(1), 24–48. https://doi.org/10.1080/15205436.2015.1045149

Bode, L. (2016b). Pruning the news feed: Unfriending and unfollowing political content on social media. *Research & Politics, 3*(3), 2053168016661873. https://doi.org/10.1177/ 2053168016661873

Bode, L. (2017). Closing the gap: Gender parity in political engagement on social media. *Information, Communication & Society, 20*(4), 587–603. https://doi.org/10.1080/1369118X.2016. 1202302

Bode, L. (2019). User correction as a tool in the battle against social media misinformation networked media ecologies & public discourse. *Georgetown Law Technology Review, 4*(2), 367–378.

Bode, L., & Vraga, E. K. (2015). In related news, that was wrong: The correction of misinformation through related stories functionality in social media. *Journal of Communication, 65*(4), 619–638. https://doi.org/10.1111/jcom.12166

Bode, L., & Vraga, E. K. (2018). See something, say something: Correction of global health misinformation on social media. *Health Communication, 33*(9), 1131–1140. https://doi.org/10. 1080/10410236.2017.1331312

Bode, L., & Vraga, E. K. (2021a). Correction experiences on social media during COVID-19. *Social Media + Society, 7*(2), 205630512110088. https://doi.org/10/gr6kxc

Bode, L., & Vraga, E. K. (2021b). People-powered correction: Fixing misinformation on social media. In H. Tumber, & S. Waisbord (Eds.), *The Routledge Companion to Media Disinformation and Populism* (pp. 498–506). Routledge.

Bode, L., & Vraga, E. (2021c). The Swiss cheese model for mitigating online misinformation. *Bulletin of the Atomic Scientists, 77*(3), 129–133. https://doi.org/10.1080/00963402.2021. 1912170

Bode, L., & Vraga, E. K. (2021d). Value for correction: Documenting perceptions about peer correction of misinformation on social media in the context of COVID-19. *Journal of Quantitative Description: Digital Media, 1*. https://doi.org/10/gr6kzp

Bode, L., Vraga, E. K., & Tang, R. (2024). User correction. *Current Opinion in Psychology, 56*, 101786. https://doi.org/10.1016/j.copsyc.2023.101786

Bode, L., Vraga, E. K., & Troller-Renfree, S. (2017). Skipping politics: Measuring avoidance of political content in social media. *Research & Politics*, 4(2), 2053168017702990. https://doi.org/10/gn9846

Bode, L., Vraga, E. K., & Tully, M. (2020). Correcting misperceptions about genetically modified food on social media: Examining the impact of experts, social media heuristics, and the gateway belief model. *Science Communication*, 1075547020981375. https://doi.org/10.1177/1075547020981375

Böhm, R., & Betsch, C. (2022). Prosocial vaccination. *Current Opinion in Psychology*, 43, 307–311. https://doi.org/10.1016/j.copsyc.2021.08.010

Bond, R. M., & Garrett, R. K. (2023). Engagement with fact-checked posts on Reddit. *PNAS Nexus*, 2(3), pgad018. https://doi.org/10.1093/pnasnexus/pgad018

Bond, S. (2020, October 30). Black and Latino voters flooded with disinformation in election's final days. NPR. https://www.npr.org/2020/10/30/929248146/black-and-latino-voters-flooded-with-disinformation-in-elections-final-days

Borgo, R., Abdul-Rahman, A., Mohamed, F., Grant, P. W., Reppa, I., Floridi, L., & Chen, M. (2012). An empirical study on using visual embellishments in visualization. *IEEE Transactions on Visualization and Computer Graphics*, 18(12), 2759–2768. IEEE Transactions on Visualization and Computer Graphics. https://doi.org/10/f4fqd3

Borkin, M. A., Bylinskii, Z., Kim, N. W., Bainbridge, C. M., Yeh, C. S., Borkin, D., Pfister, H., & Oliva, A. (2016). Beyond memorability: Visualization recognition and recall. *IEEE Transactions on Visualization and Computer Graphics*, 22(1), 519–528. IEEE Transactions on Visualization and Computer Graphics. https://doi.org/10/ggf5r3

Borkin, M. A., Vo, A. A., Bylinskii, Z., Isola, P., Sunkavalli, S., Oliva, A., & Pfister, H. (2013). What makes a visualization memorable? *IEEE Transactions on Visualization and Computer Graphics*, 19(12), 2306–2315. IEEE Transactions on Visualization and Computer Graphics. https://doi.org/10/f5h3pd

Borsari, B., & Carey, K. B. (2003). Descriptive and injunctive norms in college drinking: A meta-analytic integration. *Journal of Studies on Alcohol*, 64(3), 331–341. https://doi.org/10.15288/jsa.2003.64.331

Boulianne, S., Belland, S., Tenove, C., & Friesen, K. (2021). Misinformation across social media platforms and across countries | Research Online at MacEwan. https://roam.macewan.ca/islandora/object/gm:2822

Bradburn, N. M., Rips, L. J., & Shevell, S. K. (1987). Answering autobiographical questions: The impact of memory and inference on surveys. *Science*, 236(4798), 157–161. https://doi.org/10.1126/science.3563494

Brann, M., & Himes, K. L. (2010). Perceived credibility of male versus female television newscasters. *Communication Research Reports*, 27(3), 243–252. https://doi.org/10.1080/08824091003737869

Branswell, H. (2024, April 29). There's never a good time to drink raw milk. But now's a really bad time as bird flu infects cows. *STAT*. https://www.statnews.com/2024/04/29/bird-flu-raw-milk-h5n1-risk-us-cattle/

Brashier, N. M., & Marsh, E. J. (2020). Judging truth. *Annual Review of Psychology*, 71(1). https://doi.org/10.1146/annurev-psych-010419-050807

Brashier, N. M., & Schacter, D. L. (2020). Aging in an era of fake news. *Current Directions in Psychological Science*, 29(3), 316–323. https://doi.org/10.1177/0963721420915872

Brenan, M. (2023, October 19). Media confidence in U.S. Matches 2016 record low. Gallup.Com. https://news.gallup.com/poll/512861/media-confidence-matches-2016-record-low.aspx

Broussard, M. (2018). *Artificial unintelligence: How computers misunderstand the world*. MIT Press.

Brown, A. R. (2011). Wikipedia as a data source for political scientists: Accuracy and completeness of coverage. *PS: Political Science & Politics*, 44(2), 339–343. https://doi.org/10.1017/S1049096511000199

Brown, N. I., & Peters, J. (2018). Say this, not that: Government regulation and control of social media. *Syracuse Law Review*, 68, 521–546.

Buchanan, G., Kelly, R., Makri, S., & McKay, D. (2022). Reading between the lies: A classification scheme of types of reply to misinformation in public discussion threads. *ACM SIGIR Conference on Human Information Interaction and Retrieval*, 243–253. https://doi.org/10/gr6kts

Bucher, T. (2018). *If . . . then: Algorithmic power and politics*. Oxford University Press.

Budak, C., Nyhan, B., Rothschild, D. M., Thorson, E., & Watts, D. J. (2024). Misunderstanding the harms of online misinformation. *Nature, 630*(8015), 45–53. https://doi.org/10.1038/s41586-024-07417-w

Bullock, J. G., Gerber, A. S., Hill, S. J., & Huber, G. A. (2015). Partisan bias in factual beliefs about politics. *Quarterly Journal of Political Science, 10*(4), 519–578. https://doi.org/10/ggcvk5

Burden, B. C. (2000). Voter turnout and the national election studies. *Political Analysis, 8*(4), 389–398. https://doi.org/10/ggdjvv

Burke, R. V., Distler, A. S., McCall, T. C., Hunter, E., Dhapodkar, S., Chiari-Keith, L., & Alford, A. A. (2023). A qualitative analysis of public health officials' experience in California during COVID-19: Priorities and recommendations. *Frontiers in Public Health, 11*. https://doi.org/10.3389/fpubh.2023.1175661

Burridge, L., Winch, S., & Clavarino, A. (2007). Reluctance to care: A systematic review and development of a conceptual framework. *Cancer Nursing, 30*(2), E9. https://doi.org/10/bxrhqf

Buschman, T. J., & Miller, E. K. (2007). Top-down versus bottom-up control of attention in the prefrontal and posterior parietal cortices. *Science, 315*(5820), 1860–1862. https://doi.org/10.1126/science.1138071

Bussink-Voorend, D., Hautvast, J. L. A., Vandeberg, L., Visser, O., & Hulscher, M. E. J. L. (2022). A systematic literature review to clarify the concept of vaccine hesitancy. *Nature Human Behaviour, 6*(12), Article12. https://doi.org/10/gr6k27

Butler, L. D., Koopman, C., & Zimbardo, P. G. (1995). The psychological impact of viewing the film "JFK": Emotions, beliefs, and political behavioral intentions. *Political Psychology, 16*(2), 237–257. https://doi.org/10.2307/3791831

Bwire, G. M. (2020). Coronavirus: Why men are more vulnerable to Covid-19 than women? *SN Comprehensive Clinical Medicine, 2*(7), 874–876. https://doi.org/10.1007/s42399-020-00341-w

Bylinskii, Z., Isola, P., Bainbridge, C., Torralba, A., & Oliva, A. (2015). Intrinsic and extrinsic effects on image memorability. *Vision Research, 116*, 165–178. https://doi.org/10/f7xxh3

Cacioppo, J. T., & Petty, R. E. (1979). Effects of message repetition and position on cognitive response, recall, and persuasion. *Journal of Personality and Social Psychology, 37*, 97–109. https://doi.org/10.1037/0022-3514.37.1.97

Cadet, J., & Davies, K. J. A. (2017). Oxidative DNA damage & repair: An introduction. *Free Radical Biology & Medicine, 107*, 2–12. https://doi.org/10.1016/j.freeradbiomed.2017.03.030

Calabrese, C., & Albarracín, D. (2023). Bypassing misinformation without confrontation improves policy support as much as correcting it. *Scientific Reports, 13*(1), Article 1. https://doi.org/10.1038/s41598-023-33299-5

Calleja, N., AbdAllah, A., Abad, N., Ahmed, N., Albarracin, D., Altieri, E., Anoko, J. N., Arcos, R., Azlan, A. A., Bayer, J., Bechmann, A., Bezbaruah, S., Briand, S. C., Brooks, I., Bucci, L. M., Burzo, S., Czerniak, C., Domenico, M. D., Dunn, A. G., . . . Purnat, T. D. (2021). A public health research agenda for managing infodemics: Methods and results of the first WHO infodemiology conference. *JMIR Infodemiology, 1*(1), e30979. https://doi.org/10/gnn4c5

Camaj, L. (2019). From selective exposure to selective information processing: A motivated reasoning approach. *Media and Communication, 7*(3), 8–11. https://doi.org/10.17645/mac.v7i3.2289

Campos-Castillo, C., & Shuster, S. M. (2021). So what if they're lying to us? Comparing rhetorical strategies for discrediting sources of disinformation and misinformation using an affect-based credibility rating. *American Behavioral Scientist*, 00027642211066058. https://doi.org/10/gn26h7

Canadian Centre for Cyber Security. (2022, February 23). How to identify misinformation, disinformation, and malinformation (ITSAP.00.300). Canadian Centre for Cyber Security. https://www.cyber.gc.ca/en/guidance/how-identify-misinformation-disinformation-and-malinformation-itsap00300

Carlson, C. R., & Witt, H. (2020). Online harassment of U.S. women journalists and its impact on press freedom. *First Monday*. https://doi.org/2013

Carlson, M. (2016). Metajournalistic discourse and the meanings of journalism: Definitional control, boundary work, and legitimation. *Communication Theory*, 26(4), 349–368. https://doi.org/10.1111/comt.12088

Carlson, M., Robinson, S., & Lewis, S. C. (2021). *News after Trump: Journalism's crisis of relevance in a changed media culture*. Oxford University Press.

Carnahan, D., & Garrett, R. K. (2019). Processing style and responsiveness to corrective information. *International Journal of Public Opinion Research*, 32(3), 530–546. https://doi.org/10.1093/ijpor/edz037

CCDH. (2021). The disinformation dozen. https://252f2edd-1c8b-49f5-9bb2-cb57bb47e4ba.filesusr.com/ugd/f4d9b9_b7cedc0553604720b7137f8663366ee5.pdf

CDC. (2016, January 1). Health workers report harassment, symptoms of poor mental health, and difficult working conditions. Centers for Disease Control and Prevention. https://www.cdc.gov/media/releases/2023/s1024-Health-Worker-Mental-Health.html

CDC. (2022, December 19). Key facts about seasonal flu vaccine. Centers for Disease Control and Prevention. https://t.cdc.gov/2S4F

CDC. (2023a, April 3). Raw milk questions and answers. Centers for Disease Control and Prevention. https://www.cdc.gov/foodsafety/rawmilk/raw-milk-questions-and-answers.html

CDC. (2023b, April 18). Sun Safety: Skin Cancer. https://www.cdc.gov/cancer/skin/basic_info/sun-safety.htm

Celadin, T., Capraro, V., Pennycook, G., & Rand, D. G. (2023). Displaying news source trustworthiness ratings reduces sharing intentions for false news posts. *Journal of Online Trust and Safety*, 1(5), Article 5. https://doi.org/10.54501/jots.v1i5.100

Ceylan, G., Anderson, I. A., & Wood, W. (2023). Sharing of misinformation is habitual, not just lazy or biased. *Proceedings of the National Academy of Sciences*, 120(4), e2216614120. https://doi.org/10/grnp8h

Chadwick, A., & Vaccari, C. (2019). *News sharing on UK social media: Misinformation, disinformation, and correction* [Report]. Loughborough University. https://repository.lboro.ac.uk/articles/report/News_sharing_on_UK_social_media_misinformation_disinformation_and_correction/9471269/1

Chadwick, A., Vaccari, C., & Hall, N.-A. (2022). *New public report: Covid vaccines and online personal messaging: The challenge of challenging everyday misinformation*. Everyday Misinformation. https://www.andrewchadwick.com/blog/2022/4/7/new-public-report-from-the-everyday-misinformation-project-covid-vaccines-and-online-personal-messaging-the-challenge-of-challenging-everyday-misinformation

Chaiken, S. (1980). Heuristic versus systematic information processing and the use of source versus message cues in persuasion. *Journal of Personality and Social Psychology*, 39, 752–766. https://doi.org/10/bh88sk

Chan, M. (2024). News literacy, fake news recognition, and authentication behaviors after exposure to fake news on social media. *New Media & Society*, 26(8), 4669-4688. https://doi.org/10.1177/14614448221127675

Chan, M. S., & Albarracín, D. (2023). A meta-analysis of correction effects in science-relevant misinformation. *Nature Human Behaviour*, 7(9), Article 9. https://doi.org/10.1038/s41562-023-01623-8

Chaudhry, I., & Gruzd, A. (2020). Expressing and challenging racist discourse on Facebook: How social media weaken the "spiral of silence" theory. *Policy & Internet*, 12(1), 88–108. https://doi.org/10.1002/poi3.197

Chen, L., & Fu, L. (2022). Let's fight the infodemic: The third-person effect process of misinformation during public health emergencies. *Internet Research, 32*(4), 1357–1377. https://doi.org/10.1108/INTR-03-2021-0194

Chen, L., & Tang, H. (2023). Intention of health experts to counter health misinformation in social media: Effects of perceived threat to online users, correction efficacy, and self-affirmation. *Public Understanding of Science, 32*(3), 284–303. https://doi.org/10.1177/09636625221138357

Cheng, J., Danescu-Niculescu-Mizil, C., & Leskovec, J. (2015). Antisocial behavior in online discussion communities. *Proceedings of the International AAAI Conference on Web and Social Media, 9*(1), Article 1. https://doi.org/10.1609/icwsm.v9i1.14583

Chinn, M. D., & Fairlie, R. W. (2007). The determinants of the global digital divide: A cross-country analysis of computer and internet penetration. *Oxford Economic Papers, 59*(1), 16–44. https://doi.org/10/b3cxns

Chou, S. W. Y., Gaysynsky, A., & Cappella, J. N. (2020). Where we go from here: Health misinformation on social media. *American Journal of Public Health, 110*(S3), 273–275.

Chung, M., & Kim, N. (2021). When I learn the news is false: How fact-checking information stems the spread of fake news via third-person perception. *Human Communication Research, 47*(1), 1–24. https://doi.org/10/gk5pc6

Cialdini, R. B., Kallgren, C. A., & Reno, R. R. (1991). A focus theory of normative conduct: A theoretical refinement and reevaluation of the role of norms in human behavior. *Advances in Experimental Social Psychology, 24*, 201–234. https://doi.org/10.1016/S0065-2601(08)60330-5

Cleveland Clinic. (2022, December 20). Strep throat: Symptoms, causes, diagnosis & treatment. Cleveland Clinic. https://my.clevelandclinic.org/health/diseases/4602-strep-throat

Coles, S. M., & Lane, D. (2023). Race and ethnicity as foundational forces in political communication: Special issue introduction. *Political Communication, 40*(4), 367–376. https://doi.org/10.1080/10584609.2023.2229780

Combatting Vaccine Misinformation. (2019, March 7). Meta. https://about.fb.com/news/2019/03/combatting-vaccine-misinformation/

Compton, J. (2020). Prophylactic versus therapeutic inoculation treatments for resistance to influence. *Communication Theory, 30*(3), 330–343. https://doi.org/10.1093/ct/qtz004

Condon, M., & Holleque, M. (2013). Entering politics: General self-efficacy and voting behavior among young people: Entering politics. *Political Psychology, 34*(2), 167–181. https://doi.org/10.1111/pops.12019

Conger, K., Browning, K., & Woo, E. (2021, October 22). Eating disorders and social media prove difficult to untangle. *New York Times.* https://www.nytimes.com/2021/10/22/technology/social-media-eating-disorders.html

Congress.gov. (2022, December 15). S.1143—117th Congress (2021–2022): No TikTok on Government Devices Act (2021-04-15) [legislation]. http://www.congress.gov/bill/117th-congress/senate-bill/1143

Conrad, P. (1999). Uses of expertise: Sources, quotes, and voice in the reporting of genetics in the news. *Public Understanding of Science, 8*(4), 285. https://doi.org/10.1088/0963-6625/8/4/302

Cook, J. (2020). Deconstructing climate science denial. *Research Handbook on Communicating Climate Change*, 62–78. https://doi.org/10/gr6kt7

Coppock, A., Hill, S. J., & Vavreck, L. (2020). The small effects of political advertising are small regardless of context, message, sender, or receiver: Evidence from 59 real-time randomized experiments. *Science Advances, 6*(36), eabc4046. https://doi.org/10.1126/sciadv.abc4046

Costello, T. H., Pennycook, G., & Rand, D. (2024). *Durably reducing conspiracy beliefs through dialogues with AI.* OSF. https://doi.org/10.31234/osf.io/xcwdn

Courchesne, L., Ilhardt, J., & Shapiro, J. N. (2021). Review of social science research on the impact of countermeasures against influence operations. *Harvard Kennedy School Misinformation Review.* https://doi.org/10.37016/mr-2020-79

Craciun, C., & Baban, A. (2012). "Who will take the blame?": Understanding the reasons why Romanian mothers decline HPV vaccination for their daughters. *Vaccine, 30*(48), 6789–6793. https://doi.org/10.1016/j.vaccine.2012.09.016

Croteau, D., & Hoynes, W. (2006). *The business of media: Corporate media and the public interest.* Pine Forge Press.

Cuan-Baltazar, J. Y., Muñoz-Perez, M. J., Robledo-Vega, C., Pérez-Zepeda, M. F., & Soto-Vega, E. (2020). Misinformation of COVID-19 on the internet: Infodemiology study. *JMIR Public Health and Surveillance, 6*(2), e18444. https://doi.org/10.2196/18444

Cushion, S., Morani, M., Kyriakidou, M., & Soo, N. (2022). Why media systems matter: A fact-checking study of UK television news during the coronavirus pandemic. *Digital Journalism, 10*(5), 698–716. https://doi.org/10.1080/21670811.2021.1965490

Cutrona, C. E., & Troutman, B. R. (1986). Social support, infant temperament, and parenting self-efficacy: A mediational model of postpartum depression. *Child Development, 57*(6), 1507–1518. https://doi.org/10.2307/1130428

Cybersecurity and Infrastructure Security Agency. (n.d.). *MDM Resource Library | CISA.* Retrieved August 24, 2023 from https://www.cisa.gov/mdm-resource-library

Dambanemuya, H. K., & Diakopoulos, N. (2020). "Alexa, what is going on with the impeachment?" Evaluating smart speakers for news quality. *Proc. Computation + Journalism Symposium.* https://par.nsf.gov/biblio/10175596-alexa-what-going-impeachment-eva luating-smart-speakers-news-quality

Danner, C. (2022, December 12). Twitter's former safety head forced from home after being smeared by Elon Musk. *Intelligencer.* https://nymag.com/intelligencer/2022/12/elon-musk-smears-former-twitter-executive-yoel-roth.html

Darlenski, R., & Tsankov, N. (2020). COVID-19 pandemic and the skin: What should dermatologists know? *Clinics in Dermatology, 38*(6), 785–787. https://doi.org/10/ggs9rw

Davis, J. L., & Jurgenson, N. (2014). Context collapse: Theorizing context collusions and collisions. *Information, Communication & Society, 17*(4), 476–485. https://doi.org/10.1080/1369118X.2014.888458

Davison, W. P. (1983). The third-person effect in communication. *Public Opinion Quarterly, 47*(1), 1–15. https://doi.org/10.1086/268763

De Angelis, L., Baglivo, F., Arzilli, G., Privitera, G. P., Ferragina, P., Tozzi, A. E., & Rizzo, C. (2023). ChatGPT and the rise of large language models: The new AI-driven infodemic threat in public health. *Frontiers in Public Health, 11.* https://doi.org/10.3389/fpubh.2023.1166120

DeCook, J. R., Cotter, K., Kanthawala, S., & Foyle, K. (2022). Safe from "harm": The governance of violence by platforms. *Policy & Internet, 14*(1), 63–78. https://doi.org/10.1002/poi3.290

Department of Veterans Affairs. (2023, April 18). Content principles. https://design.va.gov/content-style-guide/content-principles

Desai, A. N., Ruidera, D., Steinbrink, J. M., Granwehr, B., & Lee, D. H. (2022). Misinformation and disinformation: The potential disadvantages of social media in infectious disease and how to combat them. *Clinical Infectious Diseases, 74*(Supplement_3), e34–e39. https://doi.org/10.1093/cid/ciac109

Descant, S. (2023, January 8). Commuter ridership is disappearing. Can mass transit adapt? Governing. https://www.governing.com/community/commuter-ridership-is-disappearing-can-mvass-transit-adapt

Destradi, S. (2017). Reluctance in international politics: A conceptualization. *European Journal of International Relations, 23*(2), 315–340. https://doi.org/10/f98b6w

DeVerna, M. R., Guess, A. M., Berinsky, A. J., Tucker, J. A., & Jost, J. T. (2022). Rumors in retweet: Ideological asymmetry in the failure to correct misinformation. *Personality and Social Psychology Bulletin,* 01461672221114222. https://doi.org/10/gr6ktv

DeVerna, M. R., Yan, H. Y., Yang, K.-C., & Menczer, F. (2023, August 21). Artificial intelligence is ineffective and potentially harmful for fact checking. arXiv.Org. https://arxiv.org/abs/2308.10800v2

Di Meco, L., & Wilfore, K. (2021, March 8). Gendered disinformation is a national security problem. Brookings. https://www.brookings.edu/techstream/gendered-disinformation-is-a-national-security-problem/

Dijk, J. van. (2020). *The digital divide*. John Wiley & Sons.

Directorate-General for Communications Networks, C. and T. (European C. (2018). A multi-dimensional approach to disinformation: Report of the independent high level group on fake news and online disinformation. Publications Office of the European Union. https://data.europa.eu/doi/10.2759/739290

Dixon, G. N., Garrett, K., Susmann, M., & Bushman, B. J. (2020). Public opinion perceptions, private support, and public actions of US adults regarding gun safety policy. *JAMA Network Open, 3*(12), e2029571. https://doi.org/10.1001/jamanetworkopen.2020.29571

Dixon, G. N., Lerner, B., & Bashian, S. (2024). Challenges to correcting pluralistic ignorance: False consensus effects, competing information environments, and anticipated social conflict. *Human Communication Research*, hqae001. https://doi.org/10.1093/hcr/hqae001

Druckman, J. N., Kang, S., Chu, J., N. Stagnaro, M., Voelkel, J. G., Mernyk, J. S., Pink, S. L., Redekopp, C., Rand, D. G., & Willer, R. (2023). Correcting misperceptions of out-partisans decreases American legislators' support for undemocratic practices. *Proceedings of the National Academy of Sciences, 120*(23), e2301836120. https://doi.org/10.1073/pnas.2301836120

Druckman, J. N., Klar, S., Krupnikov, Y., Levendusky, M., & Ryan, J. B. (2022). (Mis)estimating affective polarization. *Journal of Politics, 84*(2), 1106–1117. https://doi.org/10.1086/715603

Dubois, E., & Blank, G. (2018). The echo chamber is overstated: The moderating effect of political interest and diverse media. *Information, Communication & Society, 21*(5), 729–745. https://doi.org/10.1080/1369118X.2018.1428656

Duke Reporters' Lab. (2022, November). *Fact- checking*. Duke Reporters' Lab. https://reporterslab.org/fact-checking/

Dye, T. D., Alcantara, L., Siddiqi, S., Barbosu, M., Sharma, S., Panko, T., & Pressman, E. (2020). Risk of COVID-19-related bullying, harassment and stigma among healthcare workers: An analytical cross-sectional global study. *BMJ Open, 10*(12), e046620. https://doi.org/10.1136/bmjopen-2020-046620

Earl, J., Kimport, K., Prieto, G., Rush, C., & Reynoso, K. (2010). Changing the world one webpage at a time: Conceptualizing and explaining internet activism. *Mobilization: An International Quarterly, 15*(4), 425–446. https://doi.org/10.17813/maiq.15.4.w031232131lh37042

Ecker, U. K. H., & Antonio, L. M. (2021). Can you believe it? An investigation into the impact of retraction source credibility on the continued influence effect. *Memory & Cognition, 49*(4), 631–644. https://doi.org/10.3758/s13421-020-01129-y

Ecker, U. K. H., Butler, L. H., & Hamby, A. (2020). You don't have to tell a story! A registered report testing the effectiveness of narrative versus non-narrative misinformation corrections. *Cognitive Research: Principles and Implications, 5*(1), 64. https://doi.org/10.1186/s41235-020-00266-x

Ecker, U. K. H., Lewandowsky, S., Cook, J., Schmid, P., Fazio, L. K., Brashier, N., Kendeou, P., Vraga, E. K., & Amazeen, M. A. (2022). The psychological drivers of misinformation belief and its resistance to correction. *Nature Reviews Psychology, 1*(1), Article1. https://doi.org/10.1038/s44159-021-00006-y

Ecker, U. K. H., Lewandowsky, S., Swire, B., & Chang, D. (2011). Correcting false information in memory: Manipulating the strength of misinformation encoding and its retraction. *Psychonomic Bulletin & Review, 18*(3), 570–578. https://doi.org/10.3758/s13423-011-0065-1

Edelmann, N. (2013). Reviewing the definitions of "lurkers" and some implications for online research. *Cyberpsychology, Behavior, and Social Networking, 16*(9), 645–649. https://doi.org/10.1089/cyber.2012.0362

Eden, S. E. (1993). Individual environmental responsibility and its role in public environmental-ism. *Environment and Planning A: Economy and Space, 25*(12), 1743–1758. https://doi.org/10.1068/a251743

Edgerly, S., Mourão, M., Rachel R., Thorson, E., & Tham, S. M. (2020). When do audiences verify? How perceptions about message and source influence audience verification of news headlines. *Journalism and Mass Communication Quarterly, 97*(1), 52–71. https://doi.org/10/gh5nsv

Edwards, K., & Smith, E. E. (1996). A disconfirmation bias in the evaluation of arguments. *Journal of Personality and Social Psychology, 71*, 5–24. https://doi.org/10.1037/0022-3514.71.1.5

Eilperin, J. (2014, November 18). A handful of bills could bridge the partisan divide. But will they start a trend? *Washington Post.* https://www.washingtonpost.com/politics/a-handful-of-bills-could-bridge-the-partisan-divide/2014/11/17/b4fed0da-6e74-11e4-8808-afaa1e3a33ef_story.html

Einstein, K. L., & Glick, D. M. (2013). *Scandals, conspiracies and the vicious cycle of cynicism.* American Political Science Association.

Eismann, K. (2021). Diffusion and persistence of false rumors in social media networks: Impli-cations of searchability on rumor self-correction on Twitter. *Journal of Business Economics, 91*(9), 1299–1329. https://doi.org/10.1007/s11573-020-01022-9

Ekström, M., Lewis, S. C., & Westlund, O. (2020). Epistemologies of digital journalism and the study of misinformation. *New Media & Society, 22*(2), 205–212. https://doi.org/10.1177/1461444819856914

Ellison, N. B., Steinfield, C., & Lampe, C. (2007). The benefits of Facebook "friends:" Social capital and college students' use of online social network sites. *Journal of Computer-Mediated Communication, 12*(4), 1143–1168. https://doi.org/10.1111/j.1083-6101.2007.00367.x

Ellison, N. B., & Vitak, J. (2015). Social network site affordances and their relationship to so-cial capital processes. In S. S. Sundar (Ed.), *The handbook of the psychology of communication technology* (pp. 203–227). John Wiley & Sons.

Emigh, R. J. (2021). A historical sociology of the authentication of news. *Items.* https://items.ssrc.org/beyond-disinformation/a-historical-sociology-of-the-authentication-of-news/

eSafetyCommissioner. (2021). Online Safety Act 2021. https://www.esafety.gov.au/sites/default/files/2021-07/Online%20Safety%20Act%20-%20Fact%20sheet.pdf

European Commission. (2024a). The Digital Markets Act: Ensuring fair and open digital mar-kets. https://commission.europa.eu/strategy-and-policy/priorities-2019-2024/europe-fit-digital-age/digital-markets-act-ensuring-fair-and-open-digital-markets_en

European Commission. (2024b). Digital Services Act. https://www.consilium.europa.eu/en/policies/digital-services-act/

Evans, S. K., Pearce, K. E., Vitak, J., & Treem, J. W. (2017). Explicating affordances: A conceptual framework for understanding affordances in communication research. *Journal of Computer-Mediated Communication, 22*(1), 35–52. https://doi.org/10/f9wk33

Fazekas, P. (2023). Vividness and content. *Mind & Language, n/a*(n/a). https://doi.org/10/gr6k28

Fazio, L. K. (2020). Pausing to consider why a headline is true or false can help re-duce the sharing of false news. *Harvard Kennedy School Misinformation Review, 1*(2). https://doi.org/10.37016/mr-2020-009

Fazio, L. K., Hong, M. K., & Pillai, R. M. (2023). Combatting rumors around the French election: The memorability and effectiveness of fact-checking articles. *Cognitive Research: Principles and Implications, 8*(1), 44. https://doi.org/10.1186/s41235-023-00500-2

FDA. (2023, November 6). Barbecue basics: Tips to prevent foodborne illness. FDA. https://www.fda.gov/consumers/consumer-updates/barbecue-basics-tips-prevent-foodborne-illness

FDA. (2024). The dangers of raw milk: Unpasteurized milk can pose a serious health risk. FDA. https://www.fda.gov/food/buy-store-serve-safe-food/dangers-raw-milk-unpasteurized-milk-can-pose-serious-health-risk

Feagin, J., & Bennefield, Z. (2014). Systemic racism and U.S. health care. *Social Science & Medicine,* *103,* 7–14. https://doi.org/10/f5vrd5

Feldman, L., Myers, T. A., Hmielowski, J. D., & Leiserowitz, A. (2014). The mutual reinforcement of media selectivity and effects: Testing the reinforcing spirals framework in the context of global warming. *Journal of Communication, 64*(4), 590–611. https://doi.org/10.1111/jcom.12108

Feng, L., Hu, Y., Li, B., Stanley, H. E., Havlin, S., & Braunstein, L. A. (2015). Competing for attention in social media under information overload conditions. *PLOS ONE, 10*(7), e0126090. https://doi.org/10.1371/journal.pone.0126090

Ferrand, J., Hockensmith, R., Houghton, R. F., & Walsh-Buhi, E. R. (2020). Evaluating smart assistant responses for accuracy and misinformation regarding human papillomavirus vaccination: Content analysis study. *Journal of Medical Internet Research, 22*(8), e19018. https://doi.org/10.2196/19018

Festinger, L. (1957). *A theory of cognitive dissonance.* Stanford University Press.

Festinger, L., Riecken, H. W., & Schachter, S. (1956). *When prophecy fails.* University of Minnesota Press.

Fiorina, M. P. (2010). *Culture war? The myth of a polarized America* (3rd ed.). Longman.

Fisher, M. (2022). *The chaos machine: The inside story of how social media rewired our minds and our world.* Little, Brown and Company.

Fiske, S. T., & Taylor, S. E. (1991). *Social cognition* (2nd ed.). Mcgraw-Hill.

Fletcher, R., & Nielsen, R. K. (2018). Are people incidentally exposed to news on social media? A comparative analysis. *New Media & Society, 20*(7), 2450–2468. https://doi.org/10.1177/1461444817724170

Fletcher, R., Robertson, C. T., & Nielsen, R. K. (2021). How many people live in politically partisan online news echo chambers in different countries? *Journal of Quantitative Description: Digital Media,* 1–56. https://doi.org/10.51685/jqd.2021.020

Flynn, D. J., Nyhan, B., & Reifler, J. (2017). The nature and origins of misperceptions: Understanding false and unsupported beliefs about politics: Nature and origins of misperceptions. *Political Psychology, 38,* 127–150. https://doi.org/10.1111/pops.12394

Fombonne, E., Goin-Kochel, R. P., O'Roak, B. J., Abbeduto, L., Aberbach, G., Acampado, J., Ace, A. J., Albright, C., Alessandri, M., Amaral, D. G., Amatya, A., Anglo, C., Annett, R. D., Arriaga, I., Ashley, R., Astrovskaya, I., Baalman, K., Baer, M., Bahl, E., . . . Zick, A. (2020). Beliefs in vaccine as causes of autism among SPARK cohort caregivers. *Vaccine, 38*(7), 1794–1803. https://doi.org/10.1016/j.vaccine.2019.12.026

Forestal, J. (2021). *Designing for democracy: How to build community in digital environments.* Oxford University Press.

Fowler, E. F., & Gollust, S. E. (2015). The content and effect of politicized health controversies. *ANNALS of the American Academy of Political and Social Science, 658*(1), 155–171. https://doi.org/10.1177/0002716214555505

Freelon, D., Bossetta, M., Wells, C., Lukito, J., Xia, Y., & Adams, K. (2022). Black trolls matter: Racial and ideological asymmetries in social media disinformation. *Social Science Computer Review, 40*(3), 560–578. https://doi.org/10/gg7s2s

Freelon, D., & Lokot, T. (2020). Russian Twitter disinformation campaigns reach across the American political spectrum. *Harvard Kennedy School Misinformation Review, 1*(1). https://doi.org/10/ggns64

Freelon, D., McIlwain, C. D., & Clark, M. (2016). *Beyond the hashtags: #Ferguson, #Blacklivesmatter, and the online struggle for offline justice.* Center for Media & Social Impact. https://doi.org/10.2139/ssrn.2747066

Freelon, D., Pruden, M. L., & Malmer, D. (2023). #politicalcommunicationsowhite: Race and politics in nine communication journals, 1991–2021. *Political Communication.* https://www.tandfonline.com/doi/abs/10.1080/10584609.2023.2192187

Frost, P. (2000). The quality of false memory over time: Is memory for misinformation "remembered" or "known"? *Psychonomic Bulletin & Review, 7*(3), 531–536. https://doi.org/10.3758/BF03214367

Funk, C., Hefferon, M., Kennedy, B., & Johnson, C. (2019, August 2). Trust and mistrust in Americans' views of scientific experts. Pew Research Center Science & Society. https://www.pewresearch.org/science/2019/08/02/trust-and-mistrust-in-americans-views-of-scientific-experts/

Rainie, C., & Funk, L. (2015, January 29). Public and Scientists' Views on Science and Society. *Pew Research Center*. https://www.pewresearch.org/science/2015/01/29/public-and-scientists-views-on-science-and-society/

Gabielkov, M., Ramachandran, A., Chaintreau, A., & Legout, A. (2016). Social clicks: What and who gets read on Twitter? *Proceedings of the 2016 ACM SIGMETRICS International Conference on Measurement and Modeling of Computer Science, 179–192.* https://doi.org/10.1145/2896377.2901462

Gadarian, S. K., Goodman, S. W., & Pepinsky, T. B. (2022). *Pandemic politics: How the politicization of the pandemic endangers our lives—And our democracy.* Princeton University Press.

Gallup. (2018). *Wellcome Global Monitor 2018.* https://wellcome.org/reports/wellcome-global-monitor/2018

Garcia-Pueyo, L., Guthrie, S., Santana Schwarz, B., & Xu, B. (2022). Informative integrity frictions in social networks. *Companion Proceedings of the Web Conference 2022, 141–145.* https://doi.org/10.1145/3487553.3524221

Garrett, R. K. (2009). Politically motivated reinforcement seeking: Reframing the selective exposure debate. *Journal of Communication, 59*(4), 676–699. https://doi.org/10.1111/j.1460-2466.2009.01452.x

Garrett, R. K., & Bond, R. M. (2021). Conservatives' susceptibility to political misperceptions. *Science Advances, 7*(23), eabf1234. https://doi.org/10/gkzv8m

Garvey, M. (2022, November 17). Jimmy Fallon is asking Elon Musk to take down #RIPJimmyFallon. CNN. https://www.cnn.com/2022/11/16/entertainment/jimmy-fallon-twitter-elon-musk/index.html

Gauchat, G. (2011). The cultural authority of science: Public trust and acceptance of organized science. *Public Understanding of Science, 20*(6), 751–770. https://doi.org/10/dwr6r7

Gauchat, G. (2012). Politicization of science in the public sphere: A study of public trust in the United States, 1974 to 2010. *American Sociological Review, 77*(2), 167–187. https://doi.org/10/gc3d6j

Gearhart, S., & Zhang, W. (2015). "Was it something I said?" "No, it was something you posted!" A study of the spiral of silence theory in social media contexts. *Cyberpsychology, Behavior, and Social Networking, 18*(4), 208–213. https://doi.org/10.1089/cyber.2014.0443

Gearhart, S., & Zhang, W. (2018). Same spiral, different day? Testing the spiral of silence across issue types. *Communication Research, 45*(1), 34–54. https://doi.org/10.1177/0093650215616456

Geesaman, R., & Crissman, N. (2023). Motivation to correct misinformation: Third-person perceptions and perceived norms. *Journal of Communication and Media Studies, 8*(1), 61–74. https://doi.org/10/gr6k3h

Gibson, J. J. (1977). The theory of affordances. In J. J. Gieseking, W. Mangold, C. Katz, S. Low, & S. Saegert (Eds.), *The people, place, and space reader* (pp. 67–82), Routledge.

Gimpel, H., Heger, S., Olenberger, C., & Utz, L. (2021). The effectiveness of social norms in fighting fake news on social media. *Journal of Management Information Systems, 38*(1), 196–221. https://doi.org/10.1080/07421222.2021.1870389

Glassman, M., & Kuznetcova, I. (2022). The GameStop saga: Reddit communities and the emerging conflict between new and old media. *First Monday.* https://doi.org/2013

Goffman, E. (1959). *The presentation of self in everyday life.* Doubleday.

Goh, D. H.-L., Chua, A. Y. K., Shi, H., Wei, W., Wang, H., & Lim, E. P. (2017). An analysis of rumor and counter-rumor messages in social media. In S. Choemprayong, F. Crestani, & S. J. Cunningham (Eds.), *Digital libraries: Data, information, and knowledge for digital lives* (pp. 256–266). Springer International Publishing.

Goh, J. X., Hall, J. A., & Rosenthal, R. (2016). Mini meta-analysis of your own studies: Some arguments on why and a primer on how. *Social and Personality Psychology Compass, 10*(10), 535–549. https://doi.org/10.1111/spc3

Golebiewski, M., & Boyd, D. (2019). *Data voids: Where missing data can easily be exploited* [Report]. Data & Society Research Institute. https://apo.org.au/node/265631

Gollust, S. E., Lantz, P. M., & Ubel, P. A. (2009). The polarizing effect of news media messages about the social determinants of health. *American Journal of Public Health, 99*(12), 2160–2167. https://doi.org/10.2105/AJPH.2009.161414

Gonah, L. (2020). Key considerations for successful risk communication and community engagement (RCCE) programmes during COVID-19 pandemic and other public health emergencies. *Annals of Global Health, 86*(1), 146. https://doi.org/10.5334/aogh.3119

González-Bailón, S., Lazer, D., Barberá, P., Zhang, M., Allcott, H., Brown, T., Crespo-Tenorio, A., Freelon, D., Gentzkow, M., Guess, A. M., Iyengar, S., Kim, Y. M., Malhotra, N., Moehler, D., Nyhan, B., Pan, J., Rivera, C. V., Settle, J., Thorson, E., . . . Tucker, J. A. (2023). Asymmetric ideological segregation in exposure to political news on Facebook. *Science, 381*(6656), 392–398. https://doi.org/10.1126/science.ade7138

Goodman, B., & McPhillips, D. (2023, July 14). CDC facing major funding cuts, with direct impact on state and local health departments. CNN. https://www.cnn.com/2023/07/14/health/cdc-funding-cuts-debt-deal/index.html

Google News Initiative. (2017, July 6). Making it easier for publishers to share fact check content. Google. https://blog.google/outreach-initiatives/google-news-initiative/making-it-easier-publishers-share-fact-check-content/

Gorman, S. E., & Gorman, J. M. (2017). *Denying to the grave: Why we ignore the facts that will save us.* Oxford University Press.

Gostin, L. O. (2018). Language, science, and politics: The politicization of public health. *JAMA, 319*(6), 541–542. https://doi.org/10.1001/jama.2017.21763

Gottfried, J., & Liedke, J. (2021, August 30). Partisan divides in media trust widen, driven by a decline among Republicans. Pew Research Center. https://www.pewresearch.org/fact-tank/2021/08/30/partisan-divides-in-media-trust-widen-driven-by-a-decline-among-republicans/

Gottfried, J., Stocking, G., Grieco, E., Walker, M., Khuzam, M., & Mitchell, A. (2019, December 12). 3. Factors beyond party affiliation also connect with trust in the news media. https://www.pewresearch.org/journalism/2019/12/12/factors-beyond-party-affiliation-also-connect-with-trust-in-the-news-media/

Gøtzsche, P. C. (2000). Why we need a broad perspective on meta-analysis: It may be crucially important for patients. *BMJ, 321*(7261), 585–586. https://doi.org/10.1136/bmj.321.7261.585

Goyanes, M., Borah, P., & Gil de Zúñiga, H. (2021). Social media filtering and democracy: Effects of social media news use and uncivil political discussions on social media unfriending. *Computers in Human Behavior, 120*, 106759. https://doi.org/10.1016/j.chb.2021.106759

Graham, M., & Yair, O. (2024). Expressive responding and belief in 2020 election fraud. *Political Behavior, 46*, 1349–1374. https://doi.org/10.1007/s11109-023-09875-w

Gravelle, T. B., Phillips, J. B., Reifler, J., & Scotto, T. J. (2022). Estimating the size of "anti-vax" and vaccine hesitant populations in the US, UK, and Canada: Comparative latent class modeling of vaccine attitudes. *Human Vaccines & Immunotherapeutics, 18*(1), 2008214. https://doi.org/10/gr6kws

Graves, L. (2016). *Deciding what's true: The rise of political fact-checking in American journalism.* Columbia University Press.

Graves, L., & Anderson, C. (2020). Discipline and promote: Building infrastructure and managing algorithms in a "structured journalism" project by professional fact-checking groups. *New Media & Society, 22*(2), 342–360. https://doi.org/10/gndj9b

Gravlee, C. C. (2020). Systemic racism, chronic health inequities, and COVID-19: A syndemic in the making? *American Journal of Human Biology: The Official Journal of the Human Biology Council, 32*(5), e23482. https://doi.org/10/ghcxwk

Grewal, D., Puccinelli, N., & Monroe, K. B. (2018). Meta-analysis: Integrating accumulated knowledge. *Journal of the Academy of Marketing Science, 46*(1), 9–30. https://doi.org/10.1007/s11747-017-0570-5

Grinberg, N., Joseph, K., Friedland, L., Swire-Thompson, B., & Lazer, D. (2019). Fake news on Twitter during the 2016 U.S. presidential election. *Science, 363*(6425), 374–378. https://doi.org/10/gf3gmt

Gu, J., Dor, A., Li, K., Broniatowski, D. A., Hatheway, M., Fritz, L., & Abroms, L. C. (2022). The impact of Facebook's vaccine misinformation policy on user endorsements of vaccine content: An interrupted time series analysis. *Vaccine, 40*(14), 2209–2214. https://doi.org/10.1016/j.vaccine.2022.02.062

Guerrini, F. (2013). *Newsroom curators & independent storytellers: Content curation as a new form of journalism.* Reuters Institute for the Study of Journalism, University of Oxford.

Guess, A. M. (2015). Measure for measure: An experimental test of online political media exposure. *Political Analysis, 23*(1), 59–75. https://doi.org/10.1093/pan/mpu010

Guess, A. M., Lerner, M., Lyons, B., Montgomery, J. M., Nyhan, B., Reifler, J., & Sircar, N. (2020). A digital media literacy intervention increases discernment between mainstream and false news in the United States and India. *Proceedings of the National Academy of Sciences, 117*(27), 15536–15545. https://doi.org/10/gg87cb

Guess, A., Nagler, J., & Tucker, J. (2019). Less than you think: Prevalence and predictors of fake news dissemination on Facebook. *Science Advances, 5*(1), eaau4586. https://doi.org/10.1126/sciadv.aau4586

Guidry, J. P. D., Jin, Y., Orr, C. A., Messner, M., & Meganck, S. (2017). Ebola on Instagram and Twitter: How health organizations address the health crisis in their social media engagement. *Public Relations Review, 43*(3), 477–486. https://doi.org/10.1016/j.pubrev.2017.04.009

Guidry, J. P. D., Vraga, E. K., Laestadius, L. I., Miller, C. A., Occa, A., Nan, X., Ming, H. M., Qin, Y., Fuemmeler, B. F., & Carlyle, K. E. (2020). HPV vaccine searches on Pinterest: Before and after Pinterest's actions to moderate content. *American Journal of Public Health, 110*(S3), S305–S311. https://doi.org/10.2105/AJPH.2020.305827

Guillory, J. J., & Geraci, L. (2013). Correcting erroneous inferences in memory: The role of source credibility. *Journal of Applied Research in Memory and Cognition, 2*(4), 201–209. https://doi.org/10.1016/j.jarmac.2013.10.001

Gunther, A. C. (1995). Overrating the X-rating: The third-person perception and support for censorship of pornography. *Journal of Communication, 45*(1), 27–38. https://doi.org/10.1111/j.1460-2466.1995.tb00712.x

Hacker, P., Engel, A., & Mauer, M. (2023). Regulating ChatGPT and other large generative AI models. *Proceedings of the 2023 ACM Conference on Fairness, Accountability, and Transparency,* 1112–1123. https://doi.org/10.1145/3593013.3594067

Haidich, A. B. (2010). Meta-analysis in medical research. *Hippokratia, 14*(Suppl 1), 29–37.

Haji, A. (2020, December 7). From a lack of funding to a local news drought: How news is essential to democracy. *Brown Political Review.* https://brownpoliticalreview.org/2020/12/from-a-lack-of-funding-to-a-local-news-drought-how-news-is-essential-to-democracy/

Hallin, D. C., & Mancini, P. (2004). *Comparing media systems: Three models of media and politics.* Cambridge University Press.

Hamilton, L. C. (2015). Conservative and liberal views of science: Does trust depend on topic? *The Carsey School of Public Policy at the Scholars' Repository.* https://doi.org/10.34051/p/2020.242

Hamilton, L. C., & Safford, T. G. (2021). Elite cues and the rapid decline in trust in science agencies on COVID-19. *Sociological Perspectives, 64*(5), 988–1011. https://doi.org/10/gr6ktw

Hargittai, E. (2001). Second-level digital divide: Mapping differences in people's online skills (arXiv:cs/0109068). arXiv. https://doi.org/10.48550/arXiv.cs/0109068

Harlow, S., Brown, D. K., Salaverría, R., & García-Perdomo, V. (2020). Is the whole world watching? Building a typology of protest coverage on social media from around the world. *Journalism Studies, 21*(11), 1590–1608. https://doi.org/10/gr6kt8

Harris, E., & Bardey, A. C. (2019). Do Instagram profiles accurately portray personality? An investigation into idealized online self-presentation. *Frontiers in Psychology, 10.* https://doi.org/10.3389/fpsyg.2019.00871

Harris, J. K., Mueller, N. L., & Snider, D. (2013). Social media adoption in local health departments nationwide. *American Journal of Public Health, 103*(9), 1700–1707. https://doi.org/10.2105/AJPH.2012.301166

Hart, P. S., & Feldman, L. (2014). Threat without efficacy? Climate change on U.S. network news. *Science Communication, 36*(3), 325–351. https://doi.org/10/f6jw5h

Hart, P. S., & Feldman, L. (2016). The influence of climate change efficacy messages and efficacy beliefs on intended political participation. *PLOS ONE, 11*(8), e0157658. https://doi.org/10/gbsgvn

Hayes, A. F., Glynn, C. J., & Shanahan, J. (2005). Willingness to self-censor: A construct and measurement tool for public opinion research. *International Journal of Public Opinion Research, 17*(3), 298–323. https://doi.org/10.1093/ijpor/edh073

Haze, T., Kawano, R., Takase, H., Suzuki, S., Hirawa, N., & Tamura, K. (2023). Influence on the accuracy in ChatGPT: Differences in the amount of information per medical field. *International Journal of Medical Informatics, 180*, 105283. https://doi.org/10.1016/j.ijmedinf.2023.105283

He, B., Ahamad, M., & Kumar, S. (2023). Reinforcement learning-based counter-misinformation response generation: A case study of COVID-19 vaccine misinformation. *Proceedings of the ACM Web Conference 2023*, 2698–2709. https://doi.org/10.1145/3543507.3583388

Heikkilä, H., & Ahva, L. (2015). The relevance of journalism: Studying news audiences in a digital era. *Journalism Practice, 9*(1), 50–64. https://doi.org/10.1080/17512786.2014.928465

Heiss, R., Bode, L., Adisuryo, Z. M., Brito, L., Cuadra, A., Gao, P., Han, Y., Hearst, M., Huang, K., Kinyua, A., Lin, T., Ma, Y., Manion, T. O., Roh, Y., Salazar, A., Yue, S., & Zhang, P. (2024). Debunking mental health misperceptions in short-form social media videos: An experimental test of scientific credibility cues. *Health Communication, 39*(13), 3059–3071. https://doi.org/10.1080/10410236.2023.2301201

Helberger, N. (2020). The political power of platforms: How current attempts to regulate misinformation amplify opinion power. *Digital Journalism, 8*(6), 842–854. https://doi.org/10/gg87cc

Hern, A. (2021, June 25). Google starts warning users if search results are likely to be poor. *The Guardian.* https://www.theguardian.com/technology/2021/jun/25/google-starts-warning-users-if-search-results-are-likely-to-be-poor

Hines, J. M., Hungerford, H. R., & Tomera, A. N. (1987). Analysis and synthesis of research on responsible environmental behavior: A meta-analysis. *Journal of Environmental Education, 18*(2), 1–8. https://doi.org/10.1080/00958964.1987.9943482

Hoes, E., Altay, S., & Bermeo, J. (2023). Using ChatGPT to fight misinformation: ChatGPT nails 72% of 12,000 verified claims. https://doi.org/10.31234/osf.io/qnjkf

Holan, A. D. (2024, January 12). The principles of the truth-o-meter: How we fact-check. @politifact. https://www.politifact.com/article/2018/feb/12/principles-truth-o-meter-politifacts-methodology-i/

Hollings, J. (2013). Let the story go: The role of emotion in the decision-making process of the reluctant, vulnerable witness or whistle-blower. *Journal of Business Ethics, 114*(3), 501–512. https://doi.org/10/ggsvg9

Holton, A. E., Bélair-Gagnon, V., Bossio, D., & Molyneux, L. (2023). "Not Their Fault, but Their Problem": Organizational Responses to the Online Harassment of Journalists. *Journalism Practice, 17*(4), 859–874. https://doi.org/10.1080/17512786.2021.1946417

Hornsey, M. J., & Fielding, K. S. (2020). Understanding (and reducing) inaction on climate change. *Social Issues and Policy Review, 14*(1), 3–35. https://doi.org/10.1111/sipr.12058

Hotez, P. J. (2023). *The deadly rise of anti-science: A scientist's warning.* Johns Hopkins University Press.

Howarth, A. (2015). Exploring a curatorial turn in journalism. *M/C Journal, 18*(4), Article 4. https://doi.org/10.5204/mcj.1004

Huang, Y., & Wang, W. (2022). When a story contradicts: Correcting health misinformation on social media through different message formats and mechanisms. *Information, Communication & Society, 25*(8), 1192–1209. https://doi.org/10/gmzv9x

Huber, B., Borah, P., & Gil de Zúñiga, H. (2022). Taking corrective action when exposed to fake news: The role of fake news literacy. *Journal of Media Literacy Education, 14*(2), 1–14. https://doi.org/10/gr6kzq

Humprecht, E. (2020). How do they debunk "fake news"? A cross-national comparison of transparency in fact checks. *Digital Journalism, 8*(3), 310–327. https://doi.org/10.1080/21670811.2019.1691031

Humprecht, E., Esser, F., & Van Aelst, P. (2020). Resilience to online disinformation: A framework for cross-national comparative research. *International Journal of Press/Politics, 25*(3), 493–516. https://doi.org/10.1177/1940161219900126

International Press Institute. (2021, January 29). Rising violence against reporters in the U.S. *Ipi.Media.* https://ipi.media/rising-violence-against-reporters-in-the-u-s/

Isola, P., Xiao, J., Parikh, D., Torralba, A., & Oliva, A. (2014). What makes a photograph memorable? *IEEE Transactions on Pattern Analysis and Machine Intelligence, 36*(7), 1469–1482. https://doi.org/10/f58gfd

Iyengar, S., Lelkes, Y., Levendusky, M., Malhotra, N., & Westwood, S. J. (2019). The origins and consequences of affective polarization in the United States. *Annual Review of Political Science, 22*, 129–146. https://doi.org/10/gfv79s

Jaiswal, J., LoSchiavo, C., & Perlman, D. C. (2020). Disinformation, misinformation and inequality-driven mistrust in the time of COVID-19: Lessons unlearned from AIDS denialism. *AIDS and Behavior, 24*(10), 2776–2780. https://doi.org/10/gg9cr6

Jamieson, K. H. (1995). *Beyond the double bind: Women and leadership.* Oxford University Press.

Janmohamed, K., Walter, N., Nyhan, K., Khoshnood, K., Tucker, J. D., Sangngam, N., Altice, F. L., Ding, Q., Wong, A., Schwitzky, Z. M., Bauch, C. T., De Choudhury, M., Papakyriakopoulos, O., & Kumar, N. (2021). Interventions to mitigate COVID-19 misinformation: A systematic review and meta-analysis. *Journal of Health Communication, 26*(12), 846–857. https://doi.org/10.1080/10810730.2021.2021460

Jazbec, A., Simić, D., Corović, N., Duraković, Z., & Pavlović, M. (2003). Impact of coffee and other selected factors on general mortality and mortality due to cardiovascular disease in Croatia. *Journal of Health, Population, and Nutrition, 21*(4), 332–340.

Jaźwińska, K. (2024). The online harassment of journalists poses a threat to democracy that demands systemic solutions. Institute for Rebooting Social Media. https://rebootingsocialmedia.org/2024/02/02/the-online-harassment-of-journalists-poses-a-threat-to-democracy-that-demands-systemic-solutions/

Jennings, J., & Stroud, N. J. (2021). Asymmetric adjustment: Partisanship and correcting misinformation on Facebook. *New Media & Society,* 14614448211021720. https://doi.org/10.1177/14614448211021720

Jha, A., Lin, L., & Savoia, E. (2016). The use of social media by state health departments in the US: Analyzing health communication through Facebook. *Journal of Community Health, 41*(1), 174–179. https://doi.org/10.1007/s10900-015-0083-4

Jiang, S., & Wilson, C. (2018). Linguistic signals under misinformation and fact-checking: Evidence from user comments on social media. *Proceedings of the ACM on Human-Computer Interaction, 2*(CSCW), 82:1–82:23. https://doi.org/10.1145/3274351

Johnson, S. B., King, A. J., Warner, E. L., Aneja, S., Kann, B. H., & Bylund, C. L. (2023). Using ChatGPT to evaluate cancer myths and misconceptions: Artificial intelligence and cancer information. *JNCI Cancer Spectrum, 7*(2), pkad015. https://doi.org/10.1093/jncics/pkad015

Jolley, D., & Douglas, K. M. (2014). The social consequences of conspiracism: Exposure to conspiracy theories decreases intentions to engage in politics and to reduce one's carbon footprint. *British Journal of Psychology*, 105(1), 35–56. https://doi.org/10.1111/bjop.12018

Jolley, D., Douglas, K. M., Leite, A. C., & Schrader, T. (2019). Belief in conspiracy theories and intentions to engage in everyday crime. *British Journal of Social Psychology*, 58(3), 534–549. https://doi.org/10.1111/bjso.12311

Jones, G. M., Vraga, E. K., Hessburg, P. F., Hurteau, M. D., Allen, C. D., Keane, R. E., Spies, T. A., North, M. P., Collins, B. M., Finney, M. A., Lydersen, J. M., & Westerling, A. L. (2022). Counteracting wildfire misinformation. *Frontiers in Ecology and the Environment*, 20(7), 392–393. https://doi.org/10.1002/fee.2553

Jones, K. A., Crozier, W. E., & Strange, D. (2018). Objectivity is a myth for you but not for me or police: A bias blind spot for viewing and remembering criminal events. *Psychology, Public Policy, and Law*, 24(2), 259–270. https://doi.org/10.1037/law0000168

Jones, M. L., & Kaminski, M. E. (2020). An American's guide to the GDPR. *Denv. L. Rev.*, 98, 93–128.

Junco, R. (2013). Comparing actual and self-reported measures of Facebook use. *Computers in Human Behavior*, 29(3), 626–631. https://doi.org/10.1016/j.chb.2012.11.007

Kahan, D. M. (2015). The expressive rationality of inaccurate perceptions. SSRN Scholarly Paper 2670981. https://papers.ssrn.com/abstract=2670981

Kammerer, Y., & Gerjets, P. (2012). How search engine users evaluate and select web search results: The impact of the search engine interface on credibility assessments. In D. Lewandowski (Ed.), *Web search engine research* (pp. 251–279). Emerald Group Publishing.

Kaplan, A. M., & Haenlein, M. (2010). Users of the world, unite! The challenges and opportunities of Social Media. *Business Horizons*, 53(1), 59–68. https://doi.org/10/gzr

Karpf, D. (2019, December 10). On digital disinformation and democratic myths. MediaWell, Social Science Research Council. https://mediawell.ssrc.org/expert-reflections/on-digital-disinformation-and-democratic-myths/

Kata, A. (2010). A postmodern Pandora's box: Anti-vaccination misinformation on the Internet. *Vaccine*, 28(7), 1709–1716. https://doi.org/10.1016/j.vaccine.2009.12.022

Katz, E. (1957). The two-step flow of communication: An up-to-date report on an hypothesis. *Public Opinion Quarterly*, 21(1), 61–78. https://doi.org/10.1086/266687

Kelly, J. (2024, May 31). Google's AI recommended adding glue to pizza and other misinformation—What caused the viral blunders? *Forbes*. https://www.forbes.com/sites/jackkelly/2024/05/31/google-ai-glue-to-pizza-viral-blunders/

Kemp, P. L., Alexander, T. R., & Wahlheim, C. N. (2022). Recalling fake news during real news corrections can impair or enhance memory updating: The role of recollection-based retrieval. *Cognitive Research: Principles and Implications*, 7(1), 85. https://doi.org/10.1186/s41235-022-00434-1

Kempner, J. (2008). The Chilling Effect: How Do Researchers React to Controversy? *PLOS Medicine*, 5(11), e222. https://doi.org/10.1371/journal.pmed.0050222

Kendeou, P., Butterfuss, R., Kim, J., & Van Boekel, M. (2019). Knowledge revision through the lenses of the three-pronged approach. *Memory & Cognition*, 47(1), 33–46. https://doi.org/10.3758/s13421-018-0848-y

Kendeou, P., & O'Brien, E. J. (2014). The knowledge revision components (KReC) framework: Processes and mechanisms. In *Processing inaccurate information: Theoretical and applied perspectives from cognitive science and the educational sciences* (pp. 353–377). The MIT Press.

Kennedy, B., Tyson, A., & Funk, C. (2022, February 15). Americans' trust in scientists, other groups declines. Pew Research Center Science & Society. https://www.pewresearch.org/science/2022/02/15/americans-trust-in-scientists-other-groups-declines/

Kenski, K., & Stroud, N. J. (2006). Connections between internet use and political efficacy, knowledge, and participation. *Journal of Broadcasting & Electronic Media*, 50(2), 173–192. https://doi.org/10.1207/s15506878jobem5002_1

Kessler, G. (2024, February 22). About the fact checker. *Washington Post*. https://www.washingtonpost.com/politics/2019/01/07/about-fact-checker/

Kim, C., & Shin, W. (2022). Harassment of journalists and its aftermath: Anti-press violence, psychological suffering, and an internal chilling effect. *Digital Journalism*, 1–17. https://doi.org/10.1080/21670811.2022.2034027

Kim, D. H., Jones-Jang, S. M., & Kenski, K. (2022). Unfriending and muting during elections: The antecedents and consequences of selective avoidance on social media. *Mass Communication and Society*, 25(2), 161–184. https://doi.org/10.1080/15205436.2021.1942494

Kim, J. W., & Masullo, G. M. (2021). Exploring the influence of comment tone and content in response to misinformation in social media news. *Journalism Practice*, 15(4), 456–470. https://doi.org/10.1080/17512786.2020.1739550

Kim, M., & Cao, X. (2016). The impact of exposure to media messages promoting government conspiracy theories on distrust in the government: Evidence from a two-stage randomized experiment. *International Journal of Communication*, 10, 3808–3827.

Kim, S. C., Vraga, E. K., & Cook, J. (2021). An eye tracking approach to understanding misinformation and correction strategies on social media: The mediating role of attention and credibility to reduce HPV vaccine misperceptions. *Health Communication*, 36(13), 1687–1696. https://doi.org/10.1080/10410236.2020.1787933

King, A. J., Bol, N., Cummins, R. G., & John, K. K. (2019). Improving visual behavior research in communication science: An overview, review, and reporting recommendations for using eye-tracking methods. *Communication Methods and Measures*, 13(3), 149–177. https://doi.org/10.1080/19312458.2018.1558194

Kirzinger, A., Presiado, M., Valdes, I., Hamel, L., & Brodie, M. (2023, March 7). The COVID-19 pandemic: Insights from three years of KFF polling. KFF. https://www.kff.org/coronavirus-covid-19/poll-finding/the-covid-19-pandemic-insights-from-three-years-of-kff-polling/

Klein, E. G., Roberts, K., Manganello, J., Mcadams, R., & Mckenzie, L. (2020). When social media images and messages don't match: Attention to text versus imagery to effectively convey safety information on social media. *Journal of Health Communication*, 25(11), 879–884. https://doi.org/10.1080/10810730.2020.1853282

Kligler-Vilenchik, N. (2022). Collective social correction: Addressing misinformation through group practices of information verification on WhatsApp. *Digital Journalism*, 10(2), 300–318. https://doi.org/10.1080/21670811.2021.1972020

Knobloch-Westerwick, S. (2014). *Choice and preference in media use: Advances in selective exposure theory and research*. Routledge.

Koliska, M., & Bode, L. (2023). "I don't need a little popup to tell me:" Exploring user attitudes, perceptions, beliefs and heuristics about automated misinformation alert and detection systems. Working Paper.

Komamura, K. (2023). Japanese medical workers' sacrifice for universal health coverage. *Lancet (London, England)*, 401(10382), 1073. https://doi.org/10.1016/S0140-6736(23)00515-9

Koo, A. Z.-X., Su, M.-H., Lee, S., Ahn, S.-Y., & Rojas, H. (2021). What motivates people to correct misinformation? Examining the effects of third-person perceptions and perceived norms. *Journal of Broadcasting & Electronic Media*, 65(1), 111–134. https://doi.org/10/gmzhzr

Krause, N. M., Brossard, D., Scheufele, D. A., Xenos, M. A., & Franke, K. (2019). Trends—Americans' trust in science and scientists. *Public Opinion Quarterly*, 83(4), 817–836. https://doi.org/10/ghjrs6

Krause, N. M., Freiling, I., Beets, B., & Brossard, D. (2020). Fact-checking as risk communication: The multi-layered risk of misinformation in times of COVID-19. *Journal of Risk Research*, 23(7–8), 1052–1059. https://doi.org/10.1080/13669877.2020.1756385

Kroet, C. (2024, February 14). TikTok sets up in-app 'election centres' to fight fake news. *Euronews*. https://www.euronews.com/next/2024/02/14/tiktok-sets-up-in-app-election-centres-to-fight-election-fake-news

Krishna, A., & Amazeen, M. A. (2022). Narrative counters: Understanding the efficacy of narratives in combating anecdote-based vaccine misinformation. *Public Relations Review*, 48(5), 102251. https://doi.org/10.1016/j.pubrev.2022.102251

Krishnan, N., Gu, J., Tromble, R., & Abroms, L. C. (2021). Research note: Examining how various social media platforms have responded to COVID-19 misinformation. *Harvard Kennedy School Misinformation Review*. https://doi.org/10/gr6kzf

Krumpal, I. (2013). Determinants of social desirability bias in sensitive surveys: A literature review. *Quality & Quantity, 47*(4), 2025–2047. https://doi.org/10.1007/s11135-011-9640-9

Kubin, E., Puryear, C., Schein, C., & Gray, K. (2021). Personal experiences bridge moral and political divides better than facts. *Proceedings of the National Academy of Sciences, 118*(6), e2008389118. https://doi.org/10.1073/pnas.2008389118

Kuklinski, J. H., Quirk, P. J., Jerit, J., Schwieder, D., & Rich, R. F. (2000). Misinformation and the currency of democratic citizenship. *Journal of Politics, 62*(3), 790–816. https://doi.org/10/ctzsf9

Kunda, Z. (1990). The case for motivated reasoning. *Psychological Bulletin, 108*, 480–498. https://doi.org/10/fpphvr

Kuo, R., & Marwick, A. (2021). Critical disinformation studies: History, power, and politics. *Harvard Kennedy School Misinformation Review*. https://doi.org/10/gr6k3j

Kurtzleben, D. (2022, August 7). Republicans have long feuded with the mainstream media. Now many are shutting them out. NPR. https://www.npr.org/2022/08/07/1115949410/republicans-have-long-feuded-with-the-mainstream-media-now-many-are-shutting-the

Kuru, O., Campbell, S. W., Bayer, J. B., Baruh, L., & Ling, R. (2022). Encountering and Correcting Misinformation on WhatsApp. In H. Wasserman, & D. Madrid-Morales (Eds.), *Disinformation in the Global South* (pp. 88–107). John Wiley & Sons.

Lang, A. (2000). The limited capacity model of mediated message processing. *Journal of Communication, 50*(1), 46–70. https://doi.org/10.1111/j.1460-2466.2000.tb02833.x

Lang, A. (2006). Using the limited capacity model of motivated mediated message processing to design effective cancer communication messages. *Journal of Communication, 56*(s1), S57–S80. https://doi.org/10.1111/j.1460-2466.2006.00283.x

Lang, C., & Pearson-Merkowitz, S. (2015). Partisan sorting in the United States, 1972–2012: New evidence from a dynamic analysis. *Political Geography, 48*, 119–129. https://doi.org/10.1016/j.polgeo.2014.09.015

Langer, A. J., Ayers, T., Grass, J., Lynch, M., Angulo, F. J., & Mahon, B. E. (2012). Nonpasteurized dairy products, disease outbreaks, and state laws—United States, 1993–2006. *Emerging Infectious Diseases, 18*(3), 385–391. https://doi.org/10.3201/eid1803.111370

Larkin, H. (2021). Navigating attacks against health care workers in the COVID-19 era. *JAMA, 325*(18), 1822. https://doi.org/10.1001/jama.2021.2701

Larsen, A. (2023, August 19). Mike Lee and AOC are working together on an issue—sunscreen. What? https://www.sltrib.com/news/2023/08/19/andy-larsen-mike-lee-aoc-are/

Larson, H. J. (2020). *Stuck: How vaccine rumors start—and why they don't go away*. Oxford University Press.

Larson, R. B. (2019). Controlling social desirability bias—Ronald B. Larson, 2019. *International Journal of Market Research, 61*(5), 534–547. https://doi.org/10/ggq27d

Lasorsa, D. L. (1991). Political outspokenness: Factors working against the spiral of silence. *Journalism Quarterly, 68*(1–2), 131–140. https://doi.org/10/dqc62r

Lawson, M. A., & Kakkar, H. (2022). Of pandemics, politics, and personality: The role of conscientiousness and political ideology in the sharing of fake news. *Journal of Experimental Psychology: General, 151*(5), 1154–1177. https://doi.org/10/gnk2q8

Lazić, A., & Žeželj, I. (2021). A systematic review of narrative interventions: Lessons for countering anti-vaccination conspiracy theories and misinformation. *Public Understanding of Science, 30*(6), 644–670. https://doi.org/10.1177/09636625211011881

Leary, M. R., & Kowalski, R. M. (1990). Impression management: A literature review and two-component model. *Psychological Bulletin, 107*, 34–47. https://doi.org/10/dxcrb9

Lee, S. Y., & Seo, Y. (2023). Does tone of comments matter?: Exploring the role of uncivil comments and political orientation on weakening belief in fake news and eliciting anger. *Communication Studies, 74*(6), 515–531. https://doi.org/10.1080/10510974.2023.2246210

Lehmann, B. A., Ruiter, R. A. C., Chapman, G., & Kok, G. (2014). The intention to get vaccinated against influenza and actual vaccination uptake of Dutch healthcare personnel. *Vaccine*, 32(51), 6986–6991. https://doi.org/10.1016/j.vaccine.2014.10.034

Leiserowitz, A., Maibach, E., Rosenthal, S., Kotcher, J., Neyens, L., Marlon, J., Carman, J., Lacroix, K., & Goldberg, M. (2022, January 12). Global warming's six Americas, September 2021. Yale Program on Climate Change Communication. https://climatecommunication.yale.edu/publications/global-warmings-six-americas-september-2021/

Levendusky, M. (2023). *Our common bonds: Using what Americans share to help bridge the partisan divide*. University of Chicago Press.

Lewandowski, D., & Kammerer, Y. (2021). Factors influencing viewing behaviour on search engine results pages: A review of eye-tracking research. *Behaviour & Information Technology*, 40(14), 1485–1515. https://doi.org/10.1080/0144929X.2020.1761450

Lewandowsky, S., Cook, J., & Lombardi, D. (2020). *Debunking handbook 2020* [dataset]. Databrary. https://doi.org/10.17910/B7.1182

Lewandowsky, S., Cook, J., Schmid, P., Holford, D., Finn, A., Lombardi, D., Al-Rawi, A., Thomson, A., Leask, J., Juanchich, M., Anderson, E., Sah, S., Vraga, E. K., Gavaruzzi, T., Rapp, D., Amazeen, M., Sinatra, G., Kendeou, P., Armaos, K., . . . Hahn, U. (2022). The COVID-19 vaccine communication handbook. A practical guide for improving vaccine communication and fighting misinformation. https://open.bu.edu/handle/2144/44893

Lewandowsky, S., Ecker, U. K. H., Seifert, C. M., Schwarz, N., & Cook, J. (2012). Misinformation and its correction: Continued influence and successful debiasing. *Psychological Science in the Public Interest*, 13(3), 106–131. https://doi.org/10/gdkxfw

Lewandowsky, S., & van der Linden, S. (2021). Countering misinformation and fake news through inoculation and prebunking. *European Review of Social Psychology*, 32(2), 348–384. https://doi.org/10/gh4sd8

Lewis, S. C., Zamith, R., & Coddington, M. (2020). Online harassment and its implications for the journalist–audience relationship. *Digital Journalism*, 8(8), 1047–1067. https://doi.org/10.1080/21670811.2020.1811743

Li, J., & Wagner, M. W. (2020). The value of not knowing: Partisan cue-taking and belief updating of the uninformed, the ambiguous, and the misinformed. *Journal of Communication*, 70(5), 646–669. https://doi.org/10.1093/joc/jqaa022

Liedke, J., & Gottfried. (2022, October 27). U.S. adults under 30 now trust information from social media almost as much as from national news outlets. Pew Research Center. https://www.pewresearch.org/short-reads/2022/10/27/u-s-adults-under-30-now-trust-information-from-social-media-almost-as-much-as-from-national-news-outlets/

Lippmann, W. (1922). *Public opinion*. New York: Macmillan.

Liu, S., Guo, L., Mays, K., Betke, M., & Wijaya, D. T. (2019). Detecting Frames in News Headlines and Its Application to Analyzing News Framing Trends Surrounding U.S. Gun Violence. *Proceedings of the 23rd Conference on Computational Natural Language Learning (CoNLL)* (pp. 504–514). https://doi.org/10.18653/v1/K19-1047

Lomas, N. (2021, April 29). EU adopts rules on one-hour takedowns for terrorist content. *TechCrunch*. https://techcrunch.com/2021/04/29/eu-adopts-rules-on-one-hour-takedowns-for-terrorist-content/

London, D. A., Andelman, S. M., Christiano, A. V., Kim, J. H., Hausman, M. R., & Kim, J. M. (2019). Is Wikipedia a complete and accurate source for musculoskeletal anatomy? *Surgical and Radiologic Anatomy*, 41(10), 1187–1192. https://doi.org/10.1007/s00276-019-02280-1

Lopez, J., & Hillygus, D. S. (2018). Why so serious?: Survey trolls and misinformation. SSRN Scholarly Paper 3131087. https://doi.org/10.2139/ssrn.3131087

Lorenz-Spreen, P., Lewandowsky, S., Sunstein, C. R., & Hertwig, R. (2020). How behavioural sciences can promote truth, autonomy and democratic discourse online. *Nature Human Behaviour*, 4(11), Article 11. https://doi.org/10.1038/s41562-020-0889-7

Lukoff, K., Lyngs, U., Zade, H., Liao, J. V., Choi, J., Fan, K., Munson, S. A., & Hiniker, A. (2021). How the design of YouTube influences user sense of agency. *Proceedings of the 2021 CHI Conference on Human Factors in Computing Systems*, 1–17. https://doi.org/10.1145/3411764.3445467

Lyons, B. A., Mérola, V., Reifler, J., Spälti, A. K., Stedtnitz, C., & Stoeckel, F. (2023). When experts matter: Variations in consensus messaging for vaccine and genetically modified organism safety. *Public Understanding of Science*. https://doi.org/10.1177/09636625231188594

Lyons, B. A., Mérola, V., Reifler, J., & Stoeckel, F. (2020). How politics shape views toward fact-checking: Evidence from six European countries. *International Journal of Press/Politics, 25*(3), 469–492. https://doi.org/10.1177/1940161220921732

Ma, Y., He, B., Subrahmanian, N., & Kumar, S. (2023). Characterizing and predicting social correction on Twitter. *Proceedings of the 15th ACM Web Science Conference 2023*, 86–95. https://doi.org/10.1145/3578503.3583610

Mackay, A. I. M. (2020, December 26). The Swiss cheese infographic that went viral. *Virology Down Under*. https://virologydownunder.com/the-swiss-cheese-infographic-that-went-viral/

Maibach, E., Frumkin, H., & Ahdoot, S. (2021). Health professionals and the climate crisis: Trusted voices, essential roles. *World Medical & Health Policy, 13*(1), 137–145. https://doi.org/10/gr6kz7

Majerczak, P., & Strzelecki, A. (2022). Trust, media credibility, social ties, and the intention to share towards information verification in an age of fake news. *Behavioral Sciences, 12*(2), Article 2. https://doi.org/10.3390/bs12020051

Malhotra, P. (2023). Misinformation in WhatsApp family groups: Generational perceptions and correction considerations in a meso-news space. *Digital Journalism, 12*(5), 594–612. https://doi.org/10.1080/21670811.2023.2213731

Margolin, D. B., Hannak, A., & Weber, I. (2018). Political fact-checking on Twitter: When do corrections have an effect? *Political Communication, 35*(2), 196–219. https://doi.org/10/cv28

Marks, G. (2022, February 21). Big brands are jumping into the metaverse—will their bet pay off? *The Guardian*. https://www.theguardian.com/business/2022/feb/20/metaverse-profit-small-business-big-brands

Marsden, C., Meyer, T., & Brown, I. (2020). Platform values and democratic elections: How can the law regulate digital disinformation? *Computer Law & Security Review, 36*, 105373. https://doi.org/10/ggjt4w

Martel, C., & Rand, D. G. (2023). Misinformation warning labels are widely effective: A review of warning effects and their moderating features. *Current Opinion in Psychology, 54*, 101710. https://doi.org/10.1016/j.copsyc.2023.101710

Maruf, R. (2022, February 26). Meta and YouTube demonetize Russian state media. CNN. https://www.cnn.com/2022/02/26/tech/meta-youtube-facebook-rt-demonetize

Marwick, A. E., & boyd, D. (2011). I tweet honestly, I tweet passionately: Twitter users, context collapse, and the imagined audience. *New Media & Society, 13*(1), 114–133. https://doi.org/10/ffn6sf

Mason, L. (2018). *Uncivil agreement: How politics became our identity*. University of Chicago Press.

Masullo, G. M., & Kim, J. (2021). Exploring "angry" and "like" reactions on uncivil Facebook comments that correct misinformation in the news. *Digital Journalism, 9*(8), 1103–1122. https://doi.org/10.1080/21670811.2020.1835512

Matias, J. N., Simko, T., & Reddan. (2020, June 25). Study results: Reducing the silencing role of harassment in online feminism discussions. Citizens and Technology Lab. https://citizensandtech.org/2020/06/reducing-harassment-impacts-in-feminism-online/

Matthes, J., Knoll, J., & von Sikorski, C. (2018). The "spiral of silence" revisited: A meta-analysis on the relationship between perceptions of opinion support and political opinion expression. *Communication Research, 45*(1), 3–33. https://doi.org/10/gcv7n4

Matthes, J., Rios Morrison, K., & Schemer, C. (2010). A spiral of silence for some: Attitude certainty and the expression of political minority opinions. *Communication Research*, 37(6), 774–800. https://doi.org/10/cxj7z3

May, T. (2020). Anti-vaxxers, politicization of science, and the need for trust in pandemic response. *Journal of Health Communication*, 25(10), 761–763. https://doi.org/10.1080/10810730.2020.1864519

McCorvey, J. J. (2023, February 10). Tech layoffs shrink "trust and safety" teams, raising fears of backsliding efforts to curb online abuse. NBC News. https://www.nbcnews.com/tech/tech-news/tech-layoffs-hit-trust-safety-teams-raising-fears-backsliding-efforts-rcna69111

McDonnell, P. J., & Sanchez, C. (2018, September 21). When fake news kills: Lynchings in Mexico are linked to viral child-kidnap rumors. *Los Angeles Times*. https://www.latimes.com/world/la-fg-mexico-vigilantes-20180921-story.html

McKeever, B. W., & McKeever, R. (2019, September 13). Anti-vaccination mothers have outsized voice on social media—pro-vaccination parents could make a difference. *The Conversation*. http://theconversation.com/anti-vaccination-mothers-have-outsized-voice-on-social-media-pro-vaccination-parents-could-make-a-difference-120572

McMahon, L., Kleinman, Z., & Subramanian, C. (2025, January 7). Meta to replace "biased" fact-checkers with moderation by users. BBC. https://www.bbc.com/news/articles/cly74mpy8klo

McPhedran, R., Ratajczak, M., Mawby, M., King, E., Yang, Y., & Gold, N. (2023). Psychological inoculation protects against the social media infodemic. *Scientific Reports*, 13(1), Article 1. https://doi.org/10.1038/s41598-023-32962-1

Médecins Sans Frontières. (2015, September 4). Global health community slithers away from snakebite crisis as antivenom runs out. Médecins Sans Frontières (MSF) International. https://www.msf.org/global-health-community-slithers-away-snakebite-crisis-antivenom-runs-out

Merchant, N. (2022, December 20). Congress moves to ban TikTok from US government devices. AP News. https://apnews.com/article/technology-politics-d33e58c76bb3c13297c72816ef4e6231

Mercier, H. (2016). The argumentative theory: Predictions and empirical evidence. *Trends in Cognitive Sciences*, 20(9), 689–700. https://doi.org/10.1016/j.tics.2016.07.001

Merkley, E. (2020). Are experts (news)worthy? Balance, conflict, and mass media coverage of expert consensus. *Political Communication*, 37(4), 530–549. https://doi.org/10.1080/10584609.2020.1713269

Meta. (2023a). Bullying and harassment: Transparency Center. https://transparency.fb.com/policies/community-standards/bullying-harassment/

Meta. (2023b). Violence and incitement: Transparency Center. https://transparency.fb.com/policies/community-standards/violence-incitement/

Meta. (2024, January 9). New protections to give teens more age-appropriate experiences on our apps. https://about.fb.com/news/2024/01/teen-protections-age-appropriate-experiences-on-our-apps/

Meta. (2024, March). *Misinformation | Transparency Center*. https://transparency.fb.com/policies/community-standards/misinformation

Metz, C. (2023, November 6). Chatbots may "hallucinate" more often than many realize. *New York Times*. https://www.nytimes.com/2023/11/06/technology/chatbots-hallucination-rates.html

Micallef, N., He, B., Kumar, S., Ahamad, M., & Memon, N. (2020). The role of the crowd in countering misinformation: A case study of the COVID-19 infodemic. *2020 IEEE International Conference on Big Data (Big Data)*, 748–757. https://doi.org/10/gr6kx3

Milano, S., Taddeo, M., & Floridi, L. (2020). Recommender systems and their ethical challenges. *AI & SOCIETY*, 35(4), 957–967. https://doi.org/10.1007/s00146-020-00950-y

Miller, D. T. (2023). A century of pluralistic ignorance: What we have learned about its origins, forms, and consequences. *Frontiers in Social Psychology, 1.* https://doi.org/10.3389/frsps. 2023.1260896

Miller, K. C. (2023). Harassment's toll on democracy: The effects of harassment towards US journalists. *Journalism Practice, 17*(8), 1607–1626. https://doi.org/10.1080/17512786.2021. 2008809

Mitchell, A., Gottfried, J., Stocking, G., Walker, M., & Fedeli, S. (2019, June 5). Many Americans say made-up news is a critical problem that needs to be fixed. Pew Research Center's Journalism Project. https://www.pewresearch.org/journalism/2019/06/05/many-americans-say-made-up-news-is-a-critical-problem-that-needs-to-be-fixed/

Mo, P. K. H., Wong, C. H. W., & Lam, E. H. K. (2019). Can the health belief model and moral responsibility explain influenza vaccination uptake among nurses? *Journal of Advanced Nursing, 75*(6), 1188–1206. https://doi.org/10.1111/jan.13894

Monahan, B., & Ettinger, M. (2018). News media and disasters: Navigating old challenges and new opportunities in the digital age. In H. Rodríguez, W. Donner, & J. E. Trainor (Eds.), *Handbook of Disaster Research* (pp. 479–495). Springer International Publishing.

Montgomery, J. M., Nyhan, B., & Torres, M. (2018). How conditioning on posttreatment variables can ruin your experiment and what to do about it. *American Journal of Political Science, 62*(3), 760–775. https://doi.org/10.1111/ajps.12357

Moore, M. (2017). Inquiry into fake news. Londres: King's College London's. Centre for the Study of Media, Communication and Power. Recuperado de Https://Bit.Ly/2SlDsuM.

Morrison, S. (2023, February 23). Section 230, the internet law that's under threat, explained. *Vox.* https://www.vox.com/recode/2020/5/28/21273241/section-230-explained-supreme-court-social-media

Mosleh, M., Cole, R., & Rand, D. G. (2024). Misinformation and harmful language are interconnected, rather than distinct, challenges. *PNAS Nexus, 3*(3), pgae111. https://doi.org/10. 1093/pnasnexus/pgae111

Mourali, M., & Drake, C. (2022). The challenge of debunking health misinformation in dynamic social media conversations: Online randomized study of public masking during COVID-19. *Journal of Medical Internet Research, 24*(3), e34831. https://doi.org/10.2196/34831

Mozur, P. (2018, October 15). A genocide incited on Facebook, with posts from Myanmar's military. *New York Times.* https://www.nytimes.com/2018/10/15/technology/myanmar-facebook-genocide.html

Müller, P., & Schulz, A. (2019). Facebook or Fakebook? How users' perceptions of "fake news" are related to their evaluation and verification of news on Facebook. *Studies in Communication and Media, 8*(4), 547–559. https://doi.org/10.5771/2192-4007-2019-4-547

Mundt, M., Ross, K., & Burnett, C. M. (2018). Scaling social movements through social media: The case of Black Lives Matter. *Social Media + Society, 4*(4), 2056305118807911. https://doi.org/10/ght284

Mustafaraj, E., Finn, S., Whitlock, C., & Metaxas, P. T. (2011). Vocal minority versus silent majority: Discovering the opinions of the long tail. *2011 IEEE Third International Conference on Privacy, Security, Risk and Trust and 2011 IEEE Third International Conference on Social Computing,* 103–110. https://doi.org/10.1109/PASSAT/SocialCom.2011.188

Mutz, D. C. (1998). *Impersonal influence: How perceptions of mass collectives affect political attitudes.* Cambridge University Press.

Mutz, D. C. (2006). *Hearing the other side: Deliberative versus participatory democracy.* Cambridge University Press.

Mutz, D. C. (2008). Is deliberative democracy a falsifiable theory? *Annu. Rev. Polit. Sci., 11,* 521–538. https://doi.org/10.1146/annurev.polisci.11.081306.070308

Nadeem, R. (2022, February 9). Increasing public criticism, confusion over COVID-19 response in U.S. Pew Research Center Science & Society. https://www.pewresearch.org/science/2022/02/09/increasing-public-criticism-confusion-over-covid-19-response-in-u-s/

Nagler, R. H. (2014). Adverse outcomes associated with media exposure to contradictory nutrition messages. *Journal of Health Communication, 19*(1), 24–40. https://doi.org/10.1080/10810730.2013.798384

Nagler, R. H., Vogel, R. I., Gollust, S. E., Yzer, M. C., & Rothman, A. J. (2022). Effects of prior exposure to conflicting health information on responses to subsequent unrelated health messages: Results from a population-based longitudinal experiment. *Annals of Behavioral Medicine, 56*(5), 498–511. https://doi.org/10.1093/abm/kaab069

Nan, X., Wang, Y., & Thier, K. (2022). Why do people believe health misinformation and who is at risk? A systematic review of individual differences in susceptibility to health misinformation. *Social Science & Medicine, 314,* 115398. https://doi.org/10/gr6k3p

Naylor, B. (2017, November 29). *Trump retweets incendiary anti-Muslim videos from controversial group.* NPR. https://www.npr.org/2017/11/29/567159205/trump-retweets-incendiary-anti-muslim-videos-from-controversial-group

Nederhof, A. J. (1985). Methods of coping with social desirability bias: A review. *European Journal of Social Psychology, 15*(3), 263–280. https://doi.org/10.1002/ejsp.2420150303

Nelson, J. L. (2023). "Worse than the harassment itself." Journalists' reactions to newsroom social media policies. *Digital Journalism, 11*(8), 1456–1474. https://doi.org/10.1080/21670811.2022.2153072

Neuwirth, K., Frederick, E., & Mayo, C. (2007). The spiral of silence and fear of osolation. *Journal of Communication, 57*(3), 450–468. https://doi.org/10/cd26jw

NewsGuard Ratings. (2022). NewsGuard. https://www.newsguardtech.com/solutions/newsguard/

Neyman, C. (2017). A survey of addictive software design. *Computer Science and Software Engineering.* https://digitalcommons.calpoly.edu/cscsp/111

Nielsen, J. (2006, October 8). Participation inequality: The 90–9–1 rule for social features. Nielsen Norman Group. https://www.nngroup.com/articles/participation-inequality/

Nielsen, R. K., & Ganter, S. A. (2022). *The power of platforms: Shaping media and society.* Oxford University Press.

Nielsen, R. K., & Graves, L. (2017). "News you don't believe": Audience perspectives on fake news. Reuters Institute for the Study of Jounalism. https://ora.ox.ac.uk/objects/uuid:6eff4d14-bc72-404d-b78a-4c2573459ab8

Nielsen, U. H., Tyran, J.-R., & Wengström, E. (2014). Second thoughts on free riding. *Economics Letters, 122*(2), 136–139. https://doi.org/10.1016/j.econlet.2013.11.021

Nisbet, M. C., & Kotcher, J. E. (2009). A two-step flow of influence?: Opinion-leader campaigns on climate change. *Science Communication, 30*(3), 328–354. https://doi.org/10.1177/1075547008328797

Noble, S. U. (2018). *Algorithms of oppression: How search engines reinforce racism.* New York University Press.

Noelle-Neumann, E. (1974). The spiral of silence A theory of public opinion. *Journal of Communication, 24*(2), 43–51. https://doi.org/10.1111/j.1460-2466.1974.tb00367.x

Nölleke, D., Leonhardt, B. M., & Hanusch, F. (2023). "The chilling effect": Medical scientists' responses to audience feedback on their media appearances during the COVID-19 pandemic. *Public Understanding of Science, 32*(5), 546–560. https://doi.org/10.1177/09636625221146749

Nonnecke, B., & Preece, J. (2000). Lurker demographics: Counting the silent. *Proceedings of the SIGCHI Conference on Human Factors in Computing Systems,* 73–80. https://doi.org/10/frtbs9

Norman, P., Conner, M., & Bell, R. (1999). The theory of planned behavior and smoking cessation. *Health Psychology, 18*(1), 89–94. https://doi.org/10.1037/0278-6133.18.1.89

Norris, P. (2022). *In praise of skepticism: Trust but verify.* Oxford University Press.

Novach, M., & Ropek. (2024, May 28). The worst Google AI answers so far. Yahoo Tech. https://www.yahoo.com/tech/glue-topped-pizza-zombie-presidents-130000505.html

Nyborg, K., Anderies, J. M., Dannenberg, A., Lindahl, T., Schill, C., Schlüter, M., Adger, W. N., Arrow, K. J., Barrett, S., Carpenter, S., Chapin, F. S., Crépin, A.-S., Daily, G., Ehrlich, P.,

Folke, C., Jager, W., Kautsky, N., Levin, S. A., Madsen, O. J., . . . de Zeeuw, A. (2016). Social norms as solutions. *Science, 354*(6308), 42–43. https://doi.org/10.1126/science. aaf8317

Nyhan, B. (2021). Why the backfire effect does not explain the durability of political misperceptions. *Proceedings of the National Academy of Sciences, 118(15)*. https://doi.org/10.1073/ pnas.1912440117

Nyhan, B., Porter, E., Reifler, J., & Wood, T. J. (2020). Taking fact-checks literally but not seriously? The effects of journalistic fact-checking on factual beliefs and candidate favorability. *Political Behavior, 42*(3), 939–960. https://doi.org/10.1007/s11109-019- 09528-x

Nyhan, B., & Reifler, J. (2010). When corrections fail: The persistence of political misperceptions. *Political Behavior, 32*(2), 303–330. https://doi.org/10.1007/s11109-010-9112-2

Nyhan, B., & Reifler, J. (2015). Does correcting myths about the flu vaccine work? An experimental evaluation of the effects of corrective information. *Vaccine, 33*(3), 459–464. https://doi.org/ 10.1016/j.vaccine.2014.11.017

Ognyanova, K., Lazer, D., Baum, M. A., Druckman, J., Green, J., Perlis, R. H., Santillana, M., Lin, J., Simonson, M., & Uslu, A. (2021). Vaccine Misinformation, from Uncertainty to Resistance. The COVID States Project. https://www.covidstates.org/reports/covid-19-vaccine- misinformation-from-uncertainty-to-resistance

Ophir, Y., Romer, D., Jamieson, P. E., & Jamieson, K. H. (2020). Counteracting misleading proto-bacco YouTube videos: The effects of text-based and narrative correction interventions and the role of identification. *International Journal of Communication, 14*, 4973–4988.

Oreskes, N., & Conway, E. M. (2019). *Merchants of doubt: How a handful of scientists obscured the truth on issues from tobacco smoke to climate change* (2nd ed.). Bloomsbury Publishing.

Ortiz-Ospina, E., Roser, M., & Arriagada, P. (2024). Trust. Our World in Data. https:// ourworldindata.org/trust

Ozoma, I. (2019, August 28). Bringing authoritative vaccine results to Pinterest search. Pinterest Newsroom. https://newsroom.pinterest.com/en/post/bringing-authoritative-vaccine- results-to-pinterest-search

Pavliuc, A., George, A., Spezzano, F., Giachanou, A., Spaiser, V., & Bright, J. (2023). Editorial: Multidisciplinary approaches to mis- and disinformation studies. *Social Media + Society, 9*(1), 20563051221150405. https://doi.org/10.1177/20563051221150405

Pearce, K. E., & Malhotra, P. (2022). Inaccuracies and *Izzat*: Channel affordances for the consideration of face in misinformation correction. *Journal of Computer-Mediated Communication, 27*(2), zmac004. https://doi.org/10/gr6kvb

Pennycook, G., Epstein, Z., Mosleh, M., Arechar, A. A., Eckles, D., & Rand, D. G. (2021). Shifting attention to accuracy can reduce misinformation online. *Nature, 592*(7855), 590–595. https://doi.org/10.1038/s41586-021-03344-2

Pennycook, G., McPhetres, J., Zhang, Y., Lu, J. G., & Rand, D. G. (2020). Fighting COVID-19 misinformation on social media: Experimental evidence for a scalable accuracy-nudge intervention. *Psychological Science, 31*(7), 770–780. https://doi.org/10.1177/0956797620939054

Pennycook, G., & Rand, D. G. (2019). Lazy, not biased: Susceptibility to partisan fake news is better explained by lack of reasoning than by motivated reasoning. *Cognition, 188*, 39–50. https://doi.org/10.1016/j.cognition.2018.06.011

Perloff, R. M. (1999). The third person effect: A critical review and synthesis. *Media Psychology, 1*(4), 353–378. https://doi.org/10.1207/s1532785xmep0104_4

Peterson, J. S., Swire-Thompson, B., & Johnson, S. B. (2020). What is the alternative? Responding strategically to cancer misinformation. *Future Oncology, 16*(25), 1883–1888. https://doi. org/10.2217/fon-2020-0440

Pollard, M. S., & Davis, L. M. (2022). Decline in trust in the centers for disease control and prevention during the COVID-19 pandemic. *Rand Health Quarterly, 9*(3), 23.

Pornpitakpan, C. (2004). The persuasiveness of source credibility: A critical review of five decades' evidence. *Journal of Applied Social Psychology, 34*(2), 243–281. https://doi.org/10/bx7bgj

Porter, E., Velez, Y., & Wood, T. J. (2022). Factual corrections eliminate false beliefs about COVID-19 vaccines. *Public Opinion Quarterly, 86*(3), 762–773. https://doi.org/10.1093/poq/nfac034

Porter, E., Velez, Y., & Wood, T. J. (2023). Correcting COVID-19 vaccine misinformation in 10 countries. *Royal Society Open Science, 10*(3), 221097. https://doi.org/10/gr2nzt

Porter, E., & Wood, T. J. (2019). *False alarm: The truth about political mistruths in the Trump era* (1st ed.). Cambridge University Press.

Porter, E., & Wood, T. J. (2021). The global effectiveness of fact-checking: Evidence from simultaneous experiments in Argentina, Nigeria, South Africa, and the United Kingdom. *Proceedings of the National Academy of Sciences, 118*(37), e2104235118. https://doi.org/10/gmtkzk

Posetti, J., Shabbir, N., Maynard, D., Bontcheva, K., & Aboulez, N. (2022). The chilling: Assessing big tech's response to online violence against women journalists. UNESCO. https://unesdoc.unesco.org/ark:/48223/pf0000383044.locale=en

Powers, E., Koliska, M., & Guha, P. (2019). "Shouting Matches and Echo Chambers": Perceived Identity Threats and Political Self-Censorship on Social Media. *International Journal of Communication, 13*, 3630–3649.

Priedhorsky, R., Chen, J., Lam, S. (Tony), K., Panciera, K., Terveen, L., & Riedl, J. (2007). Creating, destroying, and restoring value in wikipedia. *Proceedings of the 2007 ACM International Conference on Supporting Group Work*, 259–268. https://doi.org/10.1145/1316624.1316663

Prieger, J. E. (2003). The supply side of the digital divide: Is there equal availability in the broadband internet access market? *Economic Inquiry, 41*(2), 346–363. https://doi.org/10/cphpn6

Prior, M. (2009a). Improving media effects research through better measurement of news exposure. *Journal of Politics, 71*(3), 893–908. https://doi.org/10.1017/S0022381609090781

Prior, M. (2009b). The immensely inflated news audience: Assessing bias in self-reported news exposure. *Public Opinion Quarterly, 73*(1), 130–143. https://doi.org/10.1093/poq/nfp002

Prior, M., Sood, G., & Khanna, K. (2015). You cannot be serious: The impact of accuracy incentives on partisan bias in reports of economic perceptions. *Quarterly Journal of Political Science, 10*(4), 489–518. https://doi.org/10/f73wkr

Prosocial Design Network. (2021). Prosocial Design Network. https://www.prosocialdesign.org//

Pundir, V., Devi, E. B., & Nath, V. (2021). Arresting fake news sharing on social media: A theory of planned behavior approach. *Management Research Review, 44*(8), 1108–1138. https://doi.org/10.1108/MRR-05-2020-0286

Pyszczynski, T., & Greenberg, J. (1987). Toward an integration of cognitive and motivational perspectives on social inference: A biased hypothesis-testing model. In L. Berkowitz (Ed.), *Advances in Experimental Social Psychology* (pp. 297–340). Academic Press.

Quan-Haase, A., Mendes, K., Ho, D., Lake, O., Nau, C., & Pieber, D. (2021). Mapping #MeToo: A synthesis review of digital feminist research across social media platforms. *New Media & Society, 23*(6), 1700–1720. https://doi.org/10.1177/1461444820984457

Rademacher, C. (2016, November 9). Presidential Badgers. Wisconsin Alumni Association. https://www.uwalumni.com/news/presidential-badgers/

Rath, B., Gao, W., Ma, J., & Srivastava, J. (2018). Utilizing computational trust to identify rumor spreaders on Twitter. *Social Network Analysis and Mining, 8*(1), 64. https://doi.org/10/gh4fgf

Reason, J., Broadbent, D. E., Baddeley, A. D., & Reason, J. (1990). The contribution of latent human failures to the breakdown of complex systems. *Philosophical Transactions of the Royal Society of London. B, Biological Sciences, 327*(1241), 475–484. https://doi.org/10.1098/rstb.1990.0090

Redlawsk, D. P. (2006). Motivated reasoning, affect, and the role of memory in voter decision making. In D. P. Redlawsk (Ed.), *Feeling Politics: Emotion in Political Information Processing* (pp. 87–107). Palgrave Macmillan.

Redlawsk, D. P., Civettini, A. J. W., & Emmerson, K. M. (2010). The affective tipping point: Do motivated reasoners ever "get it"? *Political Psychology, 31*(4), 563–593. https://doi.org/10.1111/j.1467-9221.2010.00772.x

Reedy, J., Wells, C., & Gastil, J. (2014). How voters become misinformed: An investigation of the emergence and consequences of false factual beliefs. *Social Science Quarterly, 95*(5), 1399–1418. https://doi.org/10.1111/ssqu.12102

Reeves, B. (2017, April 25). Online fake news and hate speech are fueling tribal "genocide" in South Sudan. The World from PRX. https://theworld.org/stories/2017-04-25/online-fake-news-and-hate-speech-are-fueling-tribal-genocide-south-sudan

Rich, P. R., & Zaragoza, M. S. (2016). The continued influence of implied and explicitly stated misinformation in news reports. *Journal of Experimental Psychology: Learning, Memory, and Cognition, 42*(1), 62–74. https://doi.org/10.1037/xlm0000155

Riker, W. H., & Ordeshook, P. C. (1968). A theory of the calculus of voting. *American Political Science Review, 62*(1), 25–42. https://doi.org/10.2307/1953324

Robertson, R. E., Williams, E. M., Carley, K. M., & Thiel, D. (2025). Data Voids and Warning Banners on Google Search (arXiv:2502.17542). arXiv. https://doi.org/10.48550/arXiv.2502.17542

Robinson, S. (2023). *How journalists engage: A theory of trust building, identities, and care.* Oxford University Press.

Rojas, H. (2010). "Corrective" actions in the public sphere: How perceptions of media and media effects shape political behaviors. *International Journal of Public Opinion Research, 22*(3), 343–363. https://doi.org/10/b67p2g

Ronzhyn, A., Cardenal, A. S., & Batlle Rubio, A. (2022). Defining affordances in social media research: A literature review. *New Media & Society,* 146144482211351. https://doi.org/10.1177/14614448221135187

Roozenbeek, J., Linden, S. van der, & Nygren, T. (2020). Prebunking interventions based on "inoculation" theory can reduce susceptibility to misinformation across cultures. *Harvard Kennedy School Misinformation Review.* https://doi.org/10/gg8gs9

Rosenberg, J., & Egbert, N. (2011). Online impression management: Personality traits and concerns for secondary goals as predictors of self-presentation tactics on Facebook. *Journal of Computer-mediated Communication, 17*(1), 1–18.

Rosenstiel, T., Sonderman, J., Loker, K., Ivancin, M., & Kjarval, N. (2015). Twitter and the News: How people use the social network to learn about the world. American Press Institute. https://Www.Americanpressinstitute.Org/Publications/Reports/Survey-Research/How-People-Use-Twitter-News/Single-Page.

Rossini, P., Stromer-Galley, J., Baptista, E. A., & Veiga de Oliveira, V. (2021). Dysfunctional information sharing on WhatsApp and Facebook: The role of political talk, cross-cutting exposure and social corrections. *New Media & Society, 23*(8), 2430–2451. https://doi.org/10.1177/1461444820928059

Roth, E. (2023, June 2). YouTube will stop removing false presidential election fraud claims. The Verge. https://www.theverge.com/2023/6/2/23747104/youtube-election-misinformation-policy-reversal

Rousseau, A. (2021). Adolescents' selfie-activities and idealized online self-presentation: An application of the sociocultural model. *Body Image, 36,* 16–26. https://doi.org/10.1016/j.bodyim.2020.10.005

Saks, E., & Tyson, A. (2022). Americans report more engagement with science news than in 2017. Pew Research Center. https://www.pewresearch.org/short-reads/2022/11/10/americans-report-more-engagement-with-science-news-than-in-2017/

Samples, J. (2019). Why the government should not regulate content moderation of social media. Cato Institute. https://www.cato.org/policy-analysis/why-government-should-not-regulate-content-moderation-social-media

Sander, M., Sander, M., Burbidge, T., & Beecker, J. (2020). The efficacy and safety of sunscreen use for the prevention of skin cancer. *CMAJ: Canadian Medical Association Journal, 192*(50), E1802–E1808. https://doi.org/10.1503/cmaj.201085

Sanderson, J. A., Bowden, V., Swire-Thompson, B., Lewandowsky, S., & Ecker, U. K. H. (2022). Listening to misinformation while driving: Cognitive load and the effectiveness of (repeated) corrections. *Journal of Applied Research in Memory and Cognition, 12*(3), 325–334. https://doi.org/10.1037/mac0000057

Schaefer, C., Coyne, J. C., & Lazarus, R. S. (1981). The health-related functions of social support. *Journal of Behavioral Medicine, 4*(4), 381–406. https://doi.org/10.1007/BF00846149

Schäfer, T., & Schwarz, M. A. (2019). The meaningfulness of effect sizes in psychological research: Differences between sub-disciplines and the impact of potential biases. *Frontiers in Psychology, 10.* https://doi.org/10.3389/fpsyg.2019.00813

Schaffner, B. F., & Luks, S. (2018). Misinformation or expressive responding? What an inauguration crowd can tell us about the source of political misinformation in surveys. *Public Opinion Quarterly, 82*(1), 135–147. https://doi.org/10.1093/poq/nfx042

Schaffner, B. F., & Roche, C. (2017). Misinformation and motivated reasoning: Responses to economic news in a politicized environment. *Public Opinion Quarterly, 81*(1), 86–110. https://doi.org/10.1093/poq/nfw043

Scharf, N. (2024, January 11). Can the EU's Digital Services Act inspire US tech regulation? https://www.thenation.com/?post_type=article&p=480107

Schmid, P., & Betsch, C. (2019). Effective strategies for rebutting science denialism in public discussions. *Nature Human Behaviour, 3*(9), Article 9. https://doi.org/10.1038/s41562-019-0632-4

Schmid, P., Rauber, D., Betsch, C., Lidolt, G., & Denker, M.-L. (2017). Barriers of influenza vaccination intention and behavior: A systematic review of influenza vaccine hesitancy, 2005–2016. *PLOS ONE, 12*(1), e0170550. https://doi.org/10.1371/journal.pone.0170550

Schmidt, A. L., Zollo, F., Scala, A., Betsch, C., & Quattrociocchi, W. (2018). Polarization of the vaccination debate on Facebook. *Vaccine, 36*(25), 3606–3612. https://doi.org/10.1016/j.vaccine.2018.05.040

Schudson, M. (1997). Why conversation is not the soul of democracy. *Critical Studies in Mass Communication, 14*(4), 297–309. https://doi.org/10.1080/15295039709367020

Schudson, M. (2003). *The sociology of news.* Norton.

Schulz, K. F., Altman, D. G., Moher, D., & Group, for the C. (2010). CONSORT 2010 statement: Updated guidelines for reporting parallel group randomised trials. *PLOS Medicine, 7*(3), e1000251. https://doi.org/10.1371/journal.pmed.1000251

Schwarz, N., & Oyserman, D. (2001). Asking questions about behavior: Cognition, communication, and questionnaire construction. *American Journal of Evaluation, 22*(2), 127–160. https://doi.org/10/drw7jk

Sears, D. O., & Freedman, J. L. (1967). Selective exposure to information: A critical review. *Public Opinion Quarterly, 31*(2), 194–213. https://doi.org/10.1086/267513

Sears, D. O., & Valentino, N. A. (1997). Politics matters: Political events as catalysts for preadult socialization. *American Political Science Review, 91*(1), 45–65. https://doi.org/10/fcq4bp

Sepúlveda-Torres, R., Vicente, M., Saquete, E., Lloret, E., & Palomar, M. (2021). Exploring Summarization to Enhance Headline Stance Detection. In E. Métais, F. Meziane, H. Horacek, & E. Kapetanios (Eds.), *Natural Language Processing and Information Systems* (pp. 243–254). Springer International Publishing. https://doi.org/10.1007/978-3-030-80599-9_22

Seo, H., Blomberg, M., Altschwager, D., & Vu, H. T. (2021). Vulnerable populations and misinformation: A mixed-methods approach to underserved older adults' online information assessment. *New Media & Society, 23*(7), 2012–2033. https://doi.org/10/gg9gtk

Serrano, J. (2022, September 22). Why did the FDA warn about Nyquil chicken so long after it went viral? Gizmodo. https://gizmodo.com/nyquil-chicken-fda-warning-late-misinformation-tiktok-1849569728

Shabayek, S., Vincent, E., & Théro, H. (2022). Digital platforms' governance: Missing data & information to monitor, audit & investigate platforms' misinformation interventions. https://sciencespo.hal.science/hal-03711842/document

Shahin, S., Nakahara, J., & Sánchez, M. (2021). Black Lives Matter goes global: Connective action meets cultural hybridity in Brazil, India, and Japan. *New Media & Society*, 14614448211057106. https://doi.org/10.1177/14614448211057106

Shapiro, I. (2014). Why democracies need a functional definition of journalism now more than ever. *Journalism Studies*, 15(5), 555–565. https://doi.org/10.1080/1461670X.2014.882483

Sharevski, F., Alsaadi, R., Jachim, P., & Pieroni, E. (2022). Misinformation warnings: Twitter's soft moderation effects on COVID-19 vaccine belief echoes. *Computers & Security, 114*, 102577. https://doi.org/10.1016/j.cose.2021.102577

Shearer, E. (2021, January 12). More than eight-in-ten Americans get news from digital devices. Pew Research Center. https://www.pewresearch.org/short-reads/2021/01/12/more-than-eight-in-ten-americans-get-news-from-digital-devices/

Shin, J., & Thorson, K. (2017). Partisan selective sharing: The biased diffusion of fact-checking messages on social media. *Journal of Communication, 67*(2), 233–255. https://doi.org/10.1111/jcom.12284

Shu, K., Sliva, A., Wang, S., Tang, J., & Liu, H. (2017). Fake news detection on social media: A data mining perspective. *ACM SIGKDD Explorations Newsletter, 19*(1), 22–36. https://doi.org/10.1145/3137597.3137600

Silva, M., Giovanini, L., Fernandes, J., Oliveira, D., & Silva, C. S. (2023). What makes disinformation ads engaging? A case study of Facebook ads from the Russian active measures campaign. *Journal of Interactive Advertising, 23*(3), 221–240. https://doi.org/10.1080/15252019.2023.2173991

Silverman, C., Lytvynenko, J., & Pham, S. (2017, December 28). These are 50 of the biggest fake news hits on Facebook in 2017. https://www.buzzfeednews.com/article/craigsilverman/these-are-50-of-the-biggest-fake-news-hits-on-facebook-in

Simon, F., Adami, M., Kahn, G., & Fletcher, R. (2024, June 6). How AI chatbots responded to basic questions about the 2024 European elections right before the vote. Reuters Institute for the Study of Journalism. https://reutersinstitute.politics.ox.ac.uk/news/how-ai-chatbots-responded-basic-questions-about-2024-european-elections-right-vote

Singh, L., Bode, L., Budak, C., Kawintiranon, K., Padden, C., & Vraga, E. K. (2020). Understanding high-and low-quality URL Sharing on COVID-19 Twitter streams. *Journal of Computational Social Science, 3*, 343–366. https://doi.org/10/gn82jk

Smalley, A. M., Seth. (2022, November 8). Elon Musk keeps Birdwatch alive—Under a new name. *Poynter*. https://www.poynter.org/ifcn/2022/elon-musk-keeps-birdwatch-alive-under-a-new-name/

Smith, C. N., & Seitz, H. H. (2019). Correcting misinformation about neuroscience via social media. *Science Communication*, 1075547019890073. https://doi.org/10.1177/1075547019890073

Smith, J. (2017, December 20). Designing against misinformation. *Medium*. https://medium.com/designatmeta/designing-against-misinformation-e5846b3aa1e2

Smith, V. A., Coffman, C. J., & Hudgens, M. G. (2021). Interpreting the results of intention-to-treat, per-protocol, and as-treated analyses of clinical trials. *JAMA, 326*(5), 433–434. https://doi.org/10.1001/jama.2021.2825

Snapchat. (2023). When does Snapchat delete Snaps and Chats? https://support.snapchat.com/en-US/article/when-are-snaps-chats-deleted

Sobieraj, S. (2020). *Credible threat: Attacks against women online and the future of democracy*. Oxford University Press.

Solomon, D. (2022, November 21). Why a Houston-area emergency room has a "snake bucket." *Texas Monthly*. https://www.texasmonthly.com/travel/houston-area-emergency-room-snake-bucket/

Song, H., So, J., Shim, M., Kim, J., Kim, E., & Lee, K. (2023). What message features influence the intention to share misinformation about COVID-19 on social media? The role of efficacy and novelty. *Computers in Human Behavior, 138*, 107439. https://doi.org/10.1016/j.chb.2022.107439

Song, Y., Kwon, K. H., Lu, Y., Fan, Y., & Li, B. (2021). The "parallel pandemic" in the context of China: The spread of rumors and rumor-corrections during COVID-19 in Chinese social media. *American Behavioral Scientist, 65*(14), 2014–2036. https://doi.org/10/gk649x

Sørensen, K., Pelikan, J. M., Röthlin, F., Ganahl, K., Slonska, Z., Doyle, G., Fullam, J., Kondilis, B., Agrafiotis, D., Uiters, E., Falcon, M., Mensing, M., Tchamov, K., Broucke, S. van den, Brand, H., & on behalf of the HLS-EU Consortium. (2015). Health literacy in Europe: Comparative results of the European health literacy survey (HLS-EU). *European Journal of Public Health, 25*(6), 1053–1058. https://doi.org/10.1093/eurpub/ckv043

Southwell, B. G., Brennen, J. S. B., Paquin, R., Boudewyns, V., & Zeng, J. (2022). Defining and measuring scientific misinformation. *ANNALS of the American Academy of Political and Social Science, 700*(1), 98–111. https://doi.org/10.1177/00027162221084709

Southwell, B. G., Niederdeppe, J., Cappella, J. N., Gaysynsky, A., Kelley, D. E., Oh, A., Peterson, E. B., & Chou, W.-Y. S. (2019). Misinformation as a misunderstood challenge to public health. *American Journal of Preventive Medicine, 57*(2), 282–285. https://doi.org/10/gjm96b

Stabile, B., Grant, A., Purohit, H., & Harris, K. (2019). Sex, lies, and stereotypes: Gendered implications of fake news for women in politics. *Public Integrity, 21*(5), 491–502. https://doi.org/10/gh4fbd

StatCounter. (2023, February). *Search Engine Market Share Worldwide.* StatCounter Global Stats. https://gs.statcounter.com/search-engine-market-share

SteelFisher, G. K., Findling, M. G., Caporello, H. L., Lubell, K. M., Vidoloff Melville, K. G., Lane, L., Boyea, A. A., Schafer, T. J., & Ben-Porath, E. N. (2023). Trust in US federal, state, and local public health agencies during COVID-19: Responses and policy implications. *Health Affairs, 42*(3), 328–337. https://doi.org/10.1377/hlthaff.2022.01204

Stencel, M., Ryan, E., & Luther, J. (2022, June 17). Fact-checkers extend their global reach with 391 outlets, but growth has slowed. Duke Reporters' Lab. https://reporterslab.org/fact-checkers-extend-their-global-reach-with-391-outlets-but-growth-has-slowed/

Stout, D. W. (2019, July 8). Social media statistics 2020: Top networks by the numbers. https://perma.cc/C8SP-7U2F

Stromback, J., Wikforss, A., Gluer, K., Lindholm, T., & Oscarsson, H. (Eds.). (2022). Knowledge resistance in high-choice information environments. https://www.routledge.com/Knowledge-Resistance-in-High-Choice-Information-Environments/Stromback-Wikforss-Gluer-Lindholm-Oscarsson/p/book/9780367629281

Stroud, N. J. (2017). Attention as a valuable resource. *Political Communication, 34*(3), 479–489. https://doi.org/10.1080/10584609.2017.1330077

Suarez-Lledo, V., & Alvarez-Galvez, J. (2021). Prevalence of health misinformation on social media: Systematic review. *Journal of Medical Internet Research, 23*(1), e17187. https://doi.org/10/gkmq3z

Sui, Y., & Zhang, B. (2021). Determinants of the perceived credibility of rebuttals concerning health misinformation. *International Journal of Environmental Research and Public Health, 18*(3), Article 3. https://doi.org/10.3390/ijerph18031345

Suler, J. (2004). The online disinhibition effect. *CyberPsychology & Behavior, 7*(3), 321–326. https://doi.org/10.1089/1094931041291295

Sülflow, M., Schäfer, S., & Winter, S. (2019). Selective attention in the news feed: An eye-tracking study on the perception and selection of political news posts on Facebook. *New Media & Society, 21*(1), 168–190. https://doi.org/10.1177/1461444818791520

Sun, N., Rau, P. P.-L., & Ma, L. (2014). Understanding lurkers in online communities: A literature review. *Computers in Human Behavior, 38*, 110–117. https://doi.org/10.1016/j.chb.2014.05.022

Sun, Y., Oktavianus, J., Wang, S., & Lu, F. (2022). The role of influence of presumed influence and anticipated guilt in evoking social correction of COVID-19 misinformation. *Health Communication, 37*(11), 1368–1377. https://doi.org/10/gh43ws

Sun, Y., Pan, Z., & Shen, L. (2008). Understanding the third-person perception: Evidence from a meta-analysis. *Journal of Communication, 58*(2), 280–300. https://doi.org/10.1111/j.1460-2466.2008.00385.x

Sunstein, C. R. (2018). *#Republic: Divided democracy in the age of social media.* Princeton University Press.

Swami, V. (2012). Social psychological origins of conspiracy theories: The case of the Jewish conspiracy theory in Malaysia. *Frontiers in Psychology, 3,* 280. https://doi.org/10.3389/fpsyg.2012.00280

Swire-Thompson, B., Cook, J., Butler, L. H., Sanderson, J. A., Lewandowsky, S., & Ecker, U. K. H. (2021). Correction format has a limited role when debunking misinformation. *Cognitive Research: Principles and Implications, 6*(1), 83. https://doi.org/10.1186/s41235-021-00346-6

Swire-Thompson, B., Dobbs, M., Thomas, A., & DeGutis, J. (2023). Memory failure predicts belief regression after the correction of misinformation. *Cognition, 230,* 105276. https://doi.org/10.1016/j.cognition.2022.105276

Swire-Thompson, B., Ecker, U. K. H., Lewandowsky, S., & Berinsky, A. J. (2020). They might be a liar but they're my liar: Source evaluation and the prevalence of misinformation. *Political Psychology, 41*(1), 21–34. https://doi.org/10.1111/pops.12586

Swire-Thompson, B., & Lazer, D. (2020). Public health and online misinformation: Challenges and recommendations. *Annual Review of Public Health, 41*(1), 433–451. https://doi.org/10/gg8966

Swire-Thompson, B., Miklaucic, N., Wihbey, J. P., Lazer, D., & DeGutis, J. (2022). The backfire effect after correcting misinformation is strongly associated with reliability. *Journal of Experimental Psychology: General, 151*(7), 1655–1665. https://doi.org/10.1037/xge0001131

Taber, C. S., & Lodge, M. (2006). Motivated skepticism in the evaluation of political beliefs. *American Journal of Political Science, 50*(3), 755–769. https://doi.org/10.1111/j.1540-5907.2006.00214.x

Talbot, M. (2016, September 28). Trump and the Truth: The "lying" media. *The New Yorker.* https://www.newyorker.com/news/news-desk/trump-and-the-truth-the-lying-media

Tambo, E., Djuikoue, I. C., Tazemda, G. K., Fotsing, M. F., & Zhou, X.-N. (2021). Early stage risk communication and community engagement (RCCE) strategies and measures against the coronavirus disease 2019 (COVID-19) pandemic crisis. *Global Health Journal, 5*(1), 44–50. https://doi.org/10.1016/j.glohj.2021.02.009

Tandoc, E. C., Lim, D., & Ling, R. (2020). Diffusion of disinformation: How social media users respond to fake news and why. *Journalism, 21*(3), 381–398. https://doi.org/10/ggcgpc

Tandoc, E. C., Lim, Z. W., & Ling, R. (2018). Defining "fake news." *Digital Journalism, 6*(2), 137–153. https://doi.org/10.1080/21670811.2017.1360143

Tang, R., Burnley, B., Bode, L., & Vraga, E. K. (forthcoming). Corrective democracy? The relationship between correction of misinformation on social media and connective democratic norms. Social Media + Society.

Tang, R., Vraga, E. K., Bode, L., & Boulianne, S. (2024). Who reports witnessing and performing corrections on social media in the United States, United Kingdom, Canada, and France? *Harvard Kennedy School Misinformation Review.* https://doi.org/10.37016/mr-2020-145

Tapp, A., Nancarrow, C., Davis, A., & Jones, S. (2016). Vicious or virtuous circles? Exploring the vulnerability of drivers to break low urban speed limits. *Transportation Research Part A: Policy and Practice, 91,* 195–212. https://doi.org/10.1016/j.tra.2016.06.007

Tewksbury, D., Weaver, A. J., & Maddex, B. D. (2001). Accidentally informed: Incidental news exposure on the world wide web. *Journalism and Mass Communication Quarterly, 78*(3), 533–554. https://doi.org/10.1177/107769900107800309

The White House. (2023, February 27). "No TikTok on government devices" implementation guidance. https://www.whitehouse.gov/wp-content/uploads/2023/02/M-23-13-No-TikTok-on-Government-Devices-Implementation-Guidance_final.pdf

Thakur, D., & Hankerson Madrigal, D. (2022). An Unrepresentative Democracy: How Disinformation and Online Abuse Hinder Women of Color Political Candidates in the United States.

Thomas, D. D. (2020). *Design for cognitive bias*. A Book Apart.

Thomas-Hunt, M. C., & Phillips, K. W. (2004). When what you know is not enough: Expertise and gender dynamics in task groups. *Personality and Social Psychology Bulletin, 30*(12), 1585–1598. https://doi.org/10.1177/0146167204271186

Thorburn, S., & Bogart, L. M. (2005). Conspiracy beliefs about birth control: Barriers to pregnancy prevention among African Americans of reproductive age. *Health Education & Behavior, 32*(4), 474–487. https://doi.org/10.1177/1090198105276220

Thorson, E. (2016). Belief echoes: The persistent effects of corrected misinformation. *Political Communication, 33*(3), 460–480. https://doi.org/10.1080/10584609.2015.1102187

Thorson, E. (2024). *The invented state: Policy misperceptions in the American public*. Oxford University Press.

Thorson, E., & Abdelaaty, L. (2023). Misperceptions about refugee policy. *American Political Science Review, 117*(3), 1123–1129. https://doi.org/10.1017/S0003055422000910

Thorson, K. (2014). Facing an uncertain reception: Young citizens and political interaction on Facebook. *Information, Communication & Society, 17*(2), 203–216. https://doi.org/10.1080/1369118X.2013.862563

Thorson, K. (2020). Attracting the news: Algorithms, platforms, and reframing incidental exposure. *Journalism*, 1464884920915352. https://doi.org/10.1177/1464884920915352

Thorson, K., Cotter, K., Medeiros, M., & Pak, C. (2021). Algorithmic inference, political interest, and exposure to news and politics on Facebook. *Information, Communication & Society, 24*(2), 183–200. https://doi.org/10/ggkz7z

Thorson, K., & Wells, C. (2016). Curated flows: A framework for mapping media exposure in the digital age. *Communication Theory, 26*(3), 309–328. https://doi.org/10/f878cg

Timberg, C., & Stanley-Becker, I. (2020, August 26). Black voters are being targeted in disinformation campaigns, echoing the 2016 Russian playbook. *Washington Post*. https://www.washingtonpost.com/technology/2020/08/26/race-divisions-highlighted-disinformation-2016/

Toff, B., & Nielsen, R. K. (2018). "I just google it": Folk theories of distributed discovery. *Journal of Communication, 68*(3), 636–657. https://doi.org/10.1093/joc/jqy009

Torres, R., Gerhart, N., & Negahban, A. (2018). Epistemology in the era of fake news: An exploration of information verification behaviors among social networking site users. *ACM SIGMIS Database: The DATABASE for Advances in Information Systems, 49*(3), 78–97. https://doi.org/10.1145/3242734.3242740

Tourangeau, R., & Yan, T. (2007). Sensitive questions in surveys. *Psychological Bulletin, 133*(5), 859–883. https://doi.org/10/fqchjm

Treem, J. W., & Leonardi, P. M. (2013). Social media use in organizations: Exploring the affordances of visibility, editability, persistence, and association. *Annals of the International Communication Association, 36*(1), 143–189. https://doi.org/10.1080/23808985.2013.11679130

Tripepi, G., Chesnaye, N. C., Dekker, F. W., Zoccali, C., & Jager, K. J. (2020). Intention to treat and per protocol analysis in clinical trials. *Nephrology, 25*(7), 513–517. https://doi.org/10.1111/nep.13709

Tully, M., Bode, L., & Vraga, E. K. (2020). Mobilizing users: Does exposure to misinformation and its correction affect users' responses to a health misinformation post? *Social Media + Society, 6*(4), 2056305120978377. https://doi.org/10/gm77hg

Tully, M., Vraga, E. K., & Bode, L. (2020). Designing and testing news literacy messages for social media. *Mass Communication and Society, 23*(1), 22–46. https://doi.org/10/ggnd5d

Turner Lee, N. (2018). Detecting racial bias in algorithms and machine learning. *Journal of Information, Communication and Ethics in Society, 16*(3), 252–260. https://doi.org/10.1108/JICES-06-2018-0056

Twitter. (2023, April). How Twitter handles abuse and harassment. Twitter Help. https://help. twitter.com/en/rules-and-policies/abusive-behavior

Udris, R. (2014). Cyberbullying among high school students in Japan: Development and validation of the online disinhibition scale. *Computers in Human Behavior, 41*, 253–261. https:// doi.org/10.1016/j.chb.2014.09.036

Uner, O., & Roediger, H. L. (2018). Are encoding/retrieval interactions in recall driven by remembering, knowing, or both? *Journal of Memory and Language, 103*, 44–57. https://doi.org/10. 1016/j.jml.2018.07.002

UNESCO. (2022). Finding the funds for journalism to thrive: Policy options to support media viability. UNESCO Digital Library. https://unesdoc.unesco.org/ark:/48223/pf0000381146. locale=en

Urman, A., Makhortykh, M., Ulloa, R., & Kulshrestha, J. (2022). Where the earth is flat and 9/11 is an inside job: A comparative algorithm audit of conspiratorial information in web search results. *Telematics and Informatics, 72*, 101860. https://doi.org/10.1016/j.tele.2022.101860

Uscinski, J. E., & Parent, J. M. (2014). *American conspiracy theories.* Oxford University Press.

USDA. (2023, December 6). Cleanliness helps prevent foodborne illness. Food Safety and Inspection Service. http://www.fsis.usda.gov/food-safety/safe-food-handling-and-preparation/ food-safety-basics/cleanliness-helps-prevent

USDA. (2024). Washing food: Does it promote food safety? Food Safety and Inspection Service. http://www.fsis.usda.gov/food-safety/safe-food-handling-and-preparation/ food-safety-basics/washing-food-does-it-promote-food

Vaidhyanathan, S. (2022). *Antisocial media: How Facebook disconnects us and undermines democracy* (2nd ed.). Oxford University Press.

Väliverronen, E., & Saikkonen, S. (2021). Freedom of expression challenged: Scientists' perspectives on hidden forms of suppression and self-censorship. *Science, Technology, & Human Values, 46*(6), 1172–1200. https://doi.org/10.1177/0162243920978303

Van der Linden, S. (2023). *Foolproof: Why misinformation infects our minds and how to build immunity.* Norton.

van der Meer, T. G. L. A., & Jin, Y. (2020). Seeking formula for misinformation treatment in public health crises: The effects of corrective information type and source. *Health Communication, 35*(5), 560–575. https://doi.org/10/gg87kd

van Deursen, A. J., & van Dijk, J. A. (2019). The first-level digital divide shifts from inequalities in physical access to inequalities in material access. *New Media & Society, 21*(2), 354–375. https://doi.org/10/gd54dc

Van Duyn, E. (2021). *Democracy lives in darkness: How and why people keep their politics a secret.* Oxford University Press.

Van Duyn, E., Peacock, C., & Stroud, N. J. (2021). The gender gap in online news comment sections. *Social Science Computer Review, 39*(2), 181–196. https://doi.org/10/gh24vk

Van Noorden, R. (2022). Higher-profile COVID experts more likely to get online abuse. *Nature.* https://doi.org/10.1038/d41586-022-00936-4

van Nunspeet, F., & Ellemers, N. (2023). Regulating other people's moral behaviors: Turning vicious cycles into virtuous cycles. *Group Processes & Intergroup Relations,* 13684302231159577. https://doi.org/10.1177/13684302231159577

Varshney, L. R. (2020). Respect for human autonomy in recommender systems. Cornell University. https://doi.org/10.48550/arXiv.2009.02603

Venkatraman, A., Mukhija, D., Kumar, N., & Nagpal, S. J. S. (2016). Zika virus misinformation on the internet. *Travel Medicine and Infectious Disease, 14*(4), 421–422. https://doi.org/10. 1016/j.tmaid.2016.05.018

Verba, S., Schlozman, K. L., & Brady, H. E. (1995). *Voice and equality: Civic voluntarism in American politics.* Harvard University Press.

Vijaykumar, S., Rogerson, D. T., Jin, Y., & de Oliveira Costa, M. S. (2021). Dynamics of social corrections to peers sharing COVID-19 misinformation on WhatsApp in Brazil. *Journal of the American Medical Informatics Association, 29*(1), 33–42. https://doi.org/10/gr6kzs

Vlasceanu, M., & Coman, A. (2022). The impact of social norms on health-related belief update. *Applied Psychology. Health and Well-Being, 14*(2), 453–464. https://doi.org/10.1111/aphw. 12313

Vosoughi, S., Roy, D., & Aral, S. (2018). The spread of true and false news online. *Science, 359*(6380), 1146–1151. https://doi.org/10.1126/science.aap9559

Vraga, E. K., & Bode, L. (2017). Using expert sources to correct health misinformation in social media. *Science Communication, 39*(5), 621–645. https://doi.org/10.1177/1075547017731776

Vraga, E. K., & Bode, L. (2018). I do not believe you: How providing a source corrects health misperceptions across social media platforms. *Information, Communication & Society, 21*, 1337–1353. https://doi.org/10/gc7mxj

Vraga, E. K., & Bode, L. (2020a). Correction as a solution for health misinformation on social media. *American Journal of Public Health, 110*(S3), S278–S280. https://doi.org/10/gjmhgh

Vraga, E. K., & Bode, L. (2020b). Defining misinformation and understanding its bounded nature: Using expertise and evidence for describing misinformation. *Political Communication, 37*(1), 136–144. https://doi.org/10.1080/10584609.2020. 1716500

Vraga, E. K., & Bode, L. (2021). Addressing COVID-19 misinformation on social media preemptively and responsively. *Emerging Infectious Diseases, 27*(2), 396–403. https://doi.org/ 10.3201/eid2702.203139

Vraga, E. K., & Bode, L. (2022). Correcting what's true: Testing competing claims about health misinformation on social media. *American Behavioral Scientist*, 00027642221118252. https://doi.org/10/gr6kt3

Vraga, E. K., Bode, L., Smithson, A.-B., & Troller-Renfree, S. (2019). Accidentally attentive: Comparing visual, close-ended, and open-ended measures of attention on social media. *Computers in Human Behavior, 99*, 235–244. https://doi.org/10/gmv5kj

Vraga, E. K., Bode, L., & Troller-Renfree, S. (2016). Beyond self-reports: Using eye tracking to measure topic and style differences in attention to social media content. *Communication Methods and Measures, 10*(2–3), 149–164. https://doi.org/10/gdvnns

Vraga, E. K., Bode, L., & Tully, M. (2022a). Creating news literacy messages to enhance expert corrections of misinformation on Twitter. *Communication Research, 49*(2), 245–267. https:// doi.org/10/gg3tpt

Vraga, E. K., Bode, L., & Tully, M. (2022b). The effects of a news literacy video and real-time corrections to video misinformation related to sunscreen and skin cancer. *Health Communication, 37*(13), 1622–1630. https://doi.org/10/gnpg8m

Vraga, E. K., Ecker, U. K., Žeželj, I., Lazić, A., & Azlan, A. (2023). To debunk or not to debunk? Correcting (mis) information. In T. Purnat, T. Nguyen, & S. Brand (Eds.), *Managing infodemics in the 21st century* (pp. 85–98). Springer.

Vraga, E. K., Kim, S. C., & Cook, J. (2019). Testing logic-based and humor-based corrections for science, health, and political misinformation on social media. *Journal of Broadcasting & Electronic Media, 63*(3), 393–414. https://doi.org/10/ggt4gw

Vraga, E. K., Kim, S. C., Cook, J., & Bode, L. (2020). Testing the effectiveness of correction placement and type on Instagram. *International Journal of Press/Politics, 25*(4), 632–652. https:// doi.org/10/gg87jt

Vraga, E. K., Thorson, K., Kligler-Vilenchik, N., & Gee, E. (2015). How individual sensitivities to disagreement shape youth political expression on Facebook. *Computers in Human Behavior, 45*, 281–289. https://doi.org/10/f7tsqj

Vraga, E. K., Tully, M., & Bode, L. (2022). Assessing the relative merits of news literacy and corrections in responding to misinformation on Twitter. *New Media & Society, 24*(10), 2354–2371. https://doi.org/10/gndjvh

Vraga, E. K., Tully, M., Maksl, A., Craft, S., & Ashley, S. (2021). Theorizing news literacy behaviors. *Communication Theory, 31*(1), 1–21. https://doi.org/10/ghff5h

Wagner, M. W. (2023). Independence by permission. *Science, 381*(6656), 388–391. https://doi. org/10.1126/science.adi2430

Waisbord, S. (2020). Mob censorship: Online harassment of US journalists in times of digital hate and populism. *Digital Journalism, 8*(8), 1030–1046. https://doi.org/10.1080/21670811. 2020.1818111

Waisbord, S. (2022). Can journalists be safe in a violent world? *Journalism Practice, 16*(9), 1948–1954. https://doi.org/10.1080/17512786.2022.2098524

Walker, M. (2021, July 13). U.S. newsroom employment has fallen 26% since 2008. Pew Research Center. https://www.pewresearch.org/short-reads/2021/07/13/u-s-newsroom-employment-has-fallen-26-since-2008/

Walker, M., & Gottfried, J. (2019, June 27). Republicans far more likely than Democrats to say fact-checkers tend to favor one side. Pew Research Center. https://www.pewresearch.org/short-reads/2019/06/27/republicans-far-more-likely-than-democrats-to-say-fact-checkers-tend-to-favor-one-side/

Waltenberger, F., Höferlin, S., & Froehlich, M. (2023). Reddit insights: Improving online discussion culture by contextualizing user profiles. *Extended Abstracts of the 2023 CHI Conference on Human Factors in Computing Systems,* 1–6. https://doi.org/10.1145/3544549.3585671

Walter, N., Brooks, J. J., Saucier, C. J., & Suresh, S. (2021). Evaluating the impact of attempts to correct health misinformation on social media: A meta-analysis. *Health Communication, 36*(13), 1776–1784. https://doi.org/10/gg87br

Walter, N., Cohen, J., Holbert, R. L., & Morag, Y. (2020). Fact-checking: A meta-analysis of what works and for whom. *Political Communication, 37*(3), 350–375. https://doi.org/10/dknb

Walter, N., Edgerly, S., & Saucier, C. J. (2021). "Trust, then verify": When and why people fact-check partisan information. *International Journal of Communication, 15,* 4734–4754.

Walter, N., & Murphy, S. T. (2018). How to unring the bell: A meta-analytic approach to correction of misinformation. *Communication Monographs, 85*(3), 423–441. https://doi.org/10.1080/03637751.2018.1467564

Walther, J. B. (1996). Computer-mediated communication: Impersonal, interpersonal, and hyperpersonal interaction. *Communication research, 23*(1), 3–43.

Wang, G., Gao, K., Liu, Q., Wu, Y., Zhang, K., Zhou, W., & Guo, C. (2023). Potential and limitations of ChatGPT 3.5 and 4.0 as a source of COVID-19 information: Comprehensive comparative analysis of generative and authoritative information. *Journal of Medical Internet Research, 25,* e49771. https://doi.org/10.2196/49771

Wang, Y., McKee, M., Torbica, A., & Stuckler, D. (2019). Systematic literature review on the spread of health-related misinformation on social media. *Social Science & Medicine, 240,* 112552. https://doi.org/10.1016/j.socscimed.2019.112552

Ward, J. A., Stone, E. M., Mui, P., & Resnick, B. (2022). Pandemic-related workplace violence and its impact on public health officials, March 2020–January 2021. *American Journal of Public Health, 112*(5), 736–746. https://doi.org/10.2105/AJPH.2021.306649

Wardle, C. (2017, February 16). Fake news. It's complicated. *First Draft Footnotes.* https://medium.com/1st-draft/fake-news-its-complicated-d0f773766c79

Weber, L., Ungar, L., Smith, M. R., The Associated Press, Recht, H., & Barry-Jester, A. M. (2020, July 1). Hollowed-out public health system faces more cuts amid virus. *KFF Health News.* https://kffhealthnews.org/news/us-public-health-system-underfunded-under-threat-faces-more-cuts-amid-covid-pandemic/

Weinardy, L. (2019, January 15). *How important is it to wash fruits and vegetables before eating?* Ohio State University: Wexner Medical Center. https://wexnermedical.osu.edu/blog/washing-fruits-vegetables

Wells, C., Cramer, K. J., Wagner, M. W., Alvarez, G., Friedland, L. A., Shah, D. V., & Franklin, C. (2017). When we stop talking politics: The maintenance and closing of conversation in contentious times. *Journal of Communication, 67*(1), 131–157. https://doi.org/10.1111/jcom.12280

Westcott, L. (2019, September 4). Why newsrooms need a solution to end online harassment of reporters. *Committee to Protect Journalists.* https://cpj.org/2019/09/newsrooms-solution-online-harassment-canada-usa/

Wheeler, T. (2023, January 31). The Supreme Court takes up Section 230. Brookings. https://www.brookings.edu/articles/the-supreme-court-takes-up-section-230/

WHO. (2020). Risk communication and community engagement (RCCE) readiness and response to the 2019 novel coronaviruses (2019-nCoV): Interim guidance, 26 January 2020. World Health Organization. https://apps.who.int/iris/bitstream/handle/10665/330678/9789240000810-chi.pdf

WHO. (2024a). Emergencies supported by RCCE. https://www.who.int/emergencies/risk-communications

WHO. (2024b). WHO COVID-19 dashboard. Datadot. https://data.who.int/dashboards/covid19/cases

Wichmann, F. A., Sharpe, L. T., & Gegenfurtner, K. R. (2002). The contributions of color to recognition memory for natural scenes. *Journal of Experimental Psychology: Learning, Memory, and Cognition, 28*, 509–520. https://doi.org/10/dwn8kc

Williams, H. T. P., McMurray, J. R., Kurz, T., & Hugo Lambert, F. (2015). Network analysis reveals open forums and echo chambers in social media discussions of climate change. *Global Environmental Change, 32*, 126–138. https://doi.org/10/f7fd77

Winter Storm and Heavy Snow, February 21–23, 2023. Minnesota DNR. (2023, February 24). https://www.dnr.state.mn.us/climate/journal/winter-storm-february-21-23-2023.html

Wittenberg, C., Tappin, B. M., Berinsky, A. J., & Rand, D. G. (2021). The (minimal) persuasive advantage of political video over text. *Proceedings of the National Academy of Sciences, 118*(47), e2114388118. https://doi.org/10/gqh435

Wood, T., & Porter, E. (2019). The elusive backfire effect: Mass attitudes' steadfast factual adherence. *Political Behavior, 41*(1), 135–163. https://doi.org/10.1007/s11109-018-9443-y

World Bank. (2023, June 8). From double shock to double recovery: Health financing in a time of global shocks [Text/HTML]. World Bank. https://www.worldbank.org/en/topic/health/publication/from-double-shock-to-double-recovery-health-financing-in-the-time-of-covid-19

Wright, C., Williams, P., Elizarova, O., Dahne, J., Bian, J., Zhao, Y., & Tan, A. S. L. (2021). Effects of brief exposure to misinformation about e-cigarette harms on twitter: A randomised controlled experiment. *BMJ Open.* https://bmjopen.bmj.com/content/11/9/e045445.abstract

Wright, E. J., White, K. M., & Obst, P. L. (2018). Facebook false self-presentation behaviors and negative mental health. *Cyberpsychology, Behavior, and Social Networking, 21*(1), 40–49. https://doi.org/10.1089/cyber.2016.0647

Wu, T.-Y. (2021). Proactive Opinion expression avoidance about same-sex marriage on social media: Acceptance, reactance, and self-censorship. *Mass Communication and Society, 24*(6), 918–942. https://doi.org/10/gr6k3d

X Transparency Center. (2022, July 28). COVID-19. Twitter Transparency Center. https://transparency.x.com/en/reports/covid19.html

Xiao, X. (2022). Let's verify and rectify! Examining the nuanced influence of risk appraisal and norms in combatting misinformation. *New Media & Society*, 14614448221104948. https://doi.org/10.1177/14614448221104948

Yair, O., & Huber, G. A. (2020). How robust is evidence of partisan perceptual bias in survey responses? A new approach for studying expressive responding. *Public Opinion Quarterly, 84*(2), 469–492. https://doi.org/10.1093/poq/nfaa024

Yang, Y. T., Broniatowski, D. A., & Reiss, D. R. (2019). Government role in regulating vaccine misinformation on social media platforms. *JAMA Pediatrics, 173*(11), 1011–1012. https://doi.org/10/ggt4gq

Young, D. G. (2023). *Wrong: How media, politics, and identity drive our appetite for misinformation.* Johns Hopkins University Press.

YouTube. (2023a). Hate speech policy. YouTube Help. https://support.google.com/youtube/answer/2801939?hl=en&ref_topic=9282436&sjid=15333353892293277067-NA

YouTube. (2023b, June). An update on our approach to US election misinformation. https://blog.youtube/inside-youtube/us-election-misinformation-update-2023/

Yu, R. P., Ellison, N. B., McCammon, R. J., & Langa, K. M. (2016). Mapping the two levels of digital divide: Internet access and social network site adoption among older adults in the USA. *Information, Communication & Society, 19*(10), 1445–1464. https://doi.org/10/ghptcm

Yuan, L. (2018, August 6). A generation grows up in China without Google, Facebook or Twitter. *New York Times.* https://www.nytimes.com/2018/08/06/technology/china-generation-blocked-internet.html

Zelizer, B. (2005). Definitions of journalism. *Institutions of American Democracy: The Press,* 66–80.

Zhao, Y., Wu, K., Zheng, J., Zuo, R., & Li, D. (2015). Association of coffee drinking with all-cause mortality: A systematic review and meta-analysis. *Public Health Nutrition, 18*(7), 1282–1291. https://doi.org/10.1017/S1368980014001438

Zhou, X., & Gao, D.-G. (2008). Social support and money as pain management mechanisms. *Psychological Inquiry, 19*(3–4), 127–144. https://doi.org/10.1080/10478400802587679

Zhu, J., & Dawson, K. (2023). Lurkers versus posters: Perceptions of learning in informal social media-based communities. *British Journal of Educational Technology, 54*(4), 924–942. https://doi.org/10.1111/bjet.13303

Zimdars, M., & Mcleod, K. (2020). *Fake news: Understanding media and misinformation in the digital age.* The MIT Press.

Zollo, F., Bessi, A., Vicario, M. D., Scala, A., Caldarelli, G., Shekhtman, L., Havlin, S., & Quattrociocchi, W. (2017). Debunking in a world of tribes. *PLOS ONE, 12*(7), e0181821. https://doi.org/10.1371/journal.pone.0181821

Index

Tables and figures are indicated by an italic *t* and *f* following the page number.

For the benefit of digital users, indexed terms that span two pages (e.g., 52–53) may, on occasion, appear on only one of those pages.